LOVE TROUBLES

LOVE TROUBLES

Inequality in China and its Intimate Consequences

Wanning Sun

BLOOMSBURY ACADEMIC
LONDON • NEW YORK • OXFORD • NEW DELHI • SYDNEY

BLOOMSBURY ACADEMIC
Bloomsbury Publishing Plc
50 Bedford Square, London, WC1B 3DP, UK
1385 Broadway, New York, NY 10018, USA
29 Earlsfort Terrace, Dublin 2, Ireland

BLOOMSBURY, BLOOMSBURY ACADEMIC and the Diana logo are trademarks of Bloomsbury Publishing Plc

First published in Great Britain 2023

Copyright © Wanning Sun, 2023

Wanning Sun has asserted her right under the Copyright, Designs and Patents Act, 1988, to be identified as Author of this work.

For legal purposes the Acknowledgments on pp. x–xi constitute an extension of this copyright page.

Series design by Charlotte James
Cover image © Rural migrants on the move. From the photo-essay, "Rural Migrants' Love in Dongguan," 2013. Used with permission of the photographer, Zhan Youbing (published under the pseudonym Jia Zheng).

All rights reserved. No part of this publication may be reproduced or transmitted in any form or by any means, electronic or mechanical, including photocopying, recording, or any information storage or retrieval system, without prior permission in writing from the publishers.

Bloomsbury Publishing Plc does not have any control over, or responsibility for, any third-party websites referred to or in this book. All internet addresses given in this book were correct at the time of going to press. The author and publisher regret any inconvenience caused if addresses have changed or sites have ceased to exist, but can accept no responsibility for any such changes.

A catalogue record for this book is available from the British Library.

A catalog record for this book is available from the Library of Congress.

ISBN:	HB:	978-1-3503-2960-7
	ePDF:	978-1-3503-2962-1
	eBook:	978-1-3503-2961-4

Typeset by Integra Software Services Pvt. Ltd.

To find out more about our authors and books visit www.bloomsbury.com and sign up for our newsletters.

*To my sadness and my everlasting regret, my parents in
China both died in 2021, and on each occasion, I was not able to say goodbye
to them due to Covid-19 travel and quarantine restrictions. I dedicate this
book to my parents, and I know that they would be very happy to see that
the many trips I made to Shenzhen have finally led to some tangible outcome.*

CONTENTS

List of Illustrations ix
Acknowledgments x

Introduction 1

Part I
GOVERNING LOVE

Chapter 1
RURAL MIGRANTS' MARITAL PROBLEMS AND THE DISCOURSE
OF GOVERNING 23

Chapter 2
FROM REVOLUTION TO CONSUMPTION: THE CULTURAL POLITICS
OF THE FUTURE 47

Part II
DOCUMENTING PAIN

Chapter 3
"LOVE ON THE ASSEMBLY LINE": CLASS AND THE CLICHÉS OF
ROMANTIC CONSUMPTION 71

Chapter 4
DARK INTIMACY AND ITS MORAL-ECONOMIC LOGIC 93

Part III
DOING INTIMACY

Chapter 5
MAKING CHOICES OR MAKING COMPROMISES. WOMEN AND
THE ONUS OF INTIMACY WORK 117

Chapter 6
LEFTOVER MEN AND THEIR MASCULINE GRIEVANCE:
MAKING SENSE OF RURAL MIGRANT MEN'S EMOTIONAL HARDSHIPS 141

Conclusion	159
Notes	168
Bibliography	173
Index	193

ILLUSTRATIONS

1   Rural migrant workers wearing factory uniforms stealing an intimate moment outside a factory in Dongguan City, Guangdong Province. From photo-essay "Rural Migrants' Love in Dongguan," 2013. Used with permission of the photographer, Zhan Youbing (published under the pseudonym Jia Zheng)   4

2   Rural migrant workers enjoying some downtime in a park in Dongguan City, Guangdong Province. From photo-essay "Rural Migrants' Love in Dongguan," 2013. Used with permission of the photographer, Zhan Youbing (published under the pseudonym Jia Zheng)   5

ACKNOWLEDGMENTS

My first and heartfelt thanks go to the many rural migrant workers in Shenzhen who generously spent their often scarce and always precious time talking to me. The stories they told me about themselves and their parents, families, boyfriends, and girlfriends form the backbone of the narrative in this book. Many of them opened their hearts to me about the joy and sadness, the contentment and frustration they experienced in their personal, even intimate, lives. I count myself extremely fortunate and privileged to have their trust and confidence.

I also want to express my gratitude to several officers from the labor NGOs in Shenzhen, who played an essential facilitating role in connecting me with potential research participants. Without their help, my ethnographic work would have been a lot more difficult. I also benefitted greatly from conversations with these inspiring young people, whom I admire for their dedication and commitment to advocating for rural migrant workers.

Dr. Lei Wei was my research assistant for this longitudinal project. My repeated fieldwork trips in Shenzhen over the period of several years would not have been so fruitful were it not for Wei's committed and enthusiastic assistance.

I have benefitted greatly from fellow scholars whose work on inequality and social change in China has guided and inspired me. These include Anita Chan, Louise Edwards, Eric Florence, David S. G. Goodman, Fran Martin, Bingchun Meng, Weishan Miao, Pun Ngai, Ying Qian, Mark Selden, Dorothy Solinger, Jing Wang, Yan Hairong, Yuezhi Zhao, and many others. This book is a result of my ongoing conversations with them over the past two decades. I'm also privileged to have had many conversations with Yingjie Guo, with whom I co-edited *Unequal China* (Routledge, 2013), and who has been unfailingly generous in sharing with me his thinking on class formation in China.

This project was funded by an Australian Research Council Discovery Grant ("Inequality in Love: Romance and Intimacy among China's Young Migrant Workers," ARC DP150103544). An earlier iteration of some material used in this book was published in a number of journals, including *China Information*, *Modern China*, and *NAN NÜ*.

Zhan Youbing, a rural migrant worker-cum-photographer, graciously gave me permission to use some of his photos, including the image on the cover of the book. I am very grateful to him for his generosity.

My immediate family in Australia provided both moral and logistical support so that I could spend lengthy periods each year conducting ethnography in Shenzhen.

As with most of my previous books, James Beattie was my most thoughtful and meticulous editor; he has never failed to deliver high-quality editing work, as well as valuable feedback and suggestions on the content and structure of the manuscript. As always, I am indeed enormously indebted to him.

David Avital and Olivia Dellow at Bloomsbury have been a delight to work with. I thank them for their interest in and support for this book project. I'm also deeply grateful to the two reviewers who read my manuscript very carefully, and provided very supportive and detailed comments and suggestions for improving it.

INTRODUCTION

Titanic

In a stuffy room fitted with an air-conditioner that was struggling as if it was going to die any time soon, I found myself sitting in a circle with more than twenty young Foxconn workers. It was a typical sultry summer morning in Shenzhen, and the workers, now out of their factory uniforms and wearing T-shirts, shorts, and flip-flops, looked relaxed and curious. They had signed up for a regular Sunday English-study class, and on that day, I was to be their "guest teacher." The labor non-government organization (NGO) that had helped me gain access to these workers had asked me to speak on any topic that might interest the group, while also teaching them a few useful English words. Only a few of the participants in the room were already married, and there were more men than women. Most of them did not know each other well, if at all.

I introduced myself as a researcher from overseas who was now undertaking a project in Shenzhen, and that I was hoping to conduct research on love and romance among young rural migrant workers like them. To break the ice, I asked if they wanted to tell me their favorite love stories. One male worker responded by saying that he seldom watched or read love stories, and preferred fantasy, science fiction, and action movies. Another male work chimed in that "only girls like love stories," and a third man added, "I think there's little love in real life, so I feel it's all fake."[1] When he was jokingly asked by someone in the group whether he had been hurt by love, he said, "Yes." A fourth man said, "All the love stories I've heard turned out badly; the girls are no good."

At this point, a young man, who had been quiet until then, stood up and announced that *Titanic* was the most powerful love story he had ever seen. "DW,"[2] as I later referred to him, then proceeded to give an extremely detailed account of the film. It was obvious from fellow workers' responses that most workers had seen the film, and resonated with what he said:

> You all remember the scene where Jack saves Rose by stopping her from jumping into the sea? And Rose's fiancé then invites Jack to dinner to thank him? A rich lady helps him get a nice dinner suit. At the dinner, Rose's fiancé wants to

humiliate Jack, so he asks Jack where he lives, and Jack replies, "Just the other night I was sleeping under a bridge and now here I am on the grandest ship in the world."

After DW had finished his retelling and sat down, a female worker made a comment about Rose's fiancé—the son of an iron and steel tycoon—referring to him as a *fuerdai* (child of the nouveau rich). She said:

He planted the diamond to incriminate Jack … and when the ship was sinking, all he thought about was how to save himself. He was young and strong, so he wasn't qualified to go on a lifeboat, but he snatched someone's child, and pretended to be the father.

Then another young woman joined in:

Rose was saved by Jack and went on to have a good life, having several children. Normally, we'd say that if the person I loved died to save me, I should decide never to marry, to honor his memory. But she didn't. She went on to live a good life, as Jack wished.

Then a young man offered his opinion about why the story was so popular: "People now really want to see [representations of] real love because in reality, real love is impossible to find." Another male worker agreed:

Because it doesn't exist in real life, people aspire to it even more. In reality, it's all about *meng dang hu dui* [matching doors and windows—i.e., social status]. A *diaosi* [loser] marrying a *baifumei* [rich, fair-skinned, and beautiful woman] just doesn't happen. Which is why people still want to see it in stories.

This discussion about *Titanic* took place in a local community center in Shenzhen in August 2015, where I started a longitudinal study of the impact of social inequality on people's intimate lives. It was my hope that getting people to tell their favorite love stories would shift the focus away from them and onto an often fictional (and hence de-personalized) set of moral circumstances and dilemmas, as a result of which I hoped they would feel freer to talk without thinking that they were directly disclosing very private details about their own lives. Having expected to hear a plethora of different love stories from workers, I found myself continually going back to that discussion, trying to make sense of how this engaged and animated session unfolded: why had a Hollywood blockbuster, set in an entirely different world, resonated so strongly with these young workers? My reflections on what took place that morning turned out to be instrumental in shaping the direction and design of my subsequent ethnographic work.

Given the inferior socioeconomic status of rural migrant workers in contemporary Chinese society, it should not be surprising that what resonated most with these workers was the unequal social status of the lovers. Also, the story underlines the moral (and romantic) superiority of the poor man over the rich one, and this may also account for their identification with Jack. Nor should it be surprising that their moral identification was also gender-specific. To the female Chinese worker quoted above, Rose's decision to marry and live a happy life, despite the fact that Jack had died to save her life, allowed her to question the merit of the traditional Chinese value placed on female chastity and fidelity.

Yet it is worth noting that *Titanic* does not have a happy ending. The love between Jack and Rose is immortalized by Jack's death, thereby also sidestepping the messy business of how their cross-class love might have played out in real life. These workers did not necessarily see this story as proof that true love can triumph over class; nor did they see this way of preserving cross-class love through death as inevitable. Instead, the story afforded them a catalyst to comment on the absence of cross-class love in real life. It is clear that their interpretations of *Titanic* were shaped by their own experience of living in the margins, and in turn they also made sense of their marginalized experience through their comments on these cultural texts.

Workers did not use theoretically informed language such as class or status; nor did they engage with intellectual concepts such as Bourdieu's (1984) habitus or social capital. Instead, they resorted to colloquial terms—*fuerdai, diaosi, baifumei*—made popular by the wide use of the Chinese internet. The effortlessness with which workers adopted contemporary Chinese internet idioms to narrate a Hollywood romance alerts me to the fact that ethnographers need to be attuned to the class-based colloquialisms and culture-specific language with which audiences interpret such texts. They also have to be sensitive to the equivalences and connections—as well as the possible slippages—between the theoretical language of class analysis and socially and historically specific popular idioms. Like all of us, workers to some extent live out their love, intimacy, romance, and feelings through prisms constructed by the media and a variety of other narratives, public discourses, and policy statements. In view of this, it is only logical that my investigation of individuals' emotional practices and choices takes into account how the dominant cultural categories of emotion shape these practices and choices. Cultural texts, ranging from transnational products such as *Titanic* to top-down state television programs beaming out from Beijing, can serve as useful prompts for interviews and focus group discussions.

Lovers in Dongguan

While rural migrant workers in my study freely commented on popular visual media texts, they also found themselves the object of media and public commentary. From time to time, while doing fieldwork in Foxconn's industrial precinct in Shenzhen in the period from 2015 to 2017, I would notice young rural migrant lovebirds enjoying a moment of intimacy in a public place—in a quiet corner of the street, on a park bench, or over a bowl of noodles in a cheap café. So, when I came across a group of images in a photo-essay published online in 2013 with the collective title "Rural Migrants' Love in Dongguan," my reaction was, "This is all too familiar."

Figure 1 Rural migrant workers wearing factory uniforms stealing an intimate moment outside a factory in Dongguan City, Guangdong Province. From photo-essay "Rural Migrants' Love in Dongguan," 2013. Used with permission of the photographer, Zhan Youbing (published under the pseudonym Jia Zheng).

Many of these thirty images show young rural migrant workers in intimate though not overtly sexual situations: talking quietly, holding hands, kissing, embracing, or simply sitting close to each other with their limbs intertwined. Other photos show couples going about their everyday lives, sharing a moment together while looking at their phones, riding bikes, shopping, or washing clothes. These shared intimate moments all take place in public spaces in the industrial areas of Dongguan, Guangdong Province, where these workers live and work—on the lawn of a park, on a bench by the roadside, at a table outside a snack bar, in a community library, in a public phone booth, on a city street. While some women in the photos wear casual or even sexy clothes, others wear factory uniforms.

I liked the realism of these images, but I was somewhat taken aback by the phenomenal publicity they received. The photo-essay appeared on ifeng.com, an online platform for the popular cable channel Phoenix TV, and one of China's best-known internet portals. The photos quickly went viral, appearing on many websites in China and beyond. In an attempt to gauge interest in them two months after they had appeared, I conducted a Google search using the title of the photo-essay as the search term, and this yielded around 220,000 hits. By February 2015, that number had nearly doubled, reaching 437,000.

While many re-postings of the images have generated new responses from viewers, I notice that it is the photographer's own commentary accompanying

Figure 2 Rural migrant workers enjoying some downtime in a park in Dongguan City, Guangdong Province. From photo-essay "Rural Migrants' Love in Dongguan," 2013. Used with permission of the photographer, Zhan Youbing (published under the pseudonym Jia Zheng).

the original posting on ifeng.com that has generated the most sustained and spirited reaction:

> If China is the world's factory, Dongguan in south China is one of the main shop floors. This city has witnessed countless youthful lives thrive and then decline, countless dreams born and then shattered. The love of countless *dagong* [worker] individuals is ordinary yet precious.
>
> (Jia Zheng 2013)[3,4]

To this photographer, love is incontrovertibly present in these images. But online opinions diverged widely about whether rural migrants have the capacity for genuine love and romance. It seems that what constitutes an appropriate way of conducting intimacy on the part of these young rural migrants has become a matter of heated public debate. Some comments posted by registered ifeng.com users are one liners such as "So sweet"; "How romantic"; "They are so pure and innocent"; "Love doesn't discriminate against the poor"; "Life is beautiful because love exists." Some endorsement and sympathy clearly came from outside the migrant worker community: "They are so simple, so ordinary, and asking the world for so little in return; bless them"; "My heart goes out to you, my compatriots—you are the admirable workers of China!"; "They are the mainstay of the urban economy; may the flower of their love bear sweet fruit!"

However, clearly not everyone agrees. Instead of seeing romance in these images, some see pure lust. One commenter says that Shenzhen and Dongguan are full of "illicit love birds." Criticism of such intimate acts is also implied in another post, which says that "most of these couples are just after sex; love doesn't really come into it." Besides questioning the capacity of younger workers for true love, some more trenchant criticisms are voiced in terms of moral judgment, as evidenced in this comment:

> They're not interested in learning, they have no souls, they give free rein to their bodily urges. They feel no responsibility for themselves, their family, and society. They're after cheap sexual pleasure. What do they know about love? Morality and responsibility are strange concepts to them. Their existence threatens social harmony, and they're a disgrace to their parents, family, and society.

The photographer who produced the images of Dongguan lovers had clearly hoped to capture moments of loving tenderness, but it is clear that some viewers instead saw them as evidence of moral transgression. One person posted this comment:

> I'm at a loss as to what to say about these images. Putting aside whether they are good or bad, I think women should pay some attention to their display of *suzhi* [personal quality]. You don't have to wear designer brands, but it doesn't look good to reveal too much of your body.

This criticism of "immodest" women is reinforced by another post, which says: "Love is sweet indeed, but if you want romance, you should go home and do it behind closed doors. One needs to behave in a civilized way in public, especially women."

The strong and polarized reactions to these images made me wonder what rural migrant workers themselves would make of them. When I invited a number of my fieldwork participants to comment on them, their responses were mostly along the line of "So what?" To them, what was represented here was simply their own everyday lives: "These are very familiar to me; I see people like this everywhere, all the time." A few women workers told me that they personally would not behave in too immodest a way, such as kissing or being amorous in public, but that "people must understand that these acts are not obscene; they're perfectly normal."

Some even told me that they had "been there and done that," and that "it's nothing to make a fuss about." It is clear that workers neither wanted to romanticize the love lives of the individuals in the photos, nor were they scandalized by them. Their comments stand in sharp contrast to the intense and polarized responses from online viewers of the photos—whether sympathetic or hostile.

The images in the "Rural Migrants' Love in Dongguan" series, together with the photographer's statements and public responses to the images, raise questions that are central to this book: What are the intimate consequences of China's socioeconomic inequality? Can members of marginalized social groups embody legitimate desire and be trusted to engage in "appropriate" intimacy? If they have few material resources to pursue romance, love, and intimacy, what are the thoughts about what needs to be done about their love troubles on the part of everyone outside this cohort—the state, policy makers, journalists, socioeconomic elites, and middle-class consumers?

An Intimate Turn

It is now well established that more than four decades of economic reform have transformed China into one of the most unequal countries in the world (Davis and Wang 2009; Whyte 2010).[5] Yet, few consider how socioeconomic inequality impacts on the love lives of underprivileged individuals like the workers in my study—how emotional loneliness affects their sense of self-worth, and the implications this might have for society more generally when the sheer scale of the problem is better understood. The workers in my study, being at the sharp end of China's inequality, harbor what might seem to be a very modest dream: of finding a life partner, having the chance to start a family, and living with a little more dignity and less discrimination in their often bleak and harsh lives. The dearth of research in this area seems unjustifiable, given that love is believed to be one of the strongest anchors for recognition of one's dignity and social worth (Honneth 2001; Illouz 2012).

The controversy regarding the photographic depiction of Dongguan lovers drove home for me the realization that the space of personal intimacy is not just a private matter; it is also where the moral boundaries between people from different socioeconomic groups can be—and routinely are—policed and maintained. Although words such as *love*, *romance*, and *intimacy* are frequently used, their meanings are by no means simple and clear-cut, and much is at stake in controlling how they are used. I became convinced that questions about who needs to be "governed" in their private lives, how individuals can pursue intimacy effectively, and what decisions they make about romance-related consumption are inevitably questions about the intimate consequences of socioeconomic inequality. They are also about how socioeconomic inequality correlates with the unequal distribution of discursive rights, narrative power, and access to the political lingua franca. None of these questions have received adequate scholarly attention.

While an "intimate turn" in the study of China's inequality is relatively easy to justify and prescribe, it is nevertheless hard to prosecute. For instance, how should we study the emotions, which can be ineffable, personal, and notoriously good at evading the attempts of language to capture them? How do we investigate individuals' feelings, which can be ephemeral, visceral, often pre-linguistic? And how do we document intimacy, which, by its nature, usually takes place away from the gaze of the public, including researchers such as me?

In asking these questions, I am cognizant of the fact that affect, emotion, and feelings are theoretically contested concepts. How to define and differentiate them is a complex but open-ended question. I do not intend to add to the myriad and growing discussions on the definition and nature of these concepts that have emerged since the "affective turn."[6] Regardless of whether we use the term "emotion," "affect," or "feelings" to characterize this sphere, the methodological debate about how to investigate matters of the heart—be it a "sociocultural construct" approach[7] or "non-representational theory"[8]—is more directly relevant to my concerns. In the same way that the polarized responses to the images of Dongguan lovers alerted me to the importance of studying inequality and intimacy in both symbolic and material domains, the lesson I learned from my *Titanic* discussion group was the potential for a connection between telling love stories and the ethnography of emotion. As existing research suggests, love stories are cultural texts that are rich in ethnographic insight.[9] And these love stories have a role to play in constructing a politically and socially invested ethnography of practices.[10] I therefore resolved to use a wide variety of textual materials—policy statements, scholarly research papers, news stories, videos, art-house films, blockbuster movies, photo-essays, poems, novels, blogs, and social media postings—to generate further analysis based on this empirical material.[11]

Of course, interweaving critiques of textual materials taken from the media and public culture with rejoinders from rural migrants does not lead to an account of migrants' lives that is more "objective" than these materials themselves. Rather, it is intended to lay bare, wherever possible, any tensions, contradictions, ambiguities, and sometimes even complicities between and within the two bodies of material. This approach aims to pit the dominant cultural politics of love as depicted in mainstream media against the everyday experience of migrant individuals, in order to explore the possibility of constructing an alternative grammar of emotional morality, as well as to unravel the power relations that underscore the possible gaps or overlaps between these two spheres.

Premised on these assumptions, my study set out to produce two related corpora of material: first, a body of ethnographic data about rural migrants' intimate lives, set against the backdrop of the structural inequality they face; and second, a collection of the socioeconomically situated responses of individual workers to a cluster of dominant media and cultural texts on romance and love. It is my hope that these bodies of knowledge will enable me to construct both an empirical account of the intimate consequences of their marginalized lives, and a critical analysis of how socioeconomic inequality shapes the cultural politics of love and romance. My overall agenda is to contribute to, if not engender, an *intimate turn* in the study of inequality in China.

I settled on *Love Troubles* as the title for my book in order to highlight the cultural-political and cultural-sociological directions of my study. The word "love" is often used in a wide range of relational contexts, including conjugal, familial, and friendship-based. It is also a concept that can be explored from a variety of approaches—cultural, sociological, economic, religious, philosophical, and psychological. In this book, I deploy *love*—and associated concepts such as *romance* and *intimacy*—in the specific context of relationships that have a potentially romantic, intimate, sexual, and/or marital dimension between two adult individuals. Even though all the relationships that I discuss in the book are of a kind that includes an integral sexual aspect—regardless of whether the couples in question were already sexually active at the time of my research—my primary focus here is squarely on their emotional experiences rather than their sexual practices per se.

Intimacy and Inequality: Conceptual Framework

More than ever before, debates about inequality have taken center stage in the current political and intellectual life of the global West. Yet a new frontier, representing a more ineffable, much less visible, but equally crucial dimension of debates on inequality, is still missing. When it comes to China, the world has grown increasingly fond of talking about it in terms of "China's rise"—its phenomenal economic growth, and its rapidly expanding middle class. But few consider the emotional cost of these developments; nor do they reflect on the fact that those who bear the brunt of this cost are mostly rural migrant workers, each of whom humbly aspires to a fairer share of the nation's growing wealth, as they live out the unforgiving reality of their daily lives. Their existence casts a disquieting shadow over the vision of a rejuvenated China with common prosperity that is the stuff of President Xi Jinping's "China Dream." By arguing for an intimate turn in the study of China's inequality, *Love Troubles* presents a local but significant intervention in worldwide debates on this topic.

Throughout the book, I aim to engineer this intimate turn by closely engaging with three sets of conceptual connections. The first is the connection between governmentality and desire—how the state encourages and promotes certain kinds of discourses about love and intimacy, and how it chooses appropriate role models to exemplify "correct" intimate conduct. Over the past several decades, since the start of economic reforms, Chinese individuals have increasingly been living in a privatized social order, and consequently, they have had to negotiate a much more complex moral-sexual-economic order in their personal lives. Since the beginning of these reforms four decades ago, China has witnessed the gradual rollback of the Chinese state's provision of public health, education, housing, and other goods and services. Furthermore, as Ong and Zhang (2008) demonstrate, the dramatically transformative process of privatization in the material domain has also led to the substantial privatization of social relations and individual subjecthood. Individuals are now encouraged to engage in self-governing, a process that is geared toward the goal of re-embedding them within new types of social commitment and new normative ideals, including those concerning marriage, gender roles, and personal fulfillment. This practice of self-governing has become increasingly important in contemporary China. To assist individuals in their attempts to script their own biographies, experts, including emotional counselors and psychologists, have emerged to give advice on how to develop self-control and self-awareness in pursuing intimacy.[12] The question, therefore, is: Which social groups can be trusted to govern themselves, and which are considered to need paternalistic management? Further, how are members from socioeconomically disadvantaged groups such as rural migrants configured in this discourse of governing? Which social classes can be entrusted to embody morally acceptable and legitimate desires, and what kind of intimate decisions are deemed to be conducive to social harmony, or threatening to social/moral order and thus problematic to the state?

The second conceptual connection is that between capitalism and emotion. We learn from sociologists that romantic love captures the cultural contradictions of capitalism, and that capitalism is largely responsible for the creation of a "market-based romantic utopia" (Illouz 1997, 111). A few arguments are central to the theorization of emotional capitalism. In capitalist systems, romance and intimacy have become luxury goods and services that can be purchased and outsourced: the affective medium of love has become increasingly tied to the logic of the market, and romantic love is not just a cultural commodity but has been reconfigured as "rational, self-interested, strategic, and profit-maximizing" (Hochschild 1983, 2003; Illouz 1997, 188; Illouz 2014). Also, as Lauren Berlant (2011) points out, capitalism thrives on the constant stimulation of desire, and people learn to identify with love in the same way as they identify with material commodities.

Although money has always been part of the equation as far as romantic love is concerned, capitalism has indeed intensified the commercialization of human feelings to a much higher degree. Consequently, intimacy in the era of late capitalism has grown "cold" (Illouz 2007) and has been increasingly commodified; feelings have become resources that can be outsourced as "emotion work" and "emotional labor" (Hochschild 2012).

Also key to the concept of emotional capitalism is the relationship between class and emotional experience. Bourdieu (1984), for instance, argues that since the dominated classes recognize as legitimate certain cultural practices that in effect exclude them, the culture of dominated groups is, by default, deprived of a positive content of its own. Furthermore, previous sociological research (e.g., Hochschild 2003) makes it clear that people occupying different positions in the socioeconomic hierarchy have different emotional experiences, inhabit different emotional worlds, and may even have different emotional ontologies. On the other hand, the commercialized formula of romance also goes some way toward addressing class divisions, since the ritual of romantic consumption is open (to some extent) to all social groups, and speaks the "language of consumerist solidarity" (Illouz 1997, 251). These insights remain to be tested against the backdrop of socioeconomic inequality in contemporary China. To what extent are such existing theorizations about class and consumption relevant to and resonant with contemporary Chinese society, which has undergone dramatic social transformation in recent decades, and which has a class structure that is still unstable, class boundaries that are fluid, and class sensibilities that are complex and even paradoxical?

The third conceptual connection involves intimacy and modernity. As Illouz (2012, 9) argues, "To study love is not peripheral but *central* to the study of the core and foundation of modernity." Some other sociologists claim that the quest for deep emotional intimacy is at the heart of modern forms of established sexual relationships. For instance, Giddens (1992) argues that the modern notion of intimacy privileges relationships that are voluntary, personal, emotionally authentic, and love- and care-based. Individuals have become more "mobile, unsettled, and 'open'" in their behavior and feelings about sexuality and love, thereby creating "unexplored territory to be charted"—territory that is fraught with "new dangers" (Giddens 1991, 12–13). However, along with this freedom to develop a new "life politics" comes an increased level of anxiety and a sense of risk in the private sphere of love and intimate relationships; hence the newly configured importance of communication in achieving and maintaining intimacy (Illouz 2007). This capacity for self-reflexivity is widely considered to be a key dimension of becoming modern (Beck, Giddens, and Lash 1994).

Modernity in China has been experienced unevenly, with pre-modern, early modern, and late modern phases existing side by side. Transformation from an agrarian to a postindustrial society started in China from the beginning of the twentieth century, but it was during the four decades of economic reforms following the era of socialist industrialization that the pace of modernization accelerated rapidly. China, like some of its East Asian neighbors, has reaped both the benefits and the costs of "compressed modernity" (K. Chang 1999; K. Chang and M. Song 2010). The term "compressed modernity" is used to characterize the process of undergoing a high level of industrial modernization within only a few decades. Like some other East Asian societies, China's experience of modernity stands in contrast with that of the West, whose modernity has been built more slowly alongside a comparatively well-developed social welfare system that offers its citizens reasonable—though not always fair and equitable—access to social welfare goods and services. One of the consequences of compressed modernity, some scholars argue, has been the relative absence of such a safety net in these countries (see, e.g., K. Chang and M. Song 2010), thereby exposing individuals to increased levels and more diverse forms of competition, exploitation, discrimination, and risk.

Individualization is widely believed to be a key element of modernity (Beck and Beck-Gernsheim 2002). For social theorists such as Ulrich Beck, individualization takes place in late modernity when "the social order of the national state, class, ethnicity and the traditional family is in decline," in which the "ethic of individual self-fulfillment and achievement" becomes increasingly important, and in which individuals want to be the authors of their own lives, freely "choosing, deciding, shaping" their own destiny (Beck and Beck-Gernsheim 2002, 22–23). China has been no exception. However, despite evidence of increasing personal freedom and self-fulfillment within Chinese society, scholars do not always agree on the extent to which individualization has taken root in China. For instance, Yunxiang Yan's (2009) work documents the institutionalized process of individualization in China, presenting evidence of increased personal freedom and self-fulfillment within the nation's society. By contrast, other scholars (e.g., Harrell and Santos 2017) caution against exaggerating the degree of individualization in China, and, citing evidence from more recent literature (e.g., Davis and Friedman 2014), argue for the importance of examining how family and social networks continue to shape individuals' lives. What does seem clear, though, is that China has gone through a process of structural individualization that nevertheless has not led to ideological individualism (Y. Yan 2009, 2010). In light of these claims, how has China's compressed modernity and its distinct process of individualization shaped the ways in which intimacy is experienced by young migrant men and women, the core members of the China's most disadvantaged social groups?

Fieldwork

I started my fieldwork in 2015 in the newly created industrial zone of Longhua District in Shenzhen, motivated to find answers to these questions. My fieldwork mainly took the form of interacting with two groups of people and organizations, the first of which comprised rural migrant workers themselves. In each of the three years from 2015 to 2017, I spent an average of one month talking to and interacting with individuals who worked for Foxconn in the Longhua Science and Technology Park. During that period, I conducted one-to-one interviews with forty rural migrant individuals, who were chosen to reflect diversity in terms of gender, sexuality, marital status, and age, making sure to capture workers born in both the 1980s and the 1990s—decade cohorts that will figure prominently in my analysis throughout this book. These interviews mostly lasted an hour and a half, and often took place in the small, crowded rental rooms where workers lived, or occasionally in a café located in the residential areas of the industrial complex that are often described as "villages within the city" (*cheng zhong cun*).[13] This was complemented by a more sustained and intensive series of longitudinal ethnographic interactions. Having established initial rapport with the latter individuals in 2015, I returned to the same site in the two subsequent years and conducted follow-up interviews with each of them. Since Covid-19 made it impossible to travel in person to Shenzhen in more recent years, I have had to establish and maintain regular contact with as many of them as possible via WeChat, the most popular Chinese social media platform.

The main site of my fieldwork was Village Q, a "village within the city" enclave that lies outside Foxconn's plant in the Longhua District. In each of the years that I entered the site, I found that these theoretical questions were promptly overtaken by the vivid everyday lives that unfolded before me in the village. Most people here work for Foxconn's Shenzhen plant. While the dormitory accommodation is inside the Foxconn compound, rental accommodation is in what are often referred to as "handshake buildings" (*wo shou lou*).[14] Village Q exists cheek by jowl with the dramatically different world of commercial, middle-class Longhua, the two separated by nothing more than a smelly canal, and linked by a footbridge. Although workers call it the "stinking canal" (*chou shui gou*), they strongly identify with the place, and hold their annual "Stinking Canal Music Festival for Workers" there. Inside the village, the daily rhythm is predictable. Each morning, around 7:30, I would see a steady stream of workers hurrying toward the northern and western gates of the Foxconn factory, breakfast in one hand and with sleep still in their eyes, afraid to risk having their pay docked for being even a couple of minutes late. At the same time, another stream of workers going in the opposite direction would emerge from the same gates, dragging their tired bodies after a twelve-hour shift, looking pale and numb, heading for bed in their dormitory or rental accommodation. Everyone wore a lanyard with their Foxconn photo ID card hanging from it, no one being allowed to enter or leave the plant without swiping their card.

Another group of people who informed my research were volunteers and employees from local labor NGOs, whose support and assistance to me played a vital role in supporting my research. These individuals not only helped arrange initial access to rural migrant workers for the purpose of interviews and focus groups, but they also generously shared with me their own experiences and insights, drawing on their daily interactions with workers. Another important form of assistance I received from these organizations was the opportunity to take part in a variety of musical, sports, theater, educational, and training activities they organized for rural migrants—activities that engendered myriad spontaneous occasions for me to mingle and interact with workers in informal, and perhaps more natural, ways. I have relied on my numerous discussions with a dozen officers from three NGOs (two in Shenzhen, one in Guangzhou) as key—but not exclusive—points of reference, and have found it useful to pit my views and impressions against their insights and knowledge, in the interests of arriving at a more nuanced understanding. They are informants and interlocutors, as well as ethnographic partners.

Besides these one-to-one interviews and longitudinal case studies, I also facilitated a focus group discussion each year on the specific topics of love, romance, and intimacy, each of these sessions involving around twenty-five additional participants; the 2015 *Titanic* discussion analyzed earlier was from the first such session. The rural migrants who talked to me during these focus groups, and the individuals who participated in the one-to-one, in-depth interviews, were my "insider informants," revealing experiences that were available only to them. After all, only workers are allowed access to the factory, and they are not allowed to take smartphones with them onto the shop floor. So, without the comments I obtained directly from a number of male workers, I would not have known, for example, what was scribbled on the urinal walls in the men's toilets, even though the content of these scribbles is of intense ethnographic interest to me. Nor would I be privy to the lovers' tiffs or scenes of domestic violence that occurred behind closed doors, not to mention workers' interactions with their parents back in their home villages. Finally, I invited ten workers—five men and five women—to participate in the more sustained and intensive longitudinal ethnographic interactions with me that I mentioned above, over the full three-year period. During this time, I also met members of these workers' families, and generally spent as much time as possible with them—chatting, cooking, eating, shopping, and watching television, or simply "hanging out."

Inside the village, the smell of food is ubiquitous, as is the sound of popular songs lamenting the travails of unrequited love, betrayal, and loneliness. Spicy aromas of food from Hunan, Hubei, and Sichuan fill the nostrils, ameliorating the homesickness and gratifying the chili-loving palates of large cohorts of workers from these provinces. Shops selling lottery tickets, mobile phone accessories, and groceries line the streets, as do internet cafés, hair salons, and "accommodation" venues of a dubious nature, selling temporary intimacy at hourly rates. The streets are littered with promotional material in the form of cards or leaflets advertising myriad goods and services, ranging from "factory girls" who are happy to spend a night with you for a reasonable fee, to clinics offering a "quick and painless abortion." Everything that migrant workers need for subsistence can be found here. It's all cheap and cheerful, catering exclusively to workers on a wage of around 3,000 *yuan* (approximately US$440) a month.

No middle-class professionals living and working in Shenzhen have any reason to come here, even though it's only a few minutes' walk away. Workers warned me that the food in these places may not be hygienic, and that the cooking oil was "from the gutter" (*di gou you*).[15] But that did not seem to deter the many people eating there. In fact, most young workers buy a ten-*yuan* meal from these places, since they do not have the time or facilities to cook. On weekends, the internet cafés are always crowded, full of workers in search of whatever fantasy allows them to escape, if only fleetingly, from their grueling daily reality. From time to time, I would catch a glimpse of intimacy between "love birds" in public places—the sort of poignant moment of connection that is depicted in the controversial photos I discussed earlier. My conversations, interviews, focus group discussions, and encounters with workers took place mostly in this milieu, and the following chapters only represent my attempt to make sense of the lives of the people who generously shared their stories with me.

The researcher's main task in doing fieldwork is to produce ethnographic data. Although motivated and guided by a set of dispassionately and thoroughly researched questions, the process of gathering such data can often be a highly emotional process for both participants and researchers. On quite a few occasions, my interviewees became emotional and broke down in the middle of their conversations with me. Similarly, I also laughed and cried in their presence when they shared their sometimes funny, sometimes sad stories with me. However, I have always wondered what empirical status I should give to the tears and laughter that erupt at these often quite profound emotional, non-linguistic moments. In writing this book, I have tried, though perhaps not always successfully, to strike a delicate balance between the need to write these emotions—both mine and those of the rural migrant individuals who participated in my research—into and out of my ethnographic account.

Structure of the Book

In addition to this introduction, the book contains six chapters, grouped into three sections, and a conclusion. Part I, "Governing Love," investigates one crucial way of understanding how inequality shapes emotional lives, by addressing the following question: Whose love lives do the Chinese authorities consider to be in need of regulation and governing? The two chapters in this section examine the role of sociocultural elites—in this context, primarily academics and media practitioners—in producing discourses governing love. They ask how the ideology and myth of romantic love reinforces the state's management of inequality, and also evaluate the effectiveness of such governing discourses by comparing them with the personal statements of migrant workers.

In seeking to understand the anxiety underpinning the Chinese state's responses to rural migrants' marital problems, we must start with the background and context of rural-to-urban migration in China over the past few decades. Chapter 1 has three objectives. First, it establishes the "rural migrant worker" as an empirically significant figure in the study of the intimate consequences of China's social inequality. Second, it locates this empirical figure in China's socioeconomic structure so as to understand why the government considers it politically urgent to address rural migrants' marital problems. Finally, drawing on a selection of papers dealing with the topic of rural migrants' marital problems published since 2010 and retrieved from the Chinese Academic Journal Database of the China National Knowledge Infrastructure (CNKI n.d.), the chapter discusses what role China-based social sciences scholars play in the state's political project of managing inequality. The discussion demonstrates that rural migrants are caught between an urban outlook on love, marriage, and intimacy practice, on the one hand, and rural, kinship, and familial expectations, on the other. However, the causes, symptoms, and possible solutions to young rural migrants' marital troubles that both public discourses and academic literature offer are not necessarily driven by the desire to address precarity and inequality. Instead, they are mostly motivated and constrained by the state's mandate to produce knowledge that helps achieve social stability and shore up the state's political legitimacy.

Motivated by such anxiety, discourses of governmentality aiming to reconcile, or at least manage, class inequality rely on putting in place appropriate moral, cultural, and rhetorical resources. The ideology of love, complete with a new normative framework of love, must allow individuals not only to make sense of their present problems, but also—and more importantly—to acquire a way of imagining a meaningful future despite their present hardships. Chapter 2 discusses the narrative form that such discursive efforts may take, using as a launchpad a series of news reports entitled "Love on the Assembly Line" (*Liushuixian shangde aiqing*) that were screened on China Central Television (CCTV). In this chapter, I approach these love stories on a number of levels: the political economy of their production, their social semiotics, and their connection to the revolutionary discourses of love that in an earlier era were mobilized by the Communist Party of China (CPC).[16] The chapter identifies a fundamental shift from the revolution-plus-love narrative of the pre-reform era to a consumption-plus-love formula. This discursive shift marshals the CPC's classic propaganda technique of the role model, and dresses it up in the neoliberal language of choice. The resulting transformation relies on, and in turn helps to build, a new state-sponsored utopian imaginary of domestic life, thereby testifying to the state's flexibility in governing strategies and its desire to continue exerting moral guidance. Furthermore, by inviting responses to CCTV's love stories from a group of mostly male migrant workers, the chapter assesses whether this new normative framework of love, purpose-built for rural migrants, has any buy-in from China's most disenfranchised socioeconomic groups. The responses of rural migrant men and women to such a discursive maneuver range from ambivalence to total rejection, and are often informed by gender-specific experiences.

Another way into the question of inequality and its relationship with intimacy is taken up in Part II, "Documenting Pain," where I ask, first, who has the material and symbolic resources to control and contest the meaning of love; and second, whether either of two forms of artistic expression—photographic and literary— challenges or contributes to the hegemonic ideology of romantic love. The chapters in this section present two divergent approaches to expressing the pain and suffering caused by socioeconomic inequality.

Chapter 3 is concerned with the question of class and consumption. Focusing on consumption items such as the bridal dress and wedding photography— essential motifs in wedding practices in contemporary China—the chapter explores the class-specific meanings associated with these consumption activities. After a brief account of the production of professional wedding photography as an economic activity, I turn to several individuals from two socioeconomic cohorts— young rural migrants (through interviews and ethnographic interaction) and their educated urban counterparts (mainly through one-off interviews)—and investigate how they make decisions about these rituals of romantic consumption. Then, against this backdrop, the rest of the chapter offers a critical analysis of the phenomenal success of Jia Dai Tengfei's photo-essay portraying rural migrants in wedding dresses against the background of the factory shop floor. As my analysis shows, Jia, an individual from China's urban educated elite who commands ample cultural and symbolic resources, acquires social and cultural capital through his ambiguous role as both a critic of the capitalist ideology of romantic consumption and an enthusiastic exponent of it. In contrast, although the workers who appear in this photo-essay are wearing wedding dresses, they nevertheless evince pain, abandoned love, and unfulfilled longing. When the workers I interviewed were invited to comment on this photo-essay, they mostly did so by sharing their own experiences of working on the factory shop floor and living in the dormitory. Their reluctance to like these images, and their difficulty in identifying with the workers in the images, convinced me that there may be a dark side to well-meaning middle-class compassion toward the vulnerable: its intention to give visibility to marginalized workers often goes hand in hand with an expectation that workers will perform a certain kind of emotional labor (Hochschild 2012) in order to earn this benevolently intended compassion. Chapter 3 demonstrates how love and romance are unequally distributed goods, and shows that access to the rituals of romantic consumption is also stratified. Furthermore, it argues that the symbolic value generated by this emotional labor tends to bring about more opportunities for individuals from one class background than for those from the other.

Questions of why love hurts and how to make sense of emotional suffering are central to modernity, but they are also significant in empirical terms, especially when love becomes a key site of socioeconomic exchange between unequal partners or in unequal circumstances. That said, we also know that when love hurts, its suffering may be invisible to those studying it, because it is personal, private, and often eludes language. The emotional suffering of marginalized individuals can be even more elusive, and consequently difficult to document. Is it possible to make sense of workers' emotional suffering outside the governing perspective and compassionate framework adopted by urban professionals?

There are widely circulated public discourses about rural migrants' supposedly transgressive sex lives, including stories of migrant women selling sex and migrant men pursuing sex. The love lives and sexual practices of young migrants have caused concern due to their perceived threat to public health, moral order, and social stability; they are therefore both alarming to the government and offensive to middle-class sensibilities. Chapter 4 advocates a departure from a dichotomous framework of transgressive versus normative intimacy, and instead adopts a critical socioeconomic framework for understanding subaltern sexual practices in China. It explores how gender intersects with class, political power, and sexuality to produce various forms of what I call "dark intimacy," thereby questioning the moral-economic premises of the current dominant perspective on transgression. In order to get at the difficulty of documenting sexual intimacy—particularly that of a transgressive nature—I turn to media texts, literary works, and conversations with migrant women and men and NGO workers. I also discuss the alternative perspectives that emerge from the personal statements of sex workers themselves. I do so in the hope of constructing an ethnography—albeit mostly mediated and mediatized—of "anti-intimacy." More specifically, the chapter examines how a range of sexual transgressions are talked about in public and popular cultural spaces, including the controversy surrounding the phenomenon of Foxconn "factory girls" (factory workers who also sell sex on the side), and migrant men seeking casual, coercive, and even violent intimacy. This chapter shows that, although these individuals' practices are perceived as transgressive by the state, capital, and cultural traditions, there is at the same time a sociocultural and moral-economic logic to their choices and decisions.

Patriarchy negotiates with political power and social structure to reshape rural migrant men's and women's gender-based self-identification. And just as the experiences of migrant women are subject to the shaping forces of the "triple oppressions" of state, capital, and patriarchy (Pun 2005, 4), so too are the experiences of migrant men shaped by state, market, and traditional culture, albeit in different ways. Each of the two chapters in Part III, "Doing Intimacy," presents ethnographic insights into these differences between rural migrant men and women in their experiences of negotiating socioeconomic inequality.

Chapter 5 asks how cultural, political, and economic forces shape both the discourses of intimacy and rural migrant individuals' search for intimacy. Following the love lives of several migrant women longitudinally over three years, I have witnessed considerable developments and changes in their sense of self and in their romantic relationships. In this chapter I document these developments and changes as well as I can, intending this to be an account that testifies to migrant women's resilience as well as their fragility, their disappointments as well as their aspirations, and their way of approaching the future that mixes undying hope with persistent uncertainty. Migrant women's choices in intimate matters are still shaped by rural familial expectations and kinship pressures, as well as the clear socioeconomic disadvantage they face. Where relevant, this chapter situates this ethnographic account within existing sociological findings on young urban educated people's approaches to intimate relationships. This comparative perspective reveals that gender and class interact to ensure that rural migrant women do the lion's share of the intimacy work in their quest for emotional fulfillment. This chapter considers the gender- and class-specific nature of intimacy work by foregrounding the stories of four rural migrant women (two single and two married), but does this through the prism of their relationships with rural migrant men, thereby also refracting the challenges facing the latter group.

Public commentators often make the point that the 80s cohort ("*balinghou*," i.e., born in the decade of the 1980s) are very different from the 90s cohort ("*jiulinghou*") in many respects. And while these perceived differences between the two cohorts are largely constructed by researchers and the media, this view of difference is also endorsed by many rural migrants themselves. The social problem of "leftover men" among the most marginalized members of China's rural migrant population has become widely known, and is more prevalent among rural migrant men in the 80s cohort. However, there is very little understanding about how the rural migrants in this cohort talk about and make sense of their failure to secure a marriage partner. In trying to answer this question, I hope to shed important light on how socioeconomic marginalization impacts on rural migrant men's masculine identity.

Chapter 6 is a study of several unmarried rural migrant men who were born in the 1980s. This longitudinal account shows that the emotional experience of members of the latter cohort is marked by a mixture of persistent feelings of loneliness, bitterness, and dissatisfaction with the status quo of their lives, and a quiet yearning for the possibility—however remote—of "finding someone" in the future. The chapter also points to "masculine grievance" as a useful concept for understanding how unmarried migrant men rationalize their emotional hardships.

In the conclusion, I review my key empirical findings on how inequality shapes the love lives and romantic experiences of China's rural migrant workers, while also indicating how these findings may go some way toward reshaping our current thinking on the cultural politics of inequality more broadly. The study's implications include, for instance, the need to rethink the main ways in which material and symbolic structures co-produce inequality, and to articulate the conceptual potential to approach emotional inequality as both an emotional cost at the individual level and a political risk at the level of governmentality. Finally, I demonstrate the usefulness of approaching the emotional intimacy of China's subaltern from the perspective of realism and resilience rather than cruel optimism (Berlant 2011) or false hope. By seeking to "trouble" love as a discourse of governing, to trouble romance as an ideology of the market, and by presenting empirical evidence of the love troubles experienced by China's rural migrants, this book represents a modest step toward restoring—or establishing for the first time—the dignity and emotional equality that the subaltern Chinese deserve.

Part I

GOVERNING LOVE

Chapter 1

RURAL MIGRANTS' MARITAL PROBLEMS AND THE DISCOURSE OF GOVERNING

Introduction

Dr. Jiang Wenlai is a research fellow at China's Academy of Agricultural Sciences. A frequent op-ed contributor to various media outlets on rural issues, he was shocked to see himself in the firing line for a short article he had published in an online forum on October 9, 2021. Entitled "It Is Essential to Undertake a Project Aimed at 'Warming the Beds of Older Male Bachelors in Rural China,'" his article endorsed a key policy recommendation recently put forward by a local county government in Hunan Province that was aimed at solving the widespread problem of marriageable men in rural areas and rural migrants in the city not being able to find marriage partners. The local government's recommendation was to encourage young rural migrant women to stay in their village instead of migrating to the city, thereby reducing the gender ratio imbalance between men and women in the villages. Subsequently described by the media and myriad online discussions as the "Bed-Warming Project," Dr Jiang's endorsement of this proposal triggered a spate of criticism online, accusing him of "objectifying women," and "treating women as mere instruments of procreation." This controversy was subsequently reported in the newspapers, forcing Dr. Jiang to clarify and defend his position (Hongxing xinwen 2021).

Dr. Jiang is one of the many Chinese scholars who have contributed to the discussion of the problem of so called "leftover men." In early 2021, China's National Bureau of Statistics (NBS) announced its priority research projects to be undertaken in that year, in an official document known as NBS Official Edict No. 94 (NBS 2021a). Among the list of key projects was the love lives of China's rural young people. In tandem with this announcement, NBS's Humanities and Social Sciences Research Division issued an official notice calling for up-to-date statistics on marital issues among young people in rural China (NBS 2021b). These edicts from Beijing precipitated a flurry of large-scale surveys from provincial-level bureaus of statistics in a number of rural counties and townships. Many local governments posted the survey initiative on their official websites, and there was considerable media coverage reporting the findings from the surveys. And various scholars, including Dr. Jiang, were frequently called upon to make sense of the survey data and offer their views about the causes and proposed solutions to the problem.

However, it would be a mistake to assume that rural migrants' love lives suddenly became a hot topic only in 2021: this widespread issue has been front of mind for government officials, academics, journalists, and the public for more than a decade and a half, with the last ten years or so witnessing a gradual growth in the level of public interest. What is still missing is a dispassionate analysis of the politics of these public narratives. For instance, in what ways does socioeconomic inequality negatively impact on rural residents' pursuit of a fulfilling intimate life? What part do China's social scientists play in the governance of the national population, which is characterized by a sharp rural–urban inequality? How do those scholars whose research concerns sensitive social issues that involve socioeconomically disadvantaged social groups position themselves in relation to their research subjects?

This chapter focuses on these questions, and has three main objectives. First, aiming to set the scene for the book, I want to establish the "rural migrant worker" as an empirically significant figure in the study of the intimate consequences of China's social inequality. Second, I aim to locate this empirical figure in China's socioeconomic structure so as to understand why the government considers it politically urgent to address rural migrants' marital problems. Finally, drawing on a selection of papers dealing with the topic of rural migrants' marital problems published since 2010 and retrieved from the Chinese Academic Journal Database of the China National Knowledge Infrastructure (CNKI n.d.), I ask what role China-based social sciences scholars play in the state's political project of managing inequality.

Nongmingong, *Inequality, and the Rural–Urban Divide*

Rural migrant workers are often referred to as *nongmingong*. The NBS defines *nongmingong* as someone "who still holds a rural *hukou* (residential registration permit) but who, for the past six months, has either engaged in non-agricultural work or has left home to seek non-agricultural work elsewhere" (NBS 2021c). Despite its enduring staying-power in the media, academic writings, and government documents, this has never been a label that rural migrants themselves are happy to identify with.[1]

The figure of the *nongmingong* has become increasingly ubiquitous in the Chinese city, especially since the start of the economic reforms of the 1980s. Over the past four decades, the population of rural migrant workers has grown steadily. A 2016 NBS report reveals that China's internal migrants then numbered around 278 million (NBS 2016), while their 2020 survey found up to 286 million (NBS 2021c).

Rural migrants provide labor for the manufacturing and construction sector, the service and hospitality sector, small businesses, and a wide range of other areas. If the early decades of economic reforms precipitated the first generation of rural migrants in the Chinese city, by the first decade of the twenty-first century, about half of the current migrant population were younger people, born in the 1980s and 1990s. And while around 80 percent of the first-generation population were already married before going to the city, around 80 percent of the later cohorts are still single (Xu Jiaming and Wei R. 2018).[2] In January 2010, the Chinese central government issued what is known as a "No. 1 Document"—a policy edict from the highest authority—in which the government declared its intention to "step up efforts to solve the problem facing second-generation rural migrant workers." This was the first time the term "second-generation rural migrant workers" (*Xinshengdai nongmingong*) had appeared in the government's key documents (Sun R. 2010). Many of these individuals born in the 1980s and 1990s are the children of the rural migrants who went to the city to seek employment in the first two decades of economic reforms, and most of these younger workers have little or no experience in farming. The manufacturing sector in the Pearl River Delta is a major employer of China's rural migrant factory workers, most of whom belong to the 80s and 90s cohorts. They tend to be better educated and more engaged with urban consumption culture than their parents, but they also feel more stuck, angry, and disillusioned because, unlike their parents, who had always intended to go back to the village, they generally want to remain in the city. However, they see little hope of doing so, and are often unwilling even to contemplate returning to their native villages (Pun and Koo 2015).

As of 2020, workers between twenty-one and thirty make up 21 percent of this community, with those between thirty-one and forty making up another 27 percent, those aged between forty-one and fifty more than 24 percent, and those aged fifty and above more than 26 percent (NBS 2021c). The 2020 survey also found that 68 percent of rural migrants who left their native provinces for work were married, with women making up around 35 percent of all migrants, and men around 65 percent.

In the same way that race and racial difference are defining features of a person's social identity in many multicultural societies, in China, a person's socioeconomic experience and life chances have, for many decades, largely been shaped by whether they hold an urban *hukou* or a rural *hukou*. But to understand why the *hukou* system is discriminatory, we must first recognize that there are stark inequalities between urban and rural China. As early as 2006, Professor Zhang Zhenghe, director of the Rural and Regional Economics Study Center at the Chinese University of Agriculture, summarized the rural–urban disparity in terms of six dimensions (Xiong 2006).

The first of these dimensions is *income* disparity. According to Zhang, China's current urban-to-rural income disparity ratio is 3.21:1, but he is quick to point out that if the non-monetary entitlements enjoyed by urban citizens—including housing, education, health, and unemployment benefits—are also taken into account, the real disparity is in fact much greater. The second is disparity in the *level of education*, with urban populations having 43.8 times more tertiary degrees than their rural counterparts. This is compounded by the widespread phenomenon of children in rural areas dropping out of school early, despite China's policy of free education for nine years. The third dimension is differential access to *health care*, with only slightly more than 10 percent of rural populations taking up the option of health insurance, leaving the rest to pay their own medical bills. Professor Zhang stresses the close correlation between poor health and poverty. The fourth is differential levels of *consumption*, with rural populations lagging at least ten years behind urban consumers. This is followed by *employment*, with Chinese cities having an average unemployment rate of 5 percent, while rural China, where counting unemployment figures is difficult, is estimated to have only about half of its potential labor force being put to use. The last dimension Zhang identifies is a disparity in the *investment of public funds* between the city and the countryside, with Chinese cities having more access to public goods and services.

Apart from the six dimensions outlined here, rural–urban inequality can also be measured in terms of life expectancy and life span disparity. A recent study found that, while urban populations in China have an overall higher life expectancy and a lower level of gender inequality in the length of life than their rural counterparts, nevertheless, "urban–rural gaps in both life expectancy and lifespan disparity are shrinking as the rural residents are catching up fast, while the gender gaps remain large, and even widening" (Mengxue Chen and Canudas-Romo 2022, 1).

According to some experts, efforts to reduce rural–urban disparity, though high on the government agenda, have not significantly reduced the gap. For example, Professor Wei Houkai, director of the Rural Development Research Institute of the Chinese Academy of Social Sciences, has argued that, despite consistent official rhetoric directed at reducing rural–urban inequality over many decades, the gap between rural and urban China has grown bigger (Sohu 2021). Speaking at a forum in 2021, Wei said that, although the income gap between rural and urban residents has been somewhat reduced in relative terms, in absolute terms it has grown wider. He believes that rural China lags behind urban China by eleven to twelve years in terms of income level, while in terms of consumption the discrepancy is ten to thirteen years. For this reason, he argues that increasing incomes for rural residents is one of the keys to reducing the socioeconomic inequalities between rural and urban China.

Research also has proven beyond doubt that these rural–urban disparities are among the main factors driving millions of rural men and women to abandon agricultural work and seek employment in the city (Gaetano 2015; Jacka 2006; Murphy 2002; Pun 2005; Solinger 1999; W. Sun 2009; H. Yan 2008b). But ironically, this body of work has also made it clear that, despite their desire to escape from poverty or a life trajectory dictated by rural–urban inequality, many migrants find that these disparities have nevertheless followed them. In many cases, they actually experience a sharper sense of discrimination and exclusion in the city than back at home (Cao R. and Zhang L. 2020). This is largely because, although they are now living and working in the city—indeed, some of them have lived there most of their lives, or were even born in the city—they are still holders of rural *hukou*, a legacy from China's entrenched history of categorizing its population differentially, as either urban or rural. Since people's *hukou* status determines their access to public and social benefits, it means that, despite having made significant contributions to the urban economy, rural migrants are "outsiders" who are not entitled to a range of social benefits, including health care, education, housing, and employment, which residents with urban *hukou* take for granted (Liu X. 2015).

Since its implementation in the late 1950s, China's long-standing and deeply ingrained *hukou* policy has effectively divided the nation along rural–urban lines, with up to 70 percent of the population having rural *hukou*. The policy was used from the late 1950s until the late 1970s to keep villagers in the countryside, and the *hukou* system has been a critical means of ensuring population oversight and control ever since then.³ There have been gradual adjustments to the *hukou* system over the past few decades, and these adjustments have made it possible for rural residents to leave home in search of labor opportunities (K. W. Chan and Buckingham 2008; Jacka 2006; Solinger 1999; F. Wang 2005; L. Zhang 2001). Also, these adjustments were initially implemented to meet the demand for labor in export-oriented markets, and, in more recent years, as a strategy to stimulate domestic consumption and continued economic growth. While the year 2014 marked a major milestone in the *hukou* reform, the central government left it to provincial and local governments to work out the details, which resulted in many places choosing to adopt a points system that would prioritize people with higher education degrees, and those who owned property or were wealthy (Wallis 2016). If the main goal of the 2014 *hukou* reform had the broad aim of reducing the differential entitlements to social benefits of rural migrants and local permanent residents by closing the gap or deficit modestly by two percentage points by 2020, i.e., from 17.3 percent in 2012 to 15 percent in 2020, this goal clearly failed, according to Kam Wing Chan (K. W. Chan 2021a), one of the most authoritative scholars on China's *hukou* system.

The reality is that despite many reform measures, governments—both central and local—have been unwilling to abandon the system completely and permanently—a system that persistently discriminates against rural residents and rural migrants. Measuring the goal of the 2014 reform against the statistics from the 2020 Census, Kam Wing Chan concludes that "China's *hukou* reform has stalled and arguably even regressed" (K. W. Chan 2021b, 16). His assessment of *hukou* reform is that, while it has benefited a small number of migrants, "many of the reform measures in the 2014 Plan turned out to be largely cosmetic or were usurped by local governments for other purposes" (16).

Nongmingong *and the Chinese Precariat—A Dangerous Class?*

Decades of social transformation in reform-era China have brought about a dramatic change in the class structure. The Chinese worker, first transformed from the "oppressed" to the "master" in socialist discourses, is now back on the bottom rung of the social ladder (W. Sun 2016). Policy statements and scholarly literature in the post-Mao era usually consider rural migrant workers in Chinese cities as members of the "disadvantaged communities," who inhabit the space of *diceng*. "*Diceng*" means "bottom level," and the term is used as part of a metaphor of a vertically arranged social hierarchy.[4] Yet, despite their struggles and sporadic attempts at collective action for labor rights, and due to their inability to access an entire range of benefits enjoyed by urban residents, many rural migrants find themselves unable to settle in the city, but are also unable to return to their village land. In comparison with the first generation of rural migrants, the second generation is more caught in a vicious circle: "There is no hope of either transforming oneself into an urban worker or of returning to the rural community to take up life as a peasant" (Pun and Lu 2010, 503).

This paradoxical existence had led sociologists to ponder the question of how to configure China's rural migrants in class terms in the reform era. For those economic sectors that rely on rural migrant labor, their success in accumulating capital and expanding their operation options relies on a complicity between global capital and a pro-capital state, on the one hand, and a necessary process of "informalization" and "flexibilization" of labor, on the other (J. Chan 2017; Pun and J. Chan 2012). Unlike workers in the state-operated enterprises of the socialist era, rural migrant workers, especially those in the manufacturing sector, live out a reality that separates the production sphere—in the industrial regions where they currently work—from the sphere of social reproduction in rural areas. Labor sociologists Pun and Lu (2010) believe that this spatial separation determines that the proletarianization of Chinese peasant-workers can only ever be "unfinished" and "incomplete" (498), and that the pain and trauma experienced by the first generation has turned to anger and resentment in the second generation; they are best described as a "semi-proletariat" (J. Chan and Selden 2014, 600), and they exist in a "certain limbo" (601), positioned somewhere on an "arc of incomplete proletarianization" (J. Chan and Selden 2013).

In the words of Wu Xiaoying, a leading sociologist from the Chinese Academy of Social Sciences, rural migrant workers, some of them toiling endlessly in China's factories, feel that they have never enjoyed life, and that their youth has been sucked dry and run flat by the industrial machine. They move from city to city in search of work, are unable to put down roots, and therefore are forever facing the "can't stay in the city and can't return to the village" predicament (Wu Xiaoying 2017, 120). For many people in this cohort, their lives in the city are marked by an absence of predictability, security, and dignity (Pun 2016).

Socioeconomic stratification over the four decades of economic reforms poses analytical questions about class to sociologists, economists, and political scientists. Chinese scholars who are concerned with change in social structures in contemporary China use a number of labels and terms, including *jieji* (class), *jieceng* (stratum), and *qunti* (social group). Reviewing this body of Chinese-language literature, Yingjie Guo (2012) observes that in contemporary China "class" is considered to be a historical revolutionary instrument, whereas "stratum" is widely adopted as a more appropriate sociological concept to describe and analyze actual social structures. What has become clear is that the main beneficiaries and agents of China's socioeconomic growth since the early 1980s are "cadres, managers and entrepreneurs," or what have come to be described as China's "new middle class," comprising the political and economic elites who are effectively China's new "ruling classes" (Goodman 2008, 24). In contrast, the proletariat classes, comprising workers and peasants—who used to be the political "mainstream" and "backbone" of socialist China (Y. Zhao 2010, 5)—are now "losing … [their] subjectivity and legitimacy" and "can no longer be called upon by national ideology" (Lü Xinyu, quoted in Y. Zhao 2010, 6).

Regardless of how the *nongmingong* fits into the classic Marxist class analysis, China's rural migrant worker class certainly fits the description of what Guy Standing calls the "precariat class": "The precariat is a *class-in-the-making*, if not yet a *class-for-itself*, in the Marxian sense of that term" (Standing 2011, 11; italics in original). According to Standing, although the precariat experiences the "four As"—anger, anomie, anxiety, and alienation—they are not proud of themselves. In fact, Zygmunt Bauman argues that conditions of "disintegration, pulverisation, atomisation" prevent members of the precariat from uniting themselves, so consequently, "each suffers alone," even though these "individually borne sufferings are all strikingly similar" (Bauman 2017, 81). It is precisely for this reason that many scholars, including myself (W. Sun 2014), believe that a proletarian revolution with the participation of China's rural migrants is unlikely in the near future. The young rural migrant, as Pun and Lu (2010, 513) put it bluntly, "has no hope and no vision that would provide meaning to a life of dagong [working for the boss]."

At the same time, scholars concerned with precarity believe that the precariat is, as Standing describes it, a "new dangerous class," because they are angry and they are prone to listen to "ugly voices." For the same reason, as Bauman (2017) points out, both sides—capital and the precariat—eventually had to come to the conclusion that it is in both their interests to "elaborate, negotiate and observe … a mode of coexistence" (85). In order to survive, "inequality needed to invent the art of self-limitation" (87). This means limiting the degree of uncertainty facing the subordinate classes, or what Bauman calls the "levelling-up of the strength and chances of the sides engaged in the uncertainty game" (87), or, in the words of Judith Butler (2014, 115), re-distributing vulnerability and precarity across the population.

Current thinkers on precarity are very alive to the symbiotic connection between a lack of a secure, stable material life, a lack of self-esteem and social worth, and difficulty in securing stable intimate relationships. Standing (2011) believes contingency is likely to have a devastating effect on one's relationships. For instance, young people living a precarious existence may be less committed to taking care of their parents into old age in the current era of increasing longevity and shrinking state provisions; and their friendships and sexual relationships are bound to become more contingent and susceptible to instability and disruption.

The link between socioeconomic inequality and one's intimate life identified by Standing and others in precarity studies certainly can find empirical evidence in the Chinese context, and this perspective is echoed by China-based scholars. For instance, some researchers believe that China's *hukou* system directly impacts on one's chances of success in the marriage market. And the government is also clearly aware of the problem. Writing about the systemic disparity experienced by rural migrants in China in 2021, the *Guangming ribao* (*Guangming Daily*), an authoritative state-run national newspaper focusing on policy deliberations among intelligentsia, published an editorial that asserts that

> generally speaking, *hukou* is still very important. Very often in the marriage market, one's *hukou* status is still the gold standard. People still tend to judge a person's power and social position by their *hukou*. In policy terms, *hukou* status is still one of the deciding factors in determining one's education, employment, and housing outcomes. Many important decisions in people's lives are made on the basis of their *hukou* status.
>
> (Guangming.com 2021)

Rural migrant workers, especially men who are too poor to find a wife or own an apartment or car, certainly fit within the analytical category of the precariat class. But such members of the precariat in China have a more colorful and sociologically complex name—*diaosi*. The term *diaosi* is made up two Chinese characters, meaning male pubic hair. In English, the term *loser* seems to come closest to capturing the initial meaning of the term, although it has since evolved into a "dynamic, complex, and current" meme (Marquis and Yang 2013). In late 2014, one of China's most popular internet portals, Ganji.com, a nationwide online platform devoted to the provision of service and consumer information, collaborated with the Center for Market and Media Research of Peking University to produce a report on the living standards and lifestyle of young people in the lowest income bracket (Xie L. 2014). Boasting a sample of 210,000 respondents, the survey asked questions about various aspects of these low-income earners' lives, including their jobs, marriage and love lives, families, and health. According to the sixty-page survey report published in October 2014, 73.6 percent of these low-income earners were between twenty-one and thirty years old; more than half of them were single, and were living and working far away from their hometown; most had no urban *hukou*, felt discriminated against by local city people, and experienced a strong sense of being outsiders.

The report also found that most people in this cohort spent the best part of their time working, including doing extra shifts. Their main forms of recreation were sleeping and going online—including playing computer games, watching television dramas, shopping for bargain items, and sending/receiving messages on WeChat. The average monthly income of those surveyed was 2,917.7 *yuan*. They spent very little on meals (on average less than thirty-nine *yuan* per day), with 7.8 percent spending less than ten *yuan* daily on food. The majority of respondents did not own an apartment or a car, and had very little money in savings (Xie L. 2014).

The report was widely cited in the Chinese media, including mainstream Party outlets such as *China Daily*, and its use of the term *diaosi* seemed matter-of-fact, giving readers the impression that it was a neutral, widely known, and well-understood term. Public discussions in elite media stopped short of identifying rural migrants as the report's target group, although they were the one social group that objectively fitted the description in social, economic, and cultural terms. The dubious task of pointing this out was left to individual bloggers, such as this one:

> Who is a *diaosi*? Generally speaking, the most widely accepted view is that the *diaosi* community includes second-generation rural migrants, workers in the small business and manufacturing sector, discontented lowly employees, the unemployed, and those without property.
>
> (Liu Y. 2012)

Poignantly, rural migrants did not even invent the label, although the term tends to cling to them, even when it is often used to express sympathy rather than contempt.[5] An entry in Baidu Baike, China's Wikipedia, is particularly detailed about the low level of consumption typical of *diaosi*, saying, for example, that they usually use a cheaper Android phone or a fake iPhone; they wear fake designer brands bought at discounted prices; they eat at roadside food stalls; some dye their hair using cheap products; and they typically stay in rather than going out, either watching television or wasting their time going from one junk website to another. Many *diaosi* do not have girlfriends; most have no experience in dating. The few who do have a girlfriend are constantly made to feel inadequate for not having the money to meet her material expectations. Because of this, they sometimes let their girlfriends down (Baidu Baike n.d.).

Diaosi are known for their trademark refusal to drink the Kool-Aid of "chicken soup for the soul" that is often found in self-help and motivational propaganda. For them, this mentality is necessary in order to survive in a society where class stratification has intensified, and where there are few avenues of upward class mobility open to them.

While official, Party-led media have consistently refrained from using this "vulgar" term, they are nevertheless sensitive to the political and social ramifications of ignoring its existence. On November 3, 2012, the word *diaosi* did grace the pages of the *People's Daily*, the CPC's premier mouthpiece, in an article prior to the Eighteenth National People's Congress. Though not overtly condemning the term, the context in which it appeared makes it clear that Party ideologues considered the phenomenon it represents to be a cause for concern as far as social stability is concerned, and consequently a potential challenge to the Party's rule:

> Looking over the past decade, it is clear that China's social structure and its configurations of interests have undergone profound and dramatic changes. The nation has also had to deal with unprecedentedly complex factors from outside China. In addition to the aftermath of market reforms, the forces of globalization, democratization, and informationalization all crash in like tidal waves. We now live in an age of anxiety over distribution [of wealth], panic over environmental damage, a tendency towards "dad bludging"[6] (*ping die*), a *diaosi* mentality, riots, and mass protests. The relationships between individuals, society, the market, and the government are entering a "delicate and sensitive" stage.
>
> (Chen K. 2012)[7]

Despite its disapproval of the *diaosi* attitude, the Party newspaper invoked the term to make the point to its intended readers—mostly Party officials and policy makers at various levels—that the political legitimacy and longevity of the Party rested on its capacity to harness and neutralize such "unhealthy" and potentially dangerous social sentiments. After all, as Judith Butler (2014) points out in her discussion of the body and street politics, the vulnerable body is at the same time potentially an agentic body, and the vulnerable can use their bodies for purposes of resistance and mobilization, and to struggle to end precarity.

Rural Migrants' Love Lives and the Maintenance of Stability

What kind of danger does China's precariat class pose? Writing in 1987 about the urgent need for economic reforms in rural China, Deng Xiaoping warned that "the nation cannot have real political stability unless stability in rural areas is guaranteed" (Deng X. 1987). In Chinese-language scholarship on rural migrants, the link between rural migrants' marital problems and their potential for disrupting China's stability and social harmony is taken for granted, and is often used as the incontestable rationale for studying this group (Li P. 2003; Li Q. 2004). This default association between social stability, social order, and the need to address rural young people's marital difficulties is evidenced in many of the official statements released in 2021. For instance, an article on the website of a county-level government in Hunan Province underscores the importance of finding solutions to this problem, as the marital challenges facing this cohort are no longer simply "personal problems"; they are becoming a "sensitive social problem," a "big problem" that may "affect social stability," "inhibit economic growth," and jeopardize efforts to build a "harmonious society" in rural China (Hongxing xinwen 2021),

It is clear that the presence of a large cohort of unmarried and sexually repressed or sexually active young rural migrants in urban China is unsettling to the government and the state in general on a number of levels. Some young migrants are reported to engage in prostitution, commodified sex, and unprotected sex, which can lead to the spread of sexually transmitted diseases and unwanted pregnancies, posing challenges to public health and the state's birth control policy (Song Y. and Li L. 2015). Furthermore, sexual frustration is believed to have ramifications for law and order and to pose a serious threat to the moral order (Chang Z. 2010b, 44).

This widespread contemporary perception of a link between repressed sexuality on the part of unmarried rural migrant men and sex-related crimes in urban areas is not new. Historical literature also points to a connection between frustrated marital aspirations and social unrest in China (Brownell and Wasserstrom 2002; Sommers 2000). It may well have been to maintain stability that, at the end of the Cultural Revolution, many unmarried "over-age" young people received help from various government bodies to find a marriage partner when they returned to the city from the countryside (J. Zhang and P. Sun 2014). By comparison with rural migrants, urban professionals face problems finding a marriage partner that, though equally real, are perceived to be less worrisome from the point of view of social stability. Instead of direct government intervention, the market has stepped in to help urban young people (J. Zhang and P. Sun 2014).

It is reasonable to speculate that the concern with social inequality circulating in the scholarly literature and the media helps shape and sharpen the government's understanding of the political challenges such inequality poses. This is evidenced in the rhetoric of the top Party leaders. In his speech at the "two congresses" in 2015, Premier Li Keqiang referred to the need to restructure income distribution and promote social justice, so that more young people, especially those from impoverished families, would be able to "change their destiny through education," and would "have more pathways for upward social mobility" (Central Radio Network 2015). For the same reason, President Xi Jinping has also stressed the need to remove obstacles that prevent people from participating in economic activities and from enjoying the fruits of economic development. He envisioned a future when everyone would have equal opportunities to succeed and to realize their dreams. Xi also warned that unless social justice was improved, there could be "no guarantee for social harmony and stability, and people will lose faith in the economic reforms" (Wu Z. 2015).

After all, the CPC has ostensibly abandoned its original goal of leading China toward a communist utopia, and instead now openly declares its central mission to be to ensure that "our people" live a "happy life" (Xi J. 2012a). In other words, the level of happiness of the Chinese people has become a key performance indicator of satisfactory governance by the CPC. In his recommendation to the central government to improve the marriage prospects of rural migrants, Feng Gong—the well-known performance artist quoted in Chapter 2—also said that the rural migrants' dream to get married and have a happy life was "their China dream." Feng's turn of phrase is both subtle and pointed. It reminds the government that the much touted "China Dream"—the ideological brainchild of President Xi Jinping—would be devoid of moral substance and political legitimacy if members of China's marginalized social groups could not even realize their humble dream of finding a marriage partner. Given this, the statistics about rural migrants' love lives (or lack thereof) touch a raw nerve for the Party. This is especially the case given that, from its earliest revolutionary era, the CPC has sought to win the support of the rural population by promising to make marriage and family life accessible to poor male peasants (Diamant 2000; Stacey 1984). To put it more bluntly, the marital difficulties of young rural migrants is perceived to be a matter of pressing concern to the CPC, not necessarily because of these citizens' emotional unhappiness per se, but more likely because of the possible political and social ramifications of their unhappiness.

Nevertheless, while these problems in the private lives of rural migrants have become a source of anxiety for the government, the structural reforms aimed at reducing inequality may turn out to have an equally disturbing and destabilizing implication. As observed by scholars, the Party sees the middle class as a key stabilizing force in society, and consequently as politically conservative (C. Li 2013; Ren 2013). Yet, the argument for a more equitable share of resources between urban and rural citizens will have "distributive consequences" (Stiglitz 2012, 72)—consequences that are unlikely to be welcomed by either the urban middle class or vulnerable urban groups such as laid-off factory workers and recipients of minimum welfare benefits. It entails, in Butler's (2012) words, a redistribution of "vulnerability"—an outcome that is unlikely to be popular with urban middle-class citizens. Threatening the social and economic interests of the middle class by implementing social policies aimed at economic redistribution would risk instability as much as ignoring rural migrants' marital problems. This is the Catch-22 that challenges the government's stability maintenance project.

As a result of these factors, the marital problems of rural migrant workers have been a key focus for the Chinese government for some time. As early as 2010, the central government released the No. 1 Document mentioned earlier in this chapter, which precipitated a number of nationwide surveys about the lives of young rural migrants. In the same year, the All-China Federation of Trade Unions (ACFTU) released a report based on a survey of rural migrants in ten cities across several provinces, pointing out that a widespread sense of loneliness due to the lack of romantic prospects had become a "defining" aspect of the migrant experience:

> Second-generation rural migrants are mostly unmarried. This means that members of this community will experience important rites of passage—falling in love, getting married, having children, and sending their children to school—while working away from home. This forms a sharp contrast with first-generation rural migrants, 80 percent of whom were married. This is a problem we can no longer afford to ignore.
>
> (ACFTU 2010)

A similar sense of urgency was also conveyed in a report by the China Research Center for Youths and Children, which found that more than 70 percent of the construction workers surveyed considered emotional loneliness to be the most painful aspect of their migrant life (Banyuetan 2011). This impression was further reinforced in a survey conducted by *China Youth Daily* a few years later, which asked rural migrants to identity the issue that most concerned them. Up to 48 percent of rural migrant worker respondents perceived "marital problems" to be the most concerning issue, while "a strenuous work load" was chosen by 38 percent of respondents (Xiang N. 2015).

Calls to pay attention to the emotional life of rural migrant youth have come from concerned public figures, scholars, and the media, as well as from government organizations. In 2013, Feng Gong made a formal submission to the Twelfth National Congress of the CPC, highlighting the fact that many young rural migrants have trouble finding a marriage partner. Feng, the popular performance artist I mentioned above, is also a member of the national committee of the Chinese People's Political Consultative Conference, and a permanent member of the Revolutionary Committee of the Chinese Kuomintang. In his submission he argues that the government should work hard to "elevate the level of happiness of China's rural migrants" (Shao H. 2013).

China's social sciences scholars, think-tank researchers, policy makers, and media interpreted the No. 1 Document as a clear signal that rural migrants' marital difficulties had become a matter of pressing concern to the government. Discussions and analyses dealing with young rural migrants' difficulties in finding marriage partners have since appeared in a number of discursive spaces, including (1) national newspapers such as the *People's Daily* and *Guangming Daily*, which target readers in elite intellectual and policy-making circles; (2) widely circulated periodicals such as *Guancha yu sikao* (Observation and thinking) and *Kaifang shidai* (Open times), which target the general public but with a distinct concern about social issues; and (3) in academic social sciences journals.

Social Sciences Research

Starting from 2010, there has been a noticeable increase in the number of academic research publications about rural migrants and marriage. A search of the China Academic Journals Database (a part of the CNKI and the most comprehensive full-text database of Chinese journals in the world) using key words such as "new-generation rural migrants" (*Xinshengdai nongmingong*) and "marriage" (*hunyin hunlian*) highlights this sharp increase in the number of research papers on this topic. Over the thirty-two-year period from 1978 to 2009 there were 7,754 results, whereas there were 12,860 results in the six years from 2010 to 2015. In other words, before 2010 the annual average was 242 papers on the topic, compared with some 2,143 papers per year after 2010.

This gradual increase in academic output on this topic can be read as a good indication of the level of anxiety on the part of the government. To attract funding as well as to get published, the majority of social scientists in China tend to choose research topics that are prioritized by the government, as there are few alternative funding opportunities for the social sciences in China. While these academics had relatively more freedom to pursue critical research and collaborate with scholars outside China in the earlier decades of economic reforms, there has been much tighter control in the last decade, especially during Xi Jinping's regime, which began in November 2012.[8] The social sciences are expected to serve the political agenda of the Party and the government, and to conduct research within ideological and political parameters that shore up the Party's legitimacy. In 2013, Chinese universities were told by propaganda authorities not to talk about "seven things," including universal values, freedom of speech, civil society, human rights, and mistakes of the CPC (Carlson 2013). In May 2016, in his speech to an assembly of social scientists in China, President Xi reiterated these restrictions, saying that social sciences in China should have "Chinese characteristics." This included rejecting Western liberalism, supporting the political mandate of the Party, and avoiding anything that showed the CPC government and top leaders in a negative light (Xi J. 2016). Following these prescriptions, in 2016, the Chinese Academy of Social Sciences, China's key social sciences research entity, announced a new policy to scrutinize research dissertations for their ideological soundness (Cao G. 2016). In a much-cited article published in 2019, Jørgen Delman, a Danish professor of China Studies, points out that China has a "highly qualified cadre of social scientists and they are still able to publish good social sciences research, in China and abroad, as long as it addresses topics that are of interest to the Party-state and official political processes" (Delman 2019). Reframing the same point in blunter terms, Mike Gow, an academic at Coventry University in the United Kingdom, says that, in China's social sciences research, "controversial subjects will be avoided like the plague" (Sharma 2019). Given these constraints, is there any point in subjecting China's social sciences research to rigorous analysis, since it is largely state-sponsored and has to "toe the Party line"?

Here, I argue that we do need to critique China's scholarly social sciences writings, not *in spite of* but *because of* the state-imposed categories and definitions within which they are produced. As members of a disadvantaged community, rural migrants embody China's most intractable problem of inequality, and as a result they are poorly represented in both political and institutional terms (W. Sun 2014). Social scientists in China function as key intermediaries between the government and the nation's rural migrant community, and their roles are both important and ambiguous. On the one hand, these scholars are well-educated, urban, and professional individuals whose interests and views are closely aligned with the conservative state agenda on social stability (C. Li 2013; Ren 2013). On the other hand, knowledge class elites play a crucial role in shaping public opinion and policy narratives about the welfare of individuals from disadvantaged groups such as rural migrants. Their research about rural migrants' social experiences—and especially about their main problems and challenges—provides legitimation to the government's social policies, and for this reason alone it warrants careful investigation. More specifically, the Chinese government—and we, as interested observers of China—should be keenly interested in their findings about what causes these problems, and the proposed remedies that emerge from this body of scholarship. It is therefore important for us to ask questions such as: What are the political and moral impulses that propel the production of these scholarly views? And to what extent can the creation of this knowledge effectively dispel the government's anxiety?

Of course, given the constraints I have outlined, we might expect a high level of ideological uniformity in China's social sciences publications, so the main objective of this analysis is not to generate quantitative data that confirms the presence or absence of diverse or even oppositional views. Rather, it is to identify and then make sense of the principal discursive positions in this body of research, so as to interpret the "meaning" of "situation-specific" narratives (Yanow 2007, 110), in order to highlight "multiple and competing discourses in policy texts" (Taylor 2004, 433).

Hukou—*The Main Cause of Rural Migrants' Marital Problems?*

A survey of a selection of Chinese-language academic papers published since 2010 on the topic of rural migrants' marital problems leads to the impression that the authors of these works predominantly take as a given the difficulties facing young rural migrants in their attempts to establish intimate relationships or find marriage partners. The survey also points to a recurring explanation for these problems: lack of equity and access, largely as a consequence of China's long-standing *hukou* policy. Echoing the sociological and anthropological literature on *hukou* produced outside China, some Chinese social scientists also believe that *hukou* is largely responsible for the urban–rural disparity, and that it is a significant contributing factor to rural migrants' marriage problems (Guo L. 2013; Li H. and Pu K. 2011). They believe that a number of issues in the lives of rural migrants contribute to their difficulty in finding marriage partners, all of which are shaped by, as well as directly correlated with, the *hukou* policy. For instance, most young rural migrants have no permanent housing to their name, no secure employment or income, and low social status. Given their low income, they cannot afford to go on dates, let alone save enough money for an apartment, a car, wedding gifts, or a wedding itself, all of which are considered essential by urban residents (Fan Y. 2011; Zhu G. 2012).

We also learn from this literature that young rural migrants of both sexes share some common issues. Many were either born in the city or have lived in the city most of their lives. Most have few skills and little interest in farming, and most do not want to go back to the village to live (ACFTU 2010). At the same time, their prospects for settling in the city and enjoying similar entitlements to urban residents are barely better than those of their parents (Huang C. 2011). The ambiguity and uncertainty they face in terms of status (urban or rural residence) and identity (worker or peasant), plus their high level of mobility (frequently moving from one place to another to find employment) are anathema to sustained, long-term relationships (Fan Y. 2011; Song Y. and Li L. 2015). Furthermore, their employment is mostly characterized by long hours and low wages. Many young rural migrants work in gender-specific workplaces, either the male-dominated construction sector or the female-dominated toy and clothing manufacturing sector, and they therefore have few chances to meet young people of the opposite sex (Liu Jiejie 2011).

At the same time, it is also clear from this literature that *hukou*-determined socioeconomic marginality affects rural migrant women and men in different ways. In their attempts to improve their life chances through marriage by obtaining an urban *hukou*, a small percentage of rural women end up marrying urban men who themselves face some kind of disadvantage. These cross-*hukou* marriages between rural and urban residents are typically not based on romantic love, and where marriages do occur, rural migrant women mostly marry urban residents who are disabled, old, or poor (Jin, Zhang, and Yang 2016; Shen 2007). In marrying "outside" their *hukou*, these women reduce the marriage prospects of male rural migrants within the cohort (Li H. and Pu K. 2011). A small percentage of migrant women become the mistresses of urban married men (Liu Jing 2001). In both cases, these attempts to "marry up" on the part of rural migrant women (Shi Leilei 2015) are found to lack "emotional foundation," and often end in unhappiness (Guo L. 2013; Xu C. 2006). For males and females alike, then, the literature identifies two important patterns: first, rural migrant women have a much better chance than men of achieving cross-*hukou* marriages; and second, most rural migrants' marriages and intimate relationships are with someone else from their own cohort—for the vast majority of them, a successful marriage with an urban person is simply "wishful thinking" (Wu Xinhui 2011, 15).

In the meantime, while some women strive for upward mobility through marriage (often in vain), almost all of the writings surveyed for this analysis point to the fact that rural men on the bottom rung, unable to attract women of similar status, report widespread feelings of sexual frustration and low self-esteem. Not being able to afford betrothal gifts is cited as a key impediment to their finding a marriage partner (Miao T. 2012). Many rural migrant men also report being rejected on the grounds that they do not own a house, or because they have too many siblings or an impoverished family background, or because they come from a poor and remote area. So, if you are a rural migrant man who meets this description—and many of them do—your chances of finding a marriage partner are slim, especially if you are not physically attractive or do not have an engaging personality. A survey of 579 young Foxconn workers conducted by a labor-advocacy group found that up to 70 percent of male workers are single and without a girlfriend (Deng K. 2015). Older migrants—those in their late thirties and early forties—are already living with the stigma of being "men left on the shelf" (*sheng nan*). Yet, the pressure from their parents remains relentless. For this cohort, the emotional pain derives equally from loneliness and sexual frustration and from the guilt of having let their parents down.

But it is not just single young migrants who face difficulty in finding love and fulfillment. Married rural migrants are also reported to face myriad challenges. The most obvious problem is when there is a growing distrust between married couples due to long-term separation and an absence of conjugal intimacy (Du P. 2019). Married couples, many of whom live in different cities or often in separate dormitory accommodation in the same city, find it difficult to sustain conjugal relationships and therefore end up having "fast-food" romances (Song L. 2019). One nationwide survey in 2011 found that an increasing number of rural migrants get married while they are living an itinerant life, but then remain separated after marriage (Song Y., Zhang L., and Duan C. 2012). Rural migrants score much higher than their urban counterparts for divorce rates, loveless marriages, extramarital affairs, and the contraction of sexually transmitted diseases (Chongqing Report 2010).

Chang Zizhong, a research fellow at the Center for Development under the State Council, a key policy think-tank in China, could not be more explicit about the link between the happiness of individual rural migrants and the responsibility of the government:

Some people may say that marriage is a personal matter and has nothing to do with society and government. Some say that if the individual can't find someone to marry, even the mayor of the city cannot be expected to be of any help. But in reality, the obstacles preventing young rural migrants from marrying are structural. The obstacles are caused by the socioeconomic disadvantages rural migrants suffer as a result of our *hukou* system and our employment and education systems. The problems are a direct result of young migrants not having their basic rights guaranteed, and not having full access to their entitlements as citizens. Marriage is the next big problem facing rural migrants; it is also becoming a major new challenge facing urban governments.

(Chang Z. 2010a, 44)

Suzhi—*Problem or Solution?*

Although these writers believe the causes of rural migrants' marriage difficulties are structural, and some gesture toward the need to reform the *hukou* system, at the same time they make it clear that such reform cannot singlehandedly solve rural migrants' problems. Many writers draw attention to the "undesirable" attitudes, outlook, and behavior of young rural migrants, and hold the view that, typically, rural migrants suffer from inadequate *suzhi* (Song Y. and Li L. 2015; Xiao X. and Chen A. 2012). The *suzhi* discourse has become widespread since the 1980s, and it refers to the innate and nurtured physical, psychological, intellectual, moral, and ideological qualities of human bodies and their conduct (Jacka 2009). Usually translated as "personal quality," *suzhi* is an extremely resourceful "keyword" (Kipnis 2006) in the anthropological work on rural migrants conducted by scholars outside China. *Suzhi* is usually found by China's middle-class urban residents to be lacking in the behavior of peasants living in poor provinces, and migrants from these provinces (Anagnost 2008; Bakken 2000; Jacka 2009; W. Sun 2009; H. Yan 2008b).

What is broadly described as a *suzhi* deficiency is actually a catch-all expression referring to numerous dimensions of an individual's personal qualities in which they are judged to be lacking—dimensions such as emotional and psychological maturity, knowledge of the law and government policy, an understanding of "correct" moral and ethical codes of behavior, ignorance about sexual and reproductive health, social and interpersonal communication skills, and, above all, the capacity to successfully negotiate the tension between parental expectations and one's own desires, between reality and the ideals of love and romance they have absorbed from popular culture.

Many researchers see young rural migrants' emotional problems to be both a consequence and a symptom of their low *suzhi*—an upshot of their internalization of visual images of love and romance from popular culture, and of their inability to discern the difference between the real and the virtual, the possible and the unrealistic. As a result, according to these scholars, they do not have an accurate understanding of what love is, and they often date someone only to relieve boredom or loneliness, or to meet their need for companionship or sexual gratification. Young migrants are also criticized for not understanding the serious and long-term implications of getting married, and for tending to get married on impulse, thus often leading to "*shan hun, shan li*" ("shotgun weddings" and "flash divorces"), and sometimes to unwanted children (Wu Xinhui 2011; Zhu G. 2012). Furthermore, while rural migrant men are keen to take advantage of living away from family and kinship connections and commitments, alone in the city and free to engage in casual sex, they are often not prepared to accept the responsibilities associated with sexual freedom. As for young rural migrant women, many are eager to experience romance and are curious and open-minded about sex, but they can get involved in unprotected sex or become victims of sexual assault, which sometimes ends in abortion or many other injurious consequences (Huang D. and Ni X. 2020). Not surprisingly, some research suggests that young rural migrants are largely uneducated about a wide range of health-related issues to do with pregnancy, birth control, and childcare (Song Y. and Li L. 2015; Xiao X. and Chen A. 2012).

According to many researchers, low *suzhi* means that rural migrants fall victim to the myriad and cacophonous discourses on love and sexuality they encounter on the internet, and in commercial media, popular culture, and social media. These scholars judge these domains as having a negative impact on impressionable young rural migrants. As one paper observes, many rural migrants "swallow, without digesting, the cultural fast food that is readily on offer" (Xiao X. and Chen A. 2012). As noted by some researchers (e.g., Pan Q. and Ge 2014; Yang L. and Shu 2010), young rural migrants in the city are now widely exposed to urban ways of living, and many have come to expect a similar standard of consumption as city people, although this is unrealistic on their modest incomes. Internet-based popular culture is also widely blamed for the "incorrect" outlook displayed by young rural migrants, who are believed to be particularly susceptible to negative influences. Away from the supervision of teachers and parents, who would otherwise have sought to oppose or control their behavior, and too young to have a fully mature view of the world, they tend to make "irrational" decisions (Cao R. and Zhang L. 2020, 89).

In these narratives of problems, causes, and recommended remedies, we see a juxtaposition of socioeconomic and moral-cultural arguments. Policy recommendations in these writings are a mixture of critiques of the *hukou* policy, on the one hand, and arguments in favor of *suzhi* education, on the other. What is noteworthy is that these two arguments are more often than not presented as two sides of the same coin, as complementary and compatible.

Social scientists in China generally consider the link between low *suzhi* and the problems in rural migrants' love lives as natural and logical, and as part of well-established "conventional wisdom," requiring no substantiation. But the *suzhi* discourse is actually central to the very definition of the so called "disadvantaged social groups," and to the explanation of their formation: according to a common line of analysis, certain social groups become socioeconomically disadvantaged because they have low *suzhi*. Following this "logic," recommendations aimed at solving these individuals' marital problems by increasing their *suzhi* level seem equally logical and natural. Many papers express views similar to the following:

> A key factor that negatively affects rural migrants' attitudes to love and marriage is a lack of *suzhi* and capacity for moral self-discipline. Given this, a crucial pathway is education. Education will elevate their *suzhi* level, raise their awareness of civility, guide them to adopt correct values relating to marriage, and foster in them an upbeat and positive outlook in life.
> (Zhao L. 2013, 130)

If we are to follow the logic implicit in this quotation, rural migrants' lack of marital happiness is caused by their *suzhi* deficiency as well as their rural *hukou* status. As some writers argue, although rural migrants' problems manifest themselves in economic terms, they are nevertheless caused by an individual's incapacity to gain a grounded view of life. According to such critics, young migrant people need to adopt a more realistic viewpoint or—to put it more bluntly—they must cultivate lower expectations about love and the possibility of a happy marriage. Chang Zizhong, the same research fellow who highlighted structural, *hukou*-based inequality in an earlier quotation, also observes that the government needs to find a way to convince rural migrant individuals that they can enjoy the romance of dating despite their difficult material circumstances, and that they can have a happy marriage which, "though not extravagant, can still give them some warmth" (Chang Z. 2010b, 44). Evidently, then, rather than arguing for the redistribution of economic resources in order to reduce inequality between various social groups, these writers believe that rural migrants should learn to be content with whatever level of love, romance, and happiness they can achieve in their inferior status. Here, "unrealistic" expectations about love and marriage are seen as a symptom of *suzhi* deficiency. Although these writers' suggestion may be well-meaning, it nevertheless appears to betray a sense of class superiority, giving the impression of wanting to keep—or put—those in the lower classes in their place.

Another symptom widely discussed in this body of literature is rural migrants' alleged lack of self-awareness, self-reflection, and capacity for psychological "self-adjustment" in general. A typical suggestion from these scholars involves psychological counseling, which they believe to be beneficial to rural migrants whose failure in their pursuit of intimacy has left them feeling depressed, frustrated, and inadequate (Li H. and Pu K. 2011). Here, it seems that the concept of *suzhi* can be a double-edged sword: while it provides a basis for policy recommendations for the provision of skills training, sexual health education, and psychological counseling for migrant workers, it also provides a potent moral foundation on which prejudices associated with this social group can be validated and justified. An even more explicit attempt to frame workers' difficulties as an issue of individual psychological maladjustment can be found in a paper that argues that many concepts and methods in positive psychology (Seligman 1991), which is widely practiced in the United States, could be introduced to help rural migrants convert their negative feelings into positive ones, so that their sense of happiness could be improved (Li L. and Yu Q. 2014).

Young rural migrants' conjectured lack of *suzhi* is argued to have other worrisome consequences, including their frequent inability to negotiate the differences between modern and traditional attitudes and practices concerning sex and sexuality. A recurring narrative in this body of research is the tension facing young rural migrants between modern ideas of individual choice, freedom, autonomy, and romantic love, on the one hand, and pressure from their parents to get married and have children as soon as possible, on the other. Widely exposed to images and discourses of sexual freedom, young rural migrants are reported to be much more accepting than older-generation rural migrants of co-habitation, sex before marriage, extra-marital affairs, and having children out of wedlock. At the same time, unable to resist pressure from both their parents and society at large, many young rural migrants in their late teens and early twenties engage in endless rounds of speed dating arranged by relatives and friends during their visits home, which, as I have observed above, are sometimes followed by hurried weddings, unwanted pregnancies, and hasty divorces (Wu Xinhui 2011; Zhu G. 2012). Thus, these commentators appear to suggest that, rather than taking advantage of the benefits of modern attitudes toward sexuality to maximize their chances for intimacy as their urban middle-class counterparts do (W. Sun and Lei 2017), rural migrants are only interested in casual sex—usually judged to be a superficial dimension of modern relationships. Worse still, this casual attitude toward sex is now widely associated with both marriage breakdown and, worse still, the rise in rates of sexual crime and the spread of sexually transmitted diseases (Li H. and Pu K. 2011; Wu Xinhui 2011; Zhu G. 2012).

Hukou or Suzhi? *A Discussion*

This persistent view of the moral and psychological inadequacy of rural migrants is in sharp contrast to scholarship on rural migrants produced by anthropologists and sociologists outside China. There, structural inequality is not only taken to account for rural migrants' material and economic disadvantage, but it is also seen as shaping the unequal ways in which rural migrants are represented and recognized in the political and cultural domains. Rather than pointing to moral deficiency as a likely cause for the hardships facing rural migrants, this scholarship usually critiques the very discourse of moral education. In contrast to the discourse promoting *suzhi* improvement, outside China the taken-for-granted link between *suzhi* deficiency and rural migrants is widely interrogated (e.g., Anagnost 2004; Jacka 2006, 2009; W. Sun 2009; H. Yan 2008b). For instance, engaging with the Marxist notion of surplus value, Hairong Yan, an anthropologist studying China's rural migrants, argues that *suzhi* functions as an "intangible operator" in the labor contract. She argues that the *suzhi* discourse "facilitates exploitation and makes it invisible," and in so doing, becomes a central element of a neoliberal governmentality (H. Yan 2008a, 498). According to the logic of capital, *suzhi*, a concept that has been rendered measurable and quantifiable, is used to evaluate the economic worth of individuals. This is most vividly embodied in rural migrants' low wages. The systematic practice of hiring migrants as cheap labor—thus enabling profit generation and capital accumulation—is morally justified on the basis of the perceived low *suzhi* of rural people. Accordingly, Yan argues that *suzhi*, considered as an articulation of a person's value, extracts value from rural migrant workers, and this becomes crucial to the economic production of surplus value.

The *suzhi* discourse is not only important to contemporary China's booming, globally oriented market economy, but it is also essential to new post-socialist forms of state governance and state control, as argued by Tamara Jacka, another anthropologist studying rural migrants. This is because the *suzhi* discourse plays a central role in justifying the inclusion and exclusion of certain social groups from access to certain rights and responsibilities (see, e.g., Jacka 2009). Echoing these arguments, Ann Anagnost (2004) points out that *suzhi* provides a crucial means of justifying class exploitation and domination. While the urban middle class justifies its privilege on grounds of their better *suzhi* (Tomba 2014), many aspirational rural migrants internalize this perspective, and respond by trying to improve themselves and become more "cultured" and "civilized" (Jacka 2009).

Despite the seemingly natural and unquestionable ease with which these two arguments—the socioeconomic and the moral-cultural—co-exist within the Chinese-language social sciences research I have examined here, they are informed by radically different political and ideological positions, and are likely to produce vastly different socioeconomic outcomes. After all, the clearly external nature of one's *hukou* status offers a socioeconomic argument against inequality, whereas the complex and putatively internal nature of one's *suzhi* status can be marshaled to support an argument that defends and justifies inequality.

The *hukou*-driven argument made in these China-based scholars' research papers is informed by socioeconomic reality, but there is little explicit elaboration in this literature of the concrete measures that may be feasible; nor is much thought given to the likely ramifications of *hukou* reform for urban middle-class citizens. Perennial reports of vociferous opposition by Beijing and Shanghai residents to proposals granting equal rights to migrants in Beijing (e.g., Nanfang Weekend 2014) serve as a timely reminder of the likely backlash that any *hukou*-based pie-sharing policy recommendations may encounter from urban residents and socioeconomic elites. To practice the "art of self-limitation" (Bauman 2017, 97) may sound good in theory, but it is another matter when it comes to designing a policy that takes concrete steps to make this possible.

As I mentioned earlier, some cities have recently attempted to reform the *hukou* system by adopting a points system, where individuals accumulate points based on their level of education, home ownership, and payment of taxes over a certain number of years. Seen in this light, *hukou* reforms may have well be seen as a key measure for bringing about limited redistribution without fundamentally altering social relations. Indeed, in its earnest desire to uphold its political legitimacy, the CPC has sought to ameliorate social inequality "through limited redistributive intervention without having to deal with inequality-generating productive processes and relations" (Y. Guo 2012, 736). However, so far, such an intervention seems to be too slow and too limited to benefit rural migrants in the near future. This is because, on the surface, this measure appears to have done away with the rural–urban distinction, but in reality, it privileges the wealthy and the educated— those who are usually believed to have good *suzhi*—while continuing to exclude the vast majority of rural migrant workers in low-wage and unskilled jobs. This situation is particularly pronounced in big cities such as Beijing, Shanghai, and Shenzhen, where inter-provincial rural migrants tend to concentrate, and where exorbitant housing prices and living costs all but preclude the great majority of rural migrants from any viable pathways that might lead them toward becoming permanent residents (Wallis 2016).

Conclusion

This discussion about structural inequality and its intimate consequences points to the significance of the young rural migrant as a significant figure worthy of close empirical study. It also argues that this marginalized individual embodies China's most intractable problems of rural–urban inequality, and represents a social class that poses both a theoretical and practical challenge to the state's governing of inequality. We now see that connection between rural migrants' socioeconomic disadvantage and their entrenched incapacity to achieve fulfillment in marriage or intimacy is complex but incontrovertible.

However, concerns about these issues are social as well as moral and legal. Since a stable heterosexual family structure is considered to be the basic unit for the maintenance of social order (Evans 1997), a high number of broken marriages, dysfunctional families, and sexual crimes, as well as a disproportionately high number of single young rural migrants, becomes a direct threat to an orderly society in the eyes of the Chinese government.

But, as we have seen, the government's anxiety about rural migrants' marital problems goes beyond a concern with social order. After more than four decades of economic reforms, successive CPC leadership regimes have become increasingly aware of the threat that a growing level of class-based inequality poses to their political legitimacy. To a great extent, the CPC's continued grip on the nation's political reins is widely judged to rely on its capacity to minimize, if not remove, the feeling of being "stuck" that dominates the day-to-day lives of China's subaltern groups, and particularly young rural people.

It is also clear that scholarly research in China on this topic aims to address this anxiety, yet, as my discussion in this chapter makes clear, this research cannot help but highlight the paucity of effective working solutions that please both the state and their own social class. And herein lies the very root of the anxiety facing the government, China's social sciences researchers, and the country's middle class in general. If anxiety is the feeling of unease about a feared outcome as well as an inability to dispel such a fear, the problem of rural migrants' love lives is indeed a source of anxiety.

Several observations are worth highlighting here. First, academic research in China, especially in the area of the humanities and social sciences, is primarily in the service of the state, whose political agenda significantly shapes the research topics and research questions Chinese scholars choose to pursue. Second, the purpose of this research, especially in relation to current or ongoing social issues, is not just to understand and account for why these social issues exist, but also, and more importantly, to identify possible solutions, or at least to provide recommendations for governments at various levels. And third, as a consequence of the second point, social sciences researchers in China play an important role, not just in informing public discussion, but also in shaping the whole policy-making process.

This is not to say that these social scientists are unmoved by the plight of disenfranchised groups. Indeed, many China-based scholars, especially those from a rural family background such as Li De (2011), have dedicated their research careers to documenting, often with sympathy and understanding, the conundrums and frustrations experienced by rural migrants. Moreover, both the structural and cultural explanations outlined in this chapter recognize, first, that the marital difficulties facing rural migrants are widespread and their emotional needs are not being met; and second, that something needs to be done to address this problem. However, as my discussion has demonstrated, within China the production of knowledge about the problem is driven by an intention to govern vulnerable communities from the top down and to "manage" inequality, rather than by an anthropological desire to understand how social inequality shapes the emotional experiences of rural migrant individuals in their everyday lives.

There is a broad consensus that, whereas urban middle-class citizens can manage the problems in their private lives without much government intervention, the state should not ignore the private lives of rural migrants. At the same time, it is clear to all that there needs to be fundamental policy changes in areas such as social welfare, housing, healthcare, employment, and education if rural migrants' marriage prospects are ever to improve. Also clear, however, is the fact that these changes may end up alienating the urban middle class. For this reason, although the scholarly knowledge produced by China's social scientists has gone some way toward shedding important light on this pressing social issue, the politics that informs and governs the production of such knowledge can extend itself only far enough to concede the point that rural migrants have emotional needs and these needs are not currently being met.

What the discussion in this chapter brings to light is the hidden connection between structural inequality and discourses of governing. Having pointed out that the *hukou* system is a major structural cause of rural migrants' marital problems, social scientists in China nevertheless have to stop short of proposing the abolition of *hukou* as a structurally based solution, and would not even entertain the idea of criticizing the state as the instigator of such systemic inequality.

Thus, for the reasons discussed earlier, most of the policy recommendations made by these writers focus on improving the *suzhi* level of rural migrants. Here, *suzhi* is framed both as a cause of inequality and as the site for its possible solution; more specifically, we see a systematic deployment of this cultural-moral discourse for the purpose of legitimating and governing—rather than reducing or eliminating—social inequality. And, while the *hukou* system is clearly recognized as a central cause of structural inequality, it remains the elephant in the room in these researchers' attempts to grapple with possible remedies for that inequality. In its place, *suzhi* is presented as a discursive proxy for *hukou*—one that can be pitched as more actionable than *hukou* reform, especially within a prevailing neoliberal ethos that emphasizes individual responsibility. However, as we have seen here, the *suzhi* discourse results from as well as further contributes to the political and social concern surrounding rural migrants' love lives. As a result, shifting the focus away from *hukou* and onto *suzhi* is far from convincing, both as a possible cause of rural migrants' marital problems, and as a possible solution to them.

Chapter 2

FROM REVOLUTION TO CONSUMPTION: THE CULTURAL POLITICS OF THE FUTURE

Introduction

Li Yongsheng, a construction worker from rural Sichuan Province, hasn't seen his wife for more than a year. In fact, both his wife and their son are 700 kilometers away, at her mother's home in Sha'anxi Province. Spring Festival is around the corner, and Li feels the absence of his loved ones even more keenly. But the construction project on which Li is working is on a tight completion schedule. After much debating with himself, he decides to stay in Chongqing and keep working. Extra shifts mean more money, and Li wants to save money as quickly as possible to buy an apartment in Sichuan, where his wife and son can eventually settle down and have some stability. Li spends as little money as possible on himself. His daily lunch is a bowl of noodles with lots of chili, and he never buys clothes for himself. His family could come to join him, but to save the cost of the train fares he tells his wife to stay with her parents in Sha'anxi rather than come to visit him. This is an all-too-common predicament for China's rural migrant workers. But Li's story has a happy ending. His company decides to give him a surprise by secretly arranging for his family to come to Chongqing for a family reunion on the construction site, much to Li's gratitude and excitement. Li's story was broadcast on China Central Television (CCTV) on February 6, 2019, in a special annual segment of the prime-time news bulletin called "Reports from the Grassroots during the Spring Festival" (*Xinchun zou jiceng*) (CCTV 2019).

CCTV is the centerpiece of the Communist Party of China's propaganda machine. Its 7:00 p.m. daily news bulletin is widely understood to be the most authoritative and "politically correct," albeit perhaps not the most riveting, coverage of news and current affairs. For this reason, the content of CCTV's news bulletins is scrutinized most closely by the censors, and carefully studied by both ordinary viewers and Party officials—not because it is taken to present transparent and objective information, but because it is the most reliable evidence of the government's position and policies on certain issues.

Since their inception in 2011, these special reports have been part of the state television network's coordinated efforts to showcase the central and local governments' people-centered philosophy of governing. The kinds of stories included in these "Grassroots Reports" are not routine news reporting in the strict, technical sense; their suitability is judged not according to the sort of criteria of newsworthiness that are widely assumed in journalism, such as timeliness, novelty, or scale of impact—as is the case with disasters, crises, or accidents. Rather, they are stories about real, ordinary individuals whom reporters have "dug out" from the grassroots of society. Featuring everyday people who face difficult circumstances yet exemplify a "positive energy," and combining the narrative styles of documentary, reality television, and news reporting, these vignettes are intended to convert negative feelings such as frustration, discontent, and despair into hope for the future and gratitude to the government. Conceived thus, they comprise a particular news genre that attempts to renovate the old ways of doing propaganda. Many "ideological workers"—including CCTV's own news crews—now realize that the old, hackneyed sloganeering forms of propaganda do not work, and that new forms of indoctrination must, in the words of Zheng Xiuguo, head of CCTV's news team, work like "gentle rain soaking the earth without making any sound" (*xiyu run wusheng*) (Zheng Xiuguo 2013).

It is therefore clear that the discourse of governing takes concrete shape not only through elite, state-funded research in academia—as we have seen in the last chapter—but equally importantly, in the more accessible space of state media. And, as Li's story shows, national television seems to be the perfect space to propagate the state-preferred position on how individuals of limited means and resources should negotiate personal/familial relations and conduct intimate matters. The take-home message of Li's story, as the announcer says at the end of the story, is this: "Loyalty during separation over a distance of 700 kilometers is possible because of love. Li is prepared to work as hard as he can for the future of his family, and he is able to do so because of the continuing support of his loved ones."

The story of Li is one such "positive energy" story with a clear take-home message: Life is hard at the moment, and conjugal intimacy, as well as the chance of seeing one's children grow up, is impossible for the time being. But as long as there is love, distance and separation should not be a problem. What awaits us at the end of this hard work and temporary loneliness is a better life and a happy family.

What is the discursive usefulness of telling the story of rural migrant construction worker Li Yongshen, an ordinary man with few means, on national television? How is the story told in a way that assists the state's agenda of reconciling/managing class inequality? How do discourses of governmentality construct the future and encourage hope, despite the growing precarity that currently confronts people in their everyday lives, especially those in marginalized social groups? What moral, cultural, and rhetorical resources does this ideology of the future draw on, and to what extent does it represent a departure, even a rupture, from China's past—both traditional and revolutionary? Furthermore, if the political project of a "happy life for all Chinese" has become a key ingredient of the official "China Dream" rhetoric, does this project have any buy-in from China's most disenfranchised socioeconomic groups? To address these questions is a matter of urgent political concern, since they afford us a hitherto unexplored prism through which to assess the political purchase of the government's China Dream project and its prospects for stability maintenance.

Situated in an extended analysis of CCTV's love stories, this chapter pursues these questions by taking an approach that is at once analytical, ethnographic, and historical. My aim is to pinpoint a particular moment in China's state capitalism when the discourse of romantic love becomes a means of managing, if not solving, social inequality. To effectively engage with the questions raised above, I approach CCTV's love stories on a number of levels: political economy, social semiotics, viewer interpretation, and historical connection. In methodological terms, I put CCTV's love stories to a number of uses. First, these stories are part of a heuristic ethnographic device, functioning as vital conversational fodder and an interview tactic, for the purpose of generating among interviewees a set of potentially different or even contradictory statements and positions. Second, the stories themselves function as a prism through which we can understand the political, economic, and media-institutional context in which the official discourse of conjugal love is produced. Third, they present themselves as an example of the narrative forms and strategies that are deployed to construct a normative way of imagining the future. And fourth, the stories can be viewed as a textual palimpsest, containing traces of mutated past tropes and speech acts against which we can read the gaps, disruptions, and continuities in the new "consumption-plus-love" narrative framework.

The first of these uses—the ethnographic—warrants a brief explanation. Brokering an exchange between media studies and anthropology, this method is intended to produce neither an ethnography of rural migrants' media consumption—important though that is in its own right—nor an "objective" account of migrants' lives. Instead, it aims to juxtapose these two bodies of material with the aim of bringing to light the tensions, contradictions, ambiguities, and sometimes even the complicities between and within them. As I have discussed elsewhere (W. Sun 2017), using media material to generate ethnographic data has two methodological benefits: first, it shifts the focus away from the interviewees themselves and onto a fictional (depersonalized) set of moral circumstances and dilemmas; and second, it sheds light on how emotional textures, love, and feelings of intimacy are also products of particular kinds of social, political, cultural, and economic structures—thereby getting at the often complex relationship between mainstream media/cultural expressions and the subject positions of rural migrant individuals.

Love on the Assembly Line

In February 2013, around the time of the Chinese New Year, CCTV launched a series of news reports for the annual "Reports from the Grassroots during the Spring Festival," under the overall title "Love on the Assembly Line" (*Liushuixian shangde aiqing*). Each segment featured a young rural migrant couple and their relationship—some already married, others still at the courting stage. With the notable exception of one pair, none of the couples had an apartment to their name, which meant that the woman in each couple was facing social pressure against her romantic involvement with a propertyless man. As a result, their relationship was put to the test. Life was hard for all these couples at the time of the television reports, but each of their stories ended with an optimistic message: as long as they loved each other and worked hard for a future together, things would somehow work out.

Around the same time as the CCTV stories, the media, academics, and labor-advocacy groups alike also started to call on the government to address the difficulties many rural migrants faced in finding marriage partners. Feng Gong, a nationally well-known performance artist—in addition to being a member of the national committee of the Chinese People's Political Consultative Conference (CPPCC)—formally submitted a motion to the Twelfth National People's Congress in 2013, alerting the government to the fact that many young male rural migrants were having trouble finding a marriage partner, primarily because of their low socioeconomic status, but especially because of their inability to own a home. Feng argued that to be able to find conjugal love is rural migrants' "China Dream," and that the government should work hard to "elevate the level of their happiness" (Shao 2013).

While waiting for their "level of happiness" to be elevated, rural migrants—long cast in the role of cheap labor—were now expected to become better consumers. At the beginning of 2016, rural migrants were singled out as a possible solution to the problem of surplus housing stock. According to a CCTV news story on January 31, 2016, real estate totaling an area of 0.7 billion square meters lay vacant at that time, mostly in townships and small cities. The experts and policy makers quoted in the news item suggested that a key strategy for solving this problem could be to remove restrictions resulting from the *hukou* (household registration) system, so that rural migrants could afford to purchase these properties (CCTV 2016).

Meanwhile, in the big cities, housing shortages and volatility in the real estate market were stratifying the urban population, ranging from those who were desperately trying to get a foothold in the market, to those wishing to capitalize on the housing crisis as a form of investment. To ease the pressure, in early 2016 local governments issued new regulations stipulating that a couple who already owned one property but wished to purchase another must pay a larger deposit and higher assorted fees. In order to get around this regulation, some couples were resorting to "fake divorces." By late 2016, the Chinese media were brimming with stories of couples who were getting divorced in order to purchase a second apartment, but with no intention of ending their relationship—only to realize that a fake divorce could have very real consequences: some relationships fell apart as a result of this investment strategy (Xinhuanet 2016).

A few observations can be made by juxtaposing the housing issues faced by these two different social groups. As Li Zhang (2008) points out, private ownership is not merely an expression of class difference but also the very means through which class-specific subjects are formed. At the same time, notwithstanding class differences, housing is now inexorably linked to the achievement of a "happy life," yet in some cases the pursuit of the property ownership dream can end up becoming a hindrance to one's affective fulfillment—the very thing it is supposed to facilitate. For a party-state that is concerned with political legitimacy and social stability, the challenge of managing class inequality cannot merely be a matter of policy adjustment; it must also involve adjustments in the population's affect and mentality, particularly in their ways of imagining the future.

Decades of economic reforms in China, characterized by a "tense articulation between neoliberal logic and socialist sovereignty" (Ong and Zhang 2008, 2), have led to some enduring paradoxes. The state has retreated from the provision of a range of public goods and services, and clearly prefers to govern "at a distance" on issues relating to individuals. Following the transition from a socialist economy to a privatized market economy, the population is now encouraged to actively pursue a wide range of self-governing and self-enterprising practices that shape and optimize their life chances (Ong and Zhang 2008, 8).

More than ever before, the projection of a better future, or at least raising hope for such a future, is crucial to the political project of governing "from afar." Tracing the shift from the utopianism of communist China to the hedonism of the reform era, moral philosopher Jiwei Ci (2014, 206) observes that utopianism, which derives from the European notion of time as progress and the future as the realm of perfect happiness, gave the Chinese people a heightened sense of meaning and purpose. In return for that promised future happiness, people were prepared "to believe, to obey, to strive, to sacrifice, and to expect—in ways unprecedented in Chinese history" (Ci 1994, 4). However, Ci argues that by making the future the "locus of an ambitious goal" (4), this utopianism, though powerful, was dangerous and likely to lead to disappointment. When Ci was writing this in the early 1990s, that disappointment had already led to nihilism and hedonism—what he later called the "desublimation of the original utopianism" (Ci 2014, 26). Abandoning higher values of liberty and equality, the CPC, with no higher goal than to maintain stability, now declares its ultimate goal as being to meet people's "desire for a happy life" (Xi 2012b). Ci's analysis of how the future is configured in the revolutionary utopian discourse is instructive, but he stops short of addressing the question of whether the trope of the future has any continuing relevance in the CPC's contemporary project of stability maintenance. This is despite his observation (Ci 1994) that the Party, in order to justify its ongoing leadership, has had to provide moral guidance, however ineffectual and vacuous, to the Chinese population.

Of course, it is not just the Chinese people who have had to make adjustments during times of social transition. In *Cruel Optimism*, Lauren Berlant (2011, 2–4) argues that liberal–capitalist societies can no longer be counted on to deliver on their promise of prosperity, security, upward mobility, and enduring intimacy. Postwar optimism has run into an "impasse" of the present, whereby people, despite living with precarity, contingency, and crisis, remain attached to the fantasies of the good life. To Berlant, this optimism is a "scene of negotiated sustenance that makes life bearable as it presents itself ambivalently, unevenly, incoherently" (14). She argues that such optimism can be cruel because it has the power to make people believe that, despite evidence of the "instability, fragility, and dear cost" of the precarious present, life will somehow work out in the future, and that they and the world will "add up to something" (2). To Berlant, examining the "improvisation of genre" (6) as well as the "patterns of adjustment in specific aesthetic and social contexts" (7) is crucial if we want to track the "impact of neoliberal restructuring on fantasies of the good life" (18).

The politics of the future as conceived by Ci and Berlant presents a good point of departure for my pursuit of a number of questions in this chapter.

Stories, Genre, and the Context of Production

The CCTV series of love stories in 2013 consisted of five segments, each one lasting between five and fifteen minutes, and they were broadcast over five days, starting on February 4. The first, called "Home Is Where You Are," centers on a couple who had met on the assembly line in a factory in Baoding, Hebei Province. In this segment, Qiu Guoying, from Inner Mongolia, and his wife Hao Ranran, a local girl from a nearby township, talk about how they had courted. Her parents had objected to the marriage, as his family was poor. Though under a lot of pressure, Qiu went ahead and married Hao, and the couple set out to realize their dream—earning enough money to put a deposit on a flat in Baoding. They scrimped and saved every penny; Qiu worked extra shifts, and never took time off work. And their hard work finally paid off: viewers see the couple about to move into their new flat. While busy sanding the wall in their new apartment, Qiu tells the reporter that "he feels only sweet happiness in his heart, even though he has tasted a lot of bitterness." His wife, also busy furbishing the apartment, says, with obvious rapture, that she cannot wait to see the installation of a big wardrobe that can hold lots of clothes. Qiu has also been promoted from a worker to a supervisor. "He has his goals, and he's so driven to achieve them. Their story is like a motivational film," says one of Qiu's colleagues to the reporter.

Another couple featured in the series was Xiao Han and his fiancée Xiao Qing, whose story was broadcast on February 12 and 13 in 2013. Entitled "Xiao Han's Wedding," the segment is about a young man from Anhui who has brought his bride-to-be, a young woman from Sha'anxi, to get married in his parents' village home—a run-down dwelling with muddy paths. The couple are painfully aware that the groom is usually expected to build a new house for his bride—something Han cannot afford. Qing loves him, but she is under a lot of pressure; her mother objects to the marriage, and her girlfriends think that "she is selling herself short." She cries as she talks to the camera, saying that both she and her fiancé are under enormous pressure. The reporter and his camera follow the couple to the local marriage registration office in the county's township, and then to their humble but happy wedding ceremony. Han tells the reporter that he is trying to start a business back in his hometown, and hopes to save enough money to purchase a place of his own one day. He declares to his bride, "I love you. I'll take care of you forever. You will not regret marrying me" (CCTV 2013).

The final story in the series, entitled "The World Outside Is Really Wonderful," broadcast on February 16, tells the story of two young people who dare to dream. Both born in the 1990s in Fuyang, Anhui Province, the couple met on the assembly line in a factory in Ningbo, Jiangsu Province, and fell in love, although at the time of their interview they still lived in separate dormitories. Apart from the fact that they cannot afford a flat or a car, and can barely get by on their combined wages (6,000 *yuan* a month between the two of them[1]), their most immediate obstacle is that the young woman's father objects to their marriage, believing that his daughter should marry someone more skilled, someone from a more financially comfortable family or, preferably, someone with a small business of his own. Viewers see the couple going home, hoping to persuade her father. When asked by the reporter what his dream is, the young man, wearing his work uniform and standing next to his girlfriend, says, "My dream is to have enough money to put a deposit on a property somewhere in Ningbo. I don't know if it's realistic, but that's my dream."

The same optimism governs the narrative in "Chen Huan's Choice," broadcast on February 11. A married couple from rural Anhui are eking out a living in Shanghai. Chen Huan's husband came to Shanghai in 1992; he now works as a window repairer while she works on the assembly line. Their child has to stay behind in Anhui due to *hukou*-related restrictions on schooling for rural migrants' children. In order to keep the family together, her husband suggests that they go back home to start a new business. But going home would mean that Chen Huan would have to give up her job, as well as a lot of the things she likes about city life; moreover, she believes that she would need to work harder back in the village. However, she has agreed to go home even though she and her husband may have different views about what their future should be. The story ends with the couple being seen off at the long-distance bus station, with the voiceover reminding viewers that "as long as two people are together and support each other, they have a good future, even though it may be simple and ordinary."

As discussed in the last chapter, from the state's perspective of maintaining social stability through morality and law and order, the growing number of emotionally lonely and sexually unfulfilled young rural migrants of a marriageable age is deeply concerning. Thus framed, effective propaganda must be able to facilitate what Berlant (2011, 15) calls a necessary "affective adjustment" by convincing rural migrants that, despite their present "stuckness," their future will be bright, as long as they work hard.

Foxconn Workers' Perspectives

Do these stories resonate with the individuals in the cohort they seek to represent? How do migrant workers respond to the state's attempts to redefine love and marital happiness in the ways described so far? As part of my longitudinal study of the romantic experiences of young factory workers in Foxconn's Shenzhen plant,[2] I decided to use these CCTV stories as visual prompts to begin what turned out to be intimate conversations with workers about their private emotional lives.[3]

I started these conversations by showing my interviewees video clips of CCTV's "love stories" on an iPad. It turned out that, with the exception of one interviewee, none of them had seen these stories when they were broadcast by CCTV. In fact, many told me that they seldom watched CCTV news, or television in general, preferring to get their news and entertainment from digital and social media on their mobile phone.

My interviewees' responses were diverse, and considerably differentiated along lines of gender and age (the 80s cohort versus the 90s cohort). One young female work expressed surprise that CCTV would report on the love lives of people "like us." A few seemed bemused that CCTV went to such lengths to cover this topic.[4] Many respondents considered the series to have a "propaganda" purpose, although some explained the propagandistic nature of these stories more explicitly than others. But the most common response was that the stories were not "realistic." By this, workers did not mean that they did not find the stories to be true and authentic—in fact, on seeing Xiao Han and his fiancée walking along a muddy path on a rainy day to get married, more than one interviewee commented that the path in their own home village was "just as muddy." What they were reacting against was the stories' optimistic projection of the future, as well as the question of what constitutes a realistic level of consumption that rural migrants should aspire to. To be sure, rural migrants, especially from the second-generation cohort, aspire to a lifestyle and consumption standards befitting middle-class urban residents, and they exercise their agency as consumer-citizens in the enthusiastic uptake of a wide range of consumer goods including, most visibly, mobile phones and fashion items. However, when there is too great a discrepancy between what they are inspired to aim for—e.g., ownership of a property in the city—and their actual consumption power, these stories can only end up having an alienating rather than an encouraging effect.

My conversations with these workers made it clear that owning a place of their own in the city where they currently live and work was a pipe dream. In fact, it would also be beyond the dreams of many of the young, educated professionals who are struggling to gain a foothold there, it being one of the most expensive cities in China. The most that these workers could ever hope for would be to save up enough money for a deposit on an apartment in the closest township to their village, although even that would be beyond the reach of the majority of them. A handful of workers told me that this is what they are doing—putting a deposit on an apartment—but their apartments lie empty while they continue to work in Shenzhen: jobs in rural townships are scarce, and, with very little capital to their name, rural migrants have few, if any, opportunities to start a successful business there. The most affordable option, then, is to build a home on the rural land where their parents live. However, this is their least attractive prospect, given that most young people have no intention of going back to live in their village. Moreover, a not inconsiderable number of young workers I spoke to did not even have enough money to build in their own village.

At the end of the CCTV story about the hard-working Qiu Guoying and his frugal wife Hao Ranran, the announcer observes: "For rural migrant workers earning 1,000–2,000 [*yuan*] a month, the dream of buying a flat seems far-fetched.

But with their own hard work, this couple has made it possible" (CCTV 2013). Although this may be true, the rural migrants I interviewed for this study believe that the couple gave up too much in exchange for a chance to buy a house. One male worker said:

> I notice that they have no friends to help them move, and no friends to help them refurbish their place. The guy spends all his waking hours working, and has no time for friends. Who wants to live like that?

Another male worker agreed: "Happiness is not just about a man and a woman and their property. It's also about having friends and enjoying life—getting together with friends, smoking, drinking, and eating with them." And a third worker, also male, chimed in: "If this is love, it's too exhausting; I'm better off without it." It was clear that many of my male worker interviewees did not like the take-home message from this story. To some of them, friendship and homosocial ties are important, and the pursuit of a domestic utopia based exclusively on kinship-based support and conjugal love is undesirable and unworthy.

In addition, although workers typically do not object to CCTV's message of putting love before money, they do refuse to take a leap of faith, as the stories urge them to do, and accept that, even though the present is bad, the future will be better. Many workers told me that, based on their experience, it would be foolhardy to believe in the future. For Jiang YY, a man in his late twenties from Hubei Province, having walked away empty-handed from numerous blind dates arranged by matchmakers, there is every reason to be skeptical about what blind faith in the future may bring:

> Sure, Xiao Han and Xiao Qing's story ends in their happy wedding, but who knows what's going to happen after that? Xiao Han has a five-year plan, but we all know how hard it is to start a business. Would Xiao Qing still love him if (when) he fails to deliver on his promise of buying a property? I'm pretty sure the odds are against him. I haven't seen any evidence suggesting that he has what it takes to afford a property.

While fantasies of a "good life" interpellate individuals across the entire social spectrum, the cruelty of such optimism lies in the fact that rural migrants' consumption power remains woefully low, yet more than ever before, they are hailed by both the state and the market to become aspiring consumers. A 2015 survey by the National Bureau of Statistics (NBS) indicates that rural migrants' average monthly income was then 3,072 *yuan*, with those in the manufacturing sector earning an average of 2,970 *yuan* a month (NBS 2016). In addition to earning significantly less than their urban counterparts, rural migrants are also deprived of discounted housing prices, subsidized health care, free education for their children, and other public goods and services that urban-*hukou* workers and public service employees take for granted. This cruelty was vividly brought home in June 2016, when forty-six-year-old Huang Ying, a rural migrant cleaner in Hefei, Anhui Province, hit the national news. Huang and her family made an initial deposit on an apartment in Hefei using her husband's and her own lifetime savings, which they had earned by each working at two jobs, and then moved into the apartment. But they failed to pay the next installment of their loan by the due date agreed to in the contract. So, when the market value of property in Hefei skyrocketed by 300 percent and the vendor wanted to rescind the contract, Huang found that neither the law nor the market was on her side (Han and Chang 2016). Feeling trapped and desperate, and in deep debt, Huang jumped from a tall building and killed herself. Ironically, Huang's death took place just six months after the launch of the policy encouraging rural migrants to purchase surplus housing in small cities and townships, which I mentioned earlier.

CCTV's love stories represent a new speech act of promise-making, whereby the trope of a better future is conjured up to dull the pain of the present. This forms a sharp contrast to the revolutionary-era proletarian speech act of "speaking bitterness," wherein the hardships of the past would be ritualistically evoked to accentuate a happy present. In the case of the CCTV stories, however, although material deprivation, psychological insecurity, and emotional stress are very present and real, they are rationalized as a natural, teleological progression toward a better future. The consumption-plus-love formula may have eliminated the revolutionary utopia, but a trope of utopian optimism for the future still serves the CPC's efforts to produce hope. But this is not a message that young migrants like Jiang YY are prepared to buy. Workers' comments also make it clear that the notion of pursuing the kind of individualistic, romantic love promoted in these stories would not work for them. They typically do not make decisions about their love lives defiantly or independently of their parents' and peers' opinions, as the individuals in the CCTV stories appeared to do. My interviewees reminded me that, unlike their urban, middle-class professional counterparts, they can less afford to displease their parents and risk alienating themselves from their kin. Because their prospects in the city remain uncertain, their parents are, after all, the only people they can really count on.

Many of the workers I spoke to about these CCTV stories exemplified the dilemma of being caught between parental opinions and their own desires. My conversations with them made me realize this: young migrant workers crave love, but they face two possible scenarios. Some, like WJ, a female Foxconn worker from Henan Province, love someone but, facing myriad obstacles, are too scared to move to the point of putting their love to test. (I discuss WJ at greater length in Chapter 5.) Others, such as twenty-eight-year-old Qing ZB from Hubei Province, have not even been given a chance to get to first base romantically. Most of Qing's arranged dates have not gone beyond the first meeting. After several years of unsuccessful blind dates, he has become increasingly despondent. But the pressure from his parents continues unabated: "My parents are so worried that their hair has turned white." Qing recounted one of his several disappointments:

> I met this girl, as arranged by a matchmaker. We liked each other enough to exchange QQ numbers,[5] and we talked on QQ a few times. But then the

matchmaker said the girl's parents wanted 200,000 *yuan* as a betrothal gift. To raise that amount, my parents would have needed to borrow 100,000 *yuan*. The girl said to me, "Everyone else borrows money to get married. Why can't your family?" But I didn't want my parents to go into debt because of me. I have a younger brother who will have to build a home plus raise a betrothal gift in order to get married. If we're in debt now, it would be even harder to borrow money in the future. So, I said, "Forget it," and then came to Shenzhen.

Qing's experience is typical of many Foxconn workers I talked to. But despite his experience, he does not blame the girl:

She was also under a lot of pressure. If she agreed to go out with someone whose family couldn't afford a new home or betrothal gift, she would be looked down upon by others in the village. They compete with one another. Girls don't want to look like losers.

Qing's statement helped me to understand the complexity of rural migrants' responses to the CCTV narratives. On the one hand, they notice that these love stories do not realistically represent their own lives, and that their projection of an optimistic future is not convincing. On the other hand, despite their rejection of certain elements of the stories, many workers endorsed the individuals portrayed in them as role models who embodied a superior moral position to their own. After watching the story of Xiao Han's wedding to Xiao Qing, an immediate response from most rural migrant men was, "If only there were more women like Xiao Qing!" In expressing their preference for an ideal world over a present one—one in which economic considerations (ownership of a flat, the size of a betrothal gift) do not get in the way of love—these workers are not uncritically endorsing CCTV's message. Rather, it may well be because, in comparison with the love-as-consumption logic implicit in the market discourses, the official definition of love at least presents workers with a set of moral parameters that resonate with their economic circumstances and within which they can make sense of their present and future. Several single male interviewees made comments along the following lines: "Girls nowadays are too pragmatic. I would have a better chance of finding someone if there were more girls like them [the girls in the stories]." Similarly, several young women made comments similar to this one:

I think boys like to complain about us putting material things before feelings. But I think that's just their excuse for not wanting to try hard. I would be prepared to go out with someone without a property or betrothal gifts, as long as he showed a willingness and potential to acquire these things in the future, like the men do in these stories.

It seems that, despite the differences between these men and women, they all articulate a strong preference for a different world, where love trumps economic considerations.

Key Ingredients in the Love Stories

It is clear from workers' statements that the effectiveness of CCTV's love stories as government propaganda is questionable. Nevertheless, they warrant careful analysis because they present important clues to, first, what the officially acceptable framework for imagining the future is; and second, how this framework informs the ways in which inequality is narrated.

To a considerable extent, CCTV's love stories underscore the essential elements of the "modern ideology of romantic love" (Illouz 1997, 75). As befitting the mode of romantic love, the love of rural migrants in these stories is "irrational," on the one hand, and "disinterested," on the other (Illouz 1997, 75; 2007, 90). By depicting young migrants in pursuit of love in opposition to their parents, who base their notion of "romantic love" on calculations of status compatibility and profitable transactions, these stories seem to reference the anti-traditional, anti-feudal individualism that was promoted by the CPC during the revolutionary era. But my interviewees' statements make it very clear that the idea of going against the wishes of one's parents—and hence risking alienating them—in order to pursue love is both naïve and self-defeating.

At the same time, the "modern" discourse of romantic love embraced by young rural migrants in the CCTV stories is fused with a number of other key ingredients. In these stories, love is not commendable unless it is consummated through heterosexual marriage. None of the stories portray love in the form of dating without the intention to marry, and although sexual experience before and outside marriage is common among rural migrant workers, all the couples in the stories are either married or are intending to marry. In fact, this emphasis on marriage can be seen as a gesture toward what some call the "re-traditionalisation of gender norms" (Martin 2016). The emphasis on the need for romantic love to end in marriage is worth noting, since the government considers a stable heterosexual family structure to be the basic unit for the maintenance of social order (Evans 1997). The government regards marriage to be especially important for a growing number of single, unmarried men from the socioeconomic margins, due to the long-standing perceived connection between frustrated marital aspirations and social unrest at various points in Chinese history (Brownell and Wasserstrom 2002; Sommers 2000).

While the consumption–love connection is at least three decades old and is certainly not specific to China, CCTV's stories pinpoint a particular moment when this trope makes a conspicuous entry into official discourses. Furthermore, these love stories, while referencing the logic of the market, are significant for at least two additional reasons. First, they signal a discursive shift in the way rural migrants are constructed. These stories make an explicit and deliberate link between consumption and rural migrants as aspiring consumers. Far from being ideal consumers, rural migrants have until now been synonymous with cheap labor in capitalist production. But now they are positioned as the new consumer-citizens who dare to dream of a life with a bright consumerist future, all the while fulfilling their role of supplying cheap labor. Although owning a property remains a fantasy for most rural migrants, a handful of individuals who have "made it"—like Hao Ranran and her husband—are now being turned into role models. This transition in the role of rural migrants—from cheap labor to consumers—makes economic sense, given that their increased participation in consumption may help stimulate domestic production, which is key not only to sustained economic growth but also to the continuing existence of jobs for rural migrants like themselves.

The CCTV stories and others like them are also significant in that they provide a moral template according to which inequality between groups with different levels of consumption power is to be narrated. Unlike those urban middle-class consumers promoted in advertisements and myriad other cultural expressions, the individuals in these stories actually spend little money. In "Home Is Where You Are," Hao Ranran demonstrated the virtue of frugality in a way that is strikingly reminiscent of the socialist era. She racked her brains about how to cut the grocery bills. She always bought the cheapest vegetables, and at one point the couple lived on a discarded cabbage for two weeks. It is worth noting that all the individuals in this series of stories make it clear that they have no higher goal than finally being able to purchase a place of their own. In other words, they are only probationary consumer-citizens; they voluntarily adopt a frugal lifestyle now in order to realize the ultimate consumer dream of owning a home in the future. Hao and her husband are model migrant workers here, not only because they embody the achievability of the housing dream, but also because they demonstrate a willingness to live in the hope of something happening in the future while enduring their present hardship. This willingness to wait and to defer whatever present material comforts they can survive without is key to the political project of restructuring the fantasy of the good life (Berlant 2011). Furthermore, Hao and her husband are so driven by their goal of owning an apartment that they seem to have divested themselves of their regular connections with friends and colleagues. This willingness to sever extra-familial ties and draw strength only from kin-based and conjugal support is consistent with state policies that encourage not only self-enterprise but also a competitive attitude toward those outside the kinship circle. Yet, as my interviewees argue, such a strategy may not be sustainable or culturally agreeable.[6]

Clearly, these CCTV stories aim to push a new message regarding love: love does exist and you can enjoy it now, even though currently you do not own a flat, you do not have a good job, and you do not have enough money. Love is not what you feel after you succeed in getting these material things; love is what happens when both of you work toward them. Thus, rural migrants who complain about not having enough money and therefore not being happy in their present life need to make an "affective adjustment" (Berlant 2011) in their mindset. As CCTV's Zheng Xiuguo reflects, in the context of producing the story of "Xiao Han's Wedding":

> On the surface, it looks like there's nothing romantic about the love between Xiao Han and his girlfriend—they met on the factory shop floor, and even though they've dated for four years, they still don't have a place of their own. Xiao Qing's mother objects to the relationship, as she hopes her daughter will

marry someone with more resources. But Xiao Han wins her future mother-in-law over with his "five-year plan," and according to that plan, he'll build a house for his wife by the end of five years.

(Zheng Xiuguo 2013)

Although the CCTV producer sees fit to let the narrative balance hinge on the promise of what will happen in five years, none of my interviewees who were shown the story shared this sense of optimism. Just as Xiao Han made a promise about what will happen in five years, CCTV's love stories are also speech acts that make a promise about the future, when "something" may or may not happen. In this redefinition of love, individual rural migrants are not only desiring subjects but they must also pursue their desires in an appropriate fashion. Only when they do so can the state endorse their personal, mundane home-building activities as legitimate—even admirable—self-constituting activities. Both Qiu Guoying and Hao Ranran are model migrants, because they are not just desiring subjects but they also behave most responsibly in order to obtain the objects of their desire. They are thus portrayed as following the example of China's new affluent groups in their participation in consumer activities. At the same time, they adopt class-appropriate methods of going about these activities. The main message promoted here is clear: discontent and disillusion about the present, however "stuck" it is, are not commendable sentiments. Instead, individuals should be willing to "eat bitterness" for the sake of a better future.

A model rural migrant is also unencumbered by class consciousness. In the post-Mao polity, the individual who embraces consumer values and is passionate about pursuing the dream of domestic bliss is politically more "correct" than someone with a revolutionary fervor for social change. Readers of Yang Mo's revolutionary novel, *Song of Youth*, may remember that Yu Yongze lost out in a love triangle because, unlike his rival Lu Jiachuan the revolutionary, Yu was only interested in building a cozy home for his lover Lin Daojing and was not interested in the revolution. Today, the state makes it clear that China only needs individuals like Yu Yongze, and revolutionary lovers "need not apply." The individuals in CCTV's stories are exemplary because they demonstrate a capacity to channel their passion "correctly" to achieve an outcome that is consistent with the CPC's dual imperative to transition the Chinese economy from production to consumption while also promoting cross-class harmony.

The sexuality of women and men is configured differently from each other in this new consumption-plus-love formula, returning to older, deeply entrenched assumptions regarding gender roles and what can count as acceptable forms of sexuality. None of the migrant women in these stories resort to their sexual capital to equalize their economic disadvantage. There are no "gold diggers" here. Instead of aiming to "marry up," as Chinese women traditionally do (Jin, Zhang, and Yang 2016), they find romance within their own cohort. Finally, they are willing to go back to their hometown for the sake of their children and families, even though they themselves have adapted to city living and would prefer to stay. More importantly, these women demonstrate the desirable quality of being more conservative in sexual matters than their male counterparts (Choi and Peng 2016) by refusing to resort to morally questionable means of escaping poverty such as prostitution. They are also shown to be capable of turning current poverty into a positive energy, even a passion, for pursuing consumerist dreams. They demonstrate moral courage by loving a poor man, and in return, so the story goes, their courage is rewarded in the form of material gains. For these women role models, living through everyday hardships becomes a meaningful and character-building process. This way of configuring migrant women's sexuality is consistent with the state discourse's focus on the female as the agent of sexual purity. It is, however, a different story for the migrant man. "The establishment" sees the unhappiness of unmarried men in lower socioeconomic classes as posing a threat to social stability, and, by implication, to the political legitimacy of the Party. In this context, a migrant woman can demonstrate her moral worth by marrying a migrant man and making her sexuality available to him (Evans 1997, 110), thereby assisting the state in its efforts to maintain social and moral order. Here, as is the case with couples in urban China (Farrer 2014), the man's sexual drive is assumed to be natural, whereas the woman's sexuality is expected to be passive and accommodating.

Sexuality aside, the discourse of love also positions men differently from women. For a man, according to this narrative, whether you succeed in finding love depends on your attitude. Indeed, love does not come easily, and even if a woman loves you despite your poverty, your love may not last unless you work hard for a better future, provide her with a place to live, and achieve the means to support a family. So, as we saw in the previous paragraph, while rural migrant women are urged not to base their choice of partner on materialistic considerations, migrant men are told that the proof of their love lies not only in their capacity to provide for their significant other but also in their willingness to make a promise—as Xiao Han does to his fiancée.

From Revolution to Consumption: A Historical Perspective

Measured against the benchmark exemplified by the model lovers in the CCTV stories, the ardent love between two labor activists—discussed below—is unacceptable and dangerous. Toward the end of 2015, He Xiaobo was arrested, together with three other labor NGO activists in Guangzhou, in a high-profile incident that was widely reported in the international media. He's wife Yang Min took to social media to give updates on her husband's situation, but she was soon warned by the police not to say anything "irresponsible" in that forum, or else she would "face the consequences." Under intense police scrutiny, the couple resorted to publicizing their personal diary and private correspondence in order to maintain a public presence and garner moral support. These letters and diary entries, posted by the couple themselves and widely circulated on social media, were subsequently collated and distributed by various labor activist NGO newsletters.

Some parts of this material read like love letters, and one is struck by the intensely personal nature of the couple's revelations. For instance, on February 7, 2016, Yang posted a letter from her husband, complete with her own annotations. Addressing his wife as "my most beloved person," the letter dwelled on how He and his wife had first fallen in love and started courting. On February 21, Yang posted a message on social media declaring her undying love for He, saying:

> I believe in the power of love. Some people say that romantic love will turn into familial love when a couple get married, but my love for Xiaobo is still of the romantic type. It is still beautiful, like a gentle breeze and a drop of morning dew ...
>
> (China Labor Aid 2016)

The love between the two activists both harks back to and resonates with the old "revolution-plus-love" formula, wherein the personal love of revolutionary heroes—like Sister Jiang in the 1960s novel *Red Crag* (*Hong yan*), and pro-democracy student leader Chai Ling, who married her comrade in Tiananmen Square in 1989—unfolds against the backdrop of myriad revolutionary causes. With He facing jail and persecution, the re-romanticization of his relationship with his wife served an intensely political purpose. They were husband and wife, but more importantly they were comrades sharing a common political cause. The public declaration of their private feelings, carefully crafted to get around censorship, gestures—however fleetingly—toward a return to the revolution-plus-love formula. Poignantly, that formula, which dominated China's revolutionary and socialist imagination for decades, is now the "weapon of the weak," and is strategically deployed for the purpose of resistance and subterfuge. This example clearly reflects the actions and responses of only a handful of extraordinary individuals. Nevertheless, it indicates that, notwithstanding this trend toward consumption as the dominant discursive scaffolding for love, the narrative framework of revolutionary love has not died a complete death in the post-Mao polity.

We cannot appreciate the profound significance of these labor activists' gesture toward revolutionary love without a historical perspective. Left-wing writers in the 1930s, faced with the question of how to negotiate the potential tensions between individuals' erotic desires and the demands of the revolutionary cause, mostly adopted a "revolution-plus-love" formula in their representation of romantic experiences. Despite various permutations of this formula, it is clear that revolution presents itself as both a motivation and a social milieu in which lovers relate to each other while participating in revolutionary activities. In this sense, personal love is mobilized by revolution, and individual love stories necessarily unfold in the grand narrative of class, nation, and revolution.

In Liu Jianmei's (2003) view, as a literary formula, revolution-plus-love may have its origin in the political novel of the late Qing period, which is known for its concern with questions of cultural, national, and racial identity. This theme continued in the discourses of a new modern China and women's emancipation that emerged during the May Fourth period, which began in 1919. But it is the revolutionary period that saw the emergence and proliferation of writings that adopted the revolution-plus-love formula. Liu (2003, 212) sees the revolution-plus-love formula as an attempt on the part of leftist writers, who are committed to proletarian literature, to "mix utopian desires with reality anxiety."

Similarly, Haiyan Lee (2006, 256) attributes the rise of this literary genre to the radicalization of the intelligentsia in the 1920s, and their need—from both the left and right ends of the ideological spectrum—to reconcile the tension between "revolutionary fervor" and a "reluctance to relinquish the discourse of love." One particular way of resolving this tension was to postpone love and subordinate the sexual relationship to the revolutionary agenda. However, as David Der-Wei Wang (2004, 91) observes, while some—such as writer Mao Dun—see revolution and love as in conflict, others—such as Jiang Guangci—see the dynamics between the two as part of a "coherent agenda through which the revolutionary subjectivity progresses from the domain of eros to that of polis."

Literary historians believe that the heyday of the revolution-plus-love discourse was the post-1927 Revolutionary period. Although this discourse continued to inform leftist literature after that, it no longer retained the power to inspire and galvanize young people. Also, romantic love did not disappear in the post-1949 socialist literature, and the revolution-plus-love formula continued to evolve, albeit in various permutations. In Cai Xiang's (2010) account, we see how Zhao Shuli, author of *Xiao Erhei's Marriage* (*Xiao Erhei jiehun*), transplanted the revolution-plus-love formula from the social space inhabited by urban, elite intelligentsia to a rural, peasant, and grassroots milieu. Here, revolution became synonymous with "turning over the body" (*fanshen*)—a metaphorical way of describing a complete overhaul of one's world outlook—and land reforms, and political stories often took the form of love stories (Cai X. 2010, 147). Cai further observes that this framework for narrating romantic love greatly influenced the socialist fiction writing of the 1949–1966 period. While this may be true, in this particular figuration, only the "true love of the proletariat," which puts socialist values before private pleasure, is legitimate (Evans 1997, 91). This formula was again to change during the period of the Cultural Revolution (1966–1976), when class struggle became the only acceptable narrative framework, and gender relations and individual affect were submerged beneath the theme of class identity, and were portrayed only in ways that served the "repressive power of the revolutionary discourse" (Liu Jianmei 2003, 174).

It is therefore small wonder that, having emerged from the Cultural Revolution, Chinese writers, and the public in general, were eager to bid farewell to revolution and reconnect with love. In the decades since the advent of economic reforms, during which time a split has emerged between official and market-oriented cultural expressions, public discourses have all but abandoned revolution except as a trope to be parodied and deconstructed (Liu Jianmei 2003). Expressions of sexuality, private pleasure, and individual desire have tended to come more or less exclusively from the market sector. These market narratives of love feature peasants and rural migrants only as figures that are antithetical to love: perpetrators of sex crimes, homewreckers, prostitutes. With the exception of Women's Federation narratives that urge rural migrant women to become self-respecting and independent (W. Sun 2004), official discourses have largely been at a loss as to how to construct love stories involving the peasant and the worker. The proletarian protagonist, it seems, is dead.

Poignantly, the more fervent the search for love, the more elusive it has proved to be. It has been widely asserted that the market economy has gone so far as to render genuine love impossible. As one cultural commentator laments in *New Weekly* (*Xin zhoukan*), a leading chronicle of cultural trends in China: "Love suffuses our internet, dominates television dramas, and is dished up everywhere as chicken soup for the soul. But this linguistic excessiveness only highlights the fact that real love has vanished" (Sun Linlin 2015). Hence the enormous challenge facing the state propaganda machine: on the one hand, it needs to restore people's faith in the power of love; on the other hand, it must keep revolution out of the equation.

Considered against this historical backdrop, it is possible to see in the CCTV stories a decisive de-coupling of love and revolution. The trope of revolution has been demobilized, and replacing it is the indomitable force of the market—so much so that we can describe the current formula as "consumption-plus-love." Subscribing to this new formula, the love stories in CCTV's Grassroots Reports treat the lovers' commitment to each other as synonymous with their commitment to realizing a consumerist goal. What we see here is a relocation of love from a revolutionary discourse to a market discourse, which also has the desired outcome of minimizing the possibility of a revolution. Thus, while the linking of consumption and love is informed by the logic of the market, the de-linking of revolution and love in the official discourse is motivated by political as well as economic considerations.

The new discourse of domestic utopia replaces the communist vision of the common good with a fantasy of domestic happiness and individual fulfillment via the pathway of consumption. However, despite this replacement of revolution with consumption, the CPC's project of building a new moral culture still relies to a certain extent on mobilizational strategies that are often associated with the promotion of a communist utopia. A dimension of this utopian imagining, as evidenced in CCTV's love stories, is a future-oriented optimism. The current material circumstances facing the five couples featured in the CCTV love stories are unsatisfactory, to say the least. Xiao Han has no means of providing Xiao Qing with a roof under which they can live as husband and wife. In fact, they even disagree about what to do after getting married. Zhang Qianqian, the CCTV reporter who produced "Xiao Han's Wedding," wrote in her field notes:

> Fairytales usually end with the prince and princess living happily ever after, but reality is more precarious. Xiao Han and Xiao Qing in fact disagreed about their future. Xiao Han wanted to go back home and try to start a business; Xiao Qing wanted to stay in Shanghai and continue to work casually [*dagong*]. We decided

to leave this tension in the story to make it look more realistic. After all, we were not producing a fairytale.

(Zhang Q. 2013)

Similarly, Qiu Guoying and Hao Ranran have saved enough money for a down payment on a flat, but the road toward paying off the mortgage is long and arduous—Qiu will spend all of his waking hours at work instead of being with his wife, and there may be many more meals consisting mainly of discarded cabbage.

The life that these individuals now face will be mostly drudgery and hardship, and it is only made bearable by their imagination of a better future. This way of envisioning the future provides a means of making sense of as well as coping with the present. For this reason, although CCTV did not set out to write a "fairytale," the news anchorman had this to say at the end of "Xiao Han's Wedding":

Xiao Qing is wearing a bridal veil, and she looks like a princess, but Xiao Han seems a bit nervous. Perhaps reality will present many more obstacles to them, but with love in their hearts, and with their hard work, they have a bright future ahead.

(CCTV 2013)

If utopia is the "temporal locus where the future and the present, hope and reality, are supposed to meet" (Ci 1994, 221), then it is abundantly clear that today's rural migrant workers are being invited to envision a domestic utopia.

Conclusion

In a small-scale survey of 579 young Foxconn workers conducted by a labor-advocacy group, up to 70 percent of male workers were found to be single and without a girlfriend. This alarming statistic compels labor advocates to ask, somewhat rhetorically, "Who killed Foxconn workers' chance for love?" (Deng 2015). This question preoccupies labor activists as well as the left-wing intelligentsia within China. According to Marxist scholar Lü Xinyu, young rural migrants' romantic love has died a tragic death in the age of transnational capitalism—a death that has occurred in both real and symbolic senses. Up to the 1980s, love stories had provided a perennial narrative framework within which rural–urban inequality could be negotiated in moral terms. However, due to the drastically widened rural–urban gap, young rural migrants now can no longer be convincing protagonists in love stories within the framework of mainstream cultural production. In Lü's view, in today's cinema and literature the romantic love of rural migrant youth is represented only "in the form of its absence" (Lü 2015).

This discussion has uncovered a new discursive strategy by which the state propaganda machine attempts to revive the romantic love of rural migrants. And I have argued that this strategy is part of a blueprint according to which future state narratives of inequality may be constructed. The analysis in the chapter has also brought to light some new ways in which a neoliberal restructuring of the fantasy of the good life takes place in China. But situating our analysis in a historical context, we are able to see that CCTV's narratives are, very much like a bride's outfit, a mixture of something old, something new, and something borrowed. What we see is not an ideology that arrived fully formed and was made to last; rather, we see a new ideology-in-the-making, with the Party actively exploring ways of improvising and innovating its genres of storytelling. When the Party encourages rural young people to defy their parents' traditional expectations about marriage compatibility, it seems, at first glance, to be contributing to "affective individualism" (Donner and Santos 2016). But this official script of love is not about "delinking" intimacy from marriage, as is the tendency with urban educated young people in China (Farrer 2014). Nor does it advocate the hedonistic values that market discourses of romance articulate (Zavoretti 2016). Instead, it promotes a willingness to endure a frugal, or perhaps even ascetic, material life for the time being, in the hope of bringing about a happy future.

However, casting rural migrants in the positive role of hopeful lovers enjoying romantic love despite hardships does more than just proffer a corrective narrative to the widespread and worrying phenomenon among this cohort of casual or commodified sex, "shotgun weddings," high divorce rates, and "left-behind children," as has often been reported in the media and a number of research papers (e.g., Song and Li 2015). The political usefulness of these stories does not end here. Rural migrants have been brought in to play the new protagonists in a politically useful love story, within a new normative framework for narrating the present, with a redefined and reconstituted trope of the future. What the state deems in need of correction is a widespread view of sex for pleasure that detaches itself from both responsibility and commitment. Also in need of correction is the prevalent idea that love is expensive and thus available only to those with the means to purchase it. From the point of view of the state, both scenarios run the risk of further entrenching and highlighting the consequences of socioeconomic stratification, leading to social tension and social instability.

As it stands, this discursive blueprint has several political objectives. It is, first and foremost, charged with the dual goal of lowering rural migrants' expectations about love and marital happiness, on the one hand, and fueling a utopian consumerist dream, on the other. Though almost impossible to achieve, this goal is intended to replace a prevailing sense of despair with a new sense of hope and optimism for the future. Instead of young rural migrant individuals being depicted as facing the "death of love," faith in the power of love must be (re)instated as a motivating force behind individuals' desire for self-improvement. Finally, while rural migrants' desire to get married and start a family is being encouraged by the state, the passion it generates must be effectively and carefully channeled so that that it aids rather than undermines the political objective of stability maintenance. Yet again, love has been repurposed to function as what Lee (2006) describes as a "discursive technology," deployed to manage inequality in an increasingly stratified social order. If loving in the new normative way promotes social stability, enhances social harmony, and assists the political legitimation of the Party, then the Party must identify role models who demonstrate such love. Again, rural migrants are singled out to be such role models. In contrast to laid-off urban factory workers and the urban poor who are subsisting on social welfare (Solinger 2010), rural migrants are often commended in official discourses for their hard work and entrepreneurship. In the case of the CCTV stories, while it is the job of the state's propaganda workers to construct a normative love story, the task of performing the role of the authentic lover falls—once again—on the shoulders of the rural migrant.

This new normative framework for narrating love is built on the symbiotic relationship between affect and consumption—the twin engines of narrating a precarious present and projecting the fantasy of a happy life in the future. It aims to build and sustain hope, a key dimension of the Party's political project of stability maintenance. In the CCTV stories, we see a shift of the temporal locus from the present to the future, and from an experienced reality to an imaginary one. The future, by definition, has not yet arrived, so it is up for grabs, and the CCTV stories offer a good example of how this imaginary space can be colonized. The more vague the future time span is, the more room there is for political maneuvering. Xiao Han asks his fiancée to wait for five years. But, as my rural migrant interviewees remind us, there is a good chance that he will be unable to honor his promise, even though this may not be because of a lack of effort on his part.

As is clear from this discussion, rural migrant workers' moral agency shines through their capacity to bargain freely with these hegemonic messages, take what suits them, and reject what does not. On the one hand, they resonate with the lovers in the CCTV stories and express admiration for their courage, even though they are fully cognizant that these lovers have been hand-picked as role models in the state's propaganda. And they concur with the editorial message that comes with the love stories: happiness should be based on the strength of love, not on the extent of one's wealth. On the other hand, my interviewees reject the Party's speech act of promise-making, given that such a promise does not come with concrete social and economic policies that are likely to make good on it. They also refuse to feel optimistic and make the necessary "affective adjustment," even though they carry on enduring their hardships as well as they can. Individuals from this disadvantaged community may fall in love in whatever circumstances they find themselves in, get married with or without a property or a betrothal gift, and do their best to pursue happiness, however they may understand that. And they may have varying degrees of success in these pursuits. Above all, however, they know that the state is interested in neither delivering them a similar level of privilege and entitlement to their urban professional counterparts, nor recouping a proletarian subject position. Thus, if one is required to look for hope and some cause for optimism, then the resilience and realism of this group may be the best place to start.

Part II

DOCUMENTING PAIN

Chapter 3

"LOVE ON THE ASSEMBLY LINE": CLASS AND THE CLICHÉS OF ROMANTIC CONSUMPTION

Introduction

Xu Aiguo and his wife Deng Xiuzhen are both fifty-seven years of age, and both come from rural Hunan. Xu works as a cook on a construction site in Changsha City, Hunan Province, while Deng is a cleaner in the kitchen. They married thirty-five years ago, and have had a happy marriage, now with children and grandchildren. But Xu has one regret: when they married, he was too poor to afford a proper wedding photo. His wife never complains, but Xu feels bad. "Each time we see young people getting married, she is envious of their wedding photos."

Luckily, Xu is given a chance to remedy this regret. On the seventh day of the seventh month on 2020's lunar Chinese calendar—known as the "Double Seven" or "*Qixi*" Festival,[1] and widely considered to be China's Valentine Day—Xu hears news that his construction company is offering workers the chance to have their wedding photos taken free of charge. Eager not to miss this opportunity, he and his wife sign up. And so, thirty-five years after their marriage, Deng puts on a white bridal gown and stands in front of the camera, a bouquet in her hands, with her husband, dressed in a crisp white shirt and bow tie, standing beside her. Their dream has finally come true.

Stories of companies or photographic studios offering rural migrants free wedding gown photoshoots have become recurring media stories, and they tend to be timed around either the annual Spring Festival or the Chinese Valentine's Day. The story of Xu and Deng originally appeared in Rednet, an official Hunan-based provincial-level online news outlet (Zou and Li 2020), and was subsequently reposted in many outlets. Interestingly, these photoshoot opportunities are now mostly taken up by migrant workers who, like Xu and Deng, have already married, sometimes many years earlier, but who want to compensate for having missed the chance to document a significant moment in their lives, or just want to get a taste of romance.

However, it is not just construction companies that offer such opportunities. Photographing rural migrants in wedding clothes has been establishing itself as a trope for professional photographers as well. For instance, Luo Xian, a photographer with many national and international prizes to her name, won wide public recognition for her 2018–2019 project, which involved photographing sixty rural migrants in wedding clothes. Her project was widely reported by the media, including the nation's official outlets such as the *People's Daily* and the Xinhua News Agency (Ni Meng 2020).

Sociologists (e.g., Illouz 1997) tell us that making choices and decisions about "romantic consumption" is bound up with one's class positions. In the sociological literature, consumption has long been viewed as a "social, cultural and economic process of choosing goods," and as such, it constitutes an "institutional field" which bridges economic and cultural institutions, large-scale social change, and the formation of self-identity (Zukin and Maguire 2004, 173). Since individuals engage in the process of consumption as a project of expressing and forming identity, the role of consumption in constructing and shaping social identities is crucial. Viewed in this theoretical light, romance can be conceived of as a moral good that is unevenly distributed among different social groups. Sociologist of emotion and romance Eva Illouz (1997, 294) argues, for instance, that one's success in pursuing romance is largely determined by one's life conditions, income, leisure time, and level of education. In order to be free to pursue romantic love, one must therefore also be free from the burden of "necessity."

What is equally important for me in sociological terms is how class relations are negotiated between those middle-class individuals who engage in the charity of offering free photoshoots, and the rural migrants who take up such offers. In other words, the question of class inequality is not simply about differentiated levels of consumption. It is, equally importantly, about who controls the meaning of certain consumption items and practices.

In my attempt to think through these questions, I became increasingly interested in a photo-essay that was published in the *Oriental Morning Post* (*Dongfang zaobao*), a highly popular metropolitan paper in Shanghai, in February 2012. The photo-essay, timed to mark Valentine's Day, was the work of the newspaper's photojournalist Jia Dai Tengfei (2012). The photo-essay took up five pages and ran under the eye-catching headline "Love on the Assembly Line" (*Liushuixian shangde aiqing*). These photos received a sensational response. China's biggest web portal at the time, Tencent QQ, received four million hits within the first day of the photos being posted (Jia D. 2014). Youku, China's YouTube, uploaded the photos with the backing track of a popular Chinese song, "Because of Love" (*Yinwei you ai*). On February 18, 2012, China's national television network, China Central Television, reported on the publication of Jia's photos and the enthusiastic response to them. As discussed in the previous chapter, in the following year, inspired by these photographs, CCTV screened a series of mini-documentaries, also entitled "Love on the Assembly Line," as part of its prime-time news and current affairs program during the week of the Spring Festival. As well as borrowing the title of Jia's photo feature, the network's stories also featured some of the rural migrants who had posed for Jia's photographs.

The popularity of professional wedding photography as an integral part of wedding rituals in contemporary China affords me an apposite empirical context in which a number of questions can be explored: Which "conventional taxonomies of love" (Illouz 1997, 284) circulate in contemporary urban Chinese culture, how do individuals from different socioeconomic echelons participate in the "ritual" of "romantic consumption" (250), and who has the means to shape and contest hegemonic notions of romantic love? In this chapter I aim to investigate these romance-related consumption practices by considering the bridal dress and professional wedding photography from four perspectives: first, as a matrix of publicly available cultural narratives and discourses; second, as an economic activity that involves a particular form of "distributive injustice" (Whyte 2010); third, as an expression of class-specific consumer sensibility; and finally, as the product of the interaction of these three realms. The rest of this chapter proceeds in two main parts. First, I review the production of professional wedding photography as an economic activity, and as an essential component of the hegemonic "romantic industry," and then ask how individuals from two socioeconomic cohorts—young rural migrants and their educated urban counterparts—make decisions about this consumption item. My main objective here will be to unravel how exploitation of migrant workers takes place in the symbolic as well as the material domain. In the second part, I return to the political economy and social semiotics of Jia's photo-essay series. This analysis is motivated by a desire to correct a tendency in existing research to focus on the consumption of material goods and services, thereby overlooking the question of how inequality affects the distribution and consumption of symbolic goods such as respectability, status recognition, and achievement of upward social mobility. I argue that this question—whether and how the material and the symbolic are connected—is long overdue.

Jia the Photographer

Jia Dai Tengfei, a Shanghai native, is a young and highly accomplished photojournalist who has worked in many well-known media outlets in China. At the beginning of 2012, Jia was assigned to write a story on labor shortages by his then employer, the *Oriental Morning Post*. Jia visited a factory on the outskirts of Shanghai, where he got talking with some young rural migrant factory workers. He found that, under pressure from their parents, most of them had married. Some even had children, whom they had left behind in the village to be cared for by their parents. Migrant women told him that, although they had married, they had never had the opportunity to wear a bridal dress or have proper wedding photos taken. He also learned from some rural migrant men that their wives still bore a grudge against them for denying them the chance to wear a bridal gown. Back then, commercial wedding photography services—complete with a hired bridal dress and professional make-up in a romantic studio setting—were too costly for them. In recent years, these costs have fallen considerably, and today young rural migrants consider it an essential part of the wedding ritual. Since Jia happened to meet these men and women shortly before Valentine's Day, it occurred to him that he should offer to take their wedding photos retrospectively, and free of charge.

Jia wanted to photograph the couples on the factory shop floor, against the background of lathes and machines. He pitched this idea to the paper's editors, who responded enthusiastically. They offered Jia the support he needed, hiring five wedding dresses, a make-up artist, a writer, a video technician, and a small lighting team. Several hot water bottles were also purchased for workers to hold during the sessions—it was the middle of winter, and the factory shop floor was chilly. Jia's images show workers in wedding dresses and suits, posing for the camera against the dark, cold, metallic surfaces of machines on the factory shop floor. He justified his decision about the setting on the grounds that he wished to depart from the clichéd and formulaic backdrops used in commercial wedding photos, which he described as "what everybody opts for without thinking" (Jia D. 2014).

Since their publication, Jia's images have become a very apt reminder of the paradoxical process of China's march toward modernization and economic prosperity. The images of migrant individuals give a human face to the impact of China's modernization, showing its impact on individuals. Asked about Jia's "Love on the Assembly Line" series in an interview with *Changjiang ribao* (*Changjiang Daily*), James Wellford, a senior photo editor with *Newsweek*, said that the photos remind people of the resilience, hope, and faith demonstrated by China's young workers, and, for this reason, he finds these images "extremely powerful" and "moving" (Liu S. 2013).

Jia's photographs interest me not because they present evidence of the authentic feelings and emotions of rural migrant individuals or because they index romantic love—or the lack of it—among rural migrant couples. Rather, it is because their central motifs of bridal dress and wedding photography are emotionally invested visual narratives whose production, circulation, and interpretation take place in contexts of unequal power relations. For this reason, how individuals from different socioeconomic backgrounds interpret the bridal dress and professional wedding portraiture provide vital clues to what people understand and think about meanings of love and romance in general, and to how inequality shapes people's experience with romantic love.

Class and Consumption

The ways in which people from different social and cultural contexts participate in the ritual of romantic consumption has long been of interest to those who write about the relationship between class and consumption. Sociologists consider consumption to be a key class marker, and believe that class positions are negotiated through consumption in complex and often paradoxical ways. While Marx defines class in terms of one's position in relation to the means of production, Weber, on the other hand, considers consumption to be a key indicator of status group. For Weber, status is determined by the power that comes from the "social honor, or prestige" distributed within the status order (Weber [1922] 1978, 926). What confers such honor and prestige is, according to Bourdieu (1984), cultural capital. He views consumption as being bound up with taste, which manifests as one's familiarity with legitimate culture; consumption is thus a domain whereby cultural taste is used as a vehicle of class domination. Following Bourdieu, Illouz argues that the higher one's class position, the better one is able to "subvert, invert, or twist" the categories, scripts, and "clichés" that constitute the "conventional taxonomies of love" (Illouz 1997, 284).

Some sociologists have recently argued that an analytical shift away from the Marxist focus on production and toward individuals' participation in consumption—motivated by an awareness of "the far-reaching impact of the consumption variable" (Tomba 2014, 97) on China's social relations—is an effective means to the end of sidestepping class relations. As discussed in Chapter 1, despite the lack of clarity regarding the class status of *nongmingong* (rural migrant workers), what is certain is that the middle class, as a class, is widely believed to be conducive to social harmony, stability, and the political legitimacy of the Party (M. Chen and Goodman 2013). And since consumption, alongside income, occupation, and education, is a key index of middle-class membership, it is not surprising that popular media and cultural representations of the middle class are mostly associated with their consumption and lifestyles (Y. Guo 2008; Rocca 2017). In contemporary China, consumption has also presented itself as key site through which changing social structures in China in the reform era can be understood. As implied in the previous chapter, real estate markets, for instance, provides a means of "spatializing class" in urban China (L. Zhang 2010). Similarly, the retail sector affords shoppers and sales people occasions to engage in strategies of class distinction (Hanser 2008).

The analysis of the relationship between class and consumption is particularly important in times of radical social restructuring. This is because consumption affords a key site in which class-related aspirations, anxieties, and fears are simultaneously articulated and addressed. Invoking C. Wright Mills's figure of the "new middle class," Rocca points to the instability of middle-class membership in contemporary China. The new middle class are "in constant fear of losing everything. They live in an unstable world, and they are never sure where they are on the social ladder. They imitate the bourgeoisie's lifestyle and they strive to avoid falling into the category of 'workers'" (Rocca 2017, 206). For this reason, to investigate class and consumption in any given social context, we need to ask how individuals interpret consumer items and activities, and how their interpretations are imbued with class-related anxieties and aspirations. For instance, research suggests that some romantic and wedding-related consumption activities are shaped by people's desire to emulate the practices of the social class immediately above their own, thereby vividly embodying what Veblen ([1899] 2007) calls "competitive consumption."

Romantic and wedding-related activities involve the consumption of what Hirsch (2005, 10) calls "positional goods"—defined as goods that derive their economic value from their scarcity. Consumption of positional goods allows those who can afford scarce commodities, such as pristine beaches and other luxury leisure goods, to enjoy prestige and superior status. At the same time, however, consumption can also be a levelling as well as a strengthening force in the social structure, since the "democratization of luxury goods" gives lower-class consumers the feeling of moving up, while the appropriation and legitimation of "lower-class cultural practices" by the middle classes sometimes result in a merging of the cultural practices of different classes (Illouz 1997).

Bridal Photography and the Rise of the Romance Industry

Bridal gowns and professional wedding photography are indeed consumption practices that have gone through a process by which luxury goods—and, by association, romantic experience—have been democratized. One only has to see how Valentine's Day has been re-invented in China to get an idea of the extent to which romance has been commodified. Like The *Qixi* Festival, on the seventh day of the seventh month of the lunar calendar, the Western Valentine's Day is now also a booming business opportunity, with the market aggressively promoting goods and services associated with love and romance—fresh flowers, chocolates, Western-style dining, a night at the movies (Ding 2014). But none of these consumption items have been as lucrative as the bridal dress and professional bridal portraiture. This, of course, is not an exclusively Chinese phenomenon. Bonnie Adrian's study of wedding rituals in Taiwan in the 1980s and 1990s reveals bridal portraiture in Taiwan to be a "transnational visual phenomenon" (Adrian 2006, 73; see also Adrian 2003). She observes that professionally produced bridal photography service originates from Taiwan and is different from wedding photographs taken by relatives and friends.[2] In Adrian's (2006, 83) view, bridal photography represents the democratization of professionally produced "high beauty," on the one hand, and of photography as a visual genre, on the other. For this reason, we need to look beyond the "superficial outward appearances and resemblances of the photographs" and instead consider the "historical and social context in which meanings of some portraits are constructed" (Constable 2006, 46). Equally crucial is the question of how photographers and cameramen act as "agents in the social construction of marriage ritual" (Cheung 2006, 22).

Bridal portraiture came to China from Taiwan in the late 1990s, and since then has become one of the fastest growing industries in Hong Kong and China. In Hong Kong, the traditional ritual of marriage has changed considerably due to the widespread use of studio bridal photography and video recording. For middle-class women in China in the late 1990s and early 2000s, bridal photography afforded individuals an opportunity to engage in "the cosmopolitan framings of the self" (Constable 2006, 43), and as such, can be read as visual evidence of people's efforts to live out the tension between the traditional and the modern, the Chinese and the Western. Constable's discussion about this cultural phenomenon in Beijing more than a decade ago ends with several questions for further research, one of which was, "Who, among China's new under-classes, cannot afford such indulgences?" (Constable 2006, 53).

Eric Ma's discussion of "wedding imaginations" in South China includes some insights on rural migrants that go some way toward addressing Constable's question. Through an account of four wedding couples from different classes (lower versus middle) and social backgrounds (urban Chinese, rural Chinese, Hong Kong residents), Ma examines how visual competency, urban experience, and economic capital—what Ma calls the "three overlapping vectors"—intersect to shape the ways in which visuality exhibits and stabilizes class status. In comparison with other couples in Ma's study, the rural migrant couple displayed a "low level of visual competence and limited urban experience," did not subscribe to the "subtle layers of visuality in wedding romances and myths," but thought that wedding photography was a "trendy and modern thing to do" (Ma 2006, 61). By contrast, Kendall's study of wedding hall photography among rural migrant working-class Koreans in the 1980s finds that wedding photography was more about producing "necessary and important documents," and about "authenticating claims to marital respectability" (Kendall 2006, 2). She argues that, no matter how mass-produced, wedding portraits are created within and through the "authenticating context of sacred and secular rituals of getting married" (4).

A decade and a half after bridal photography reached Chinese cities and townships, bridal photography, which was then described by Constable (2006) as an "indulgence," has now become more affordable to rural migrants and other lower socioeconomic groups. In recent years, the number of professional wedding photography studios has increased by 10 percent each year, and the number of wedding dresses sold to these studios has increased by 20 percent annually (Ding 2014). A 2011 study (Ling 2011) claims that there were then 450,000 professional wedding photo studios employing around five million people in China. The same study suggests that around ten million couples get married in China each year, most of them living in small cities and townships. For these couples, wedding photoshoots consume up to 15 percent of the entire cost of their wedding.

The industry has also become increasingly stratified in terms of price, variety, professional standards, and taste. At the low end, there are packages priced at a couple of thousand *yuan* that cater to the mass market and are available through online booking and group purchases. At the high end, one can easily expect to pay more than ten thousand *yuan*, and to receive a highly personalized service in return, delivering to customers styles of romance that are increasingly individuated and technologically sophisticated. Catering mostly to millennials who are known for their more individualistic style of self-expression, the competitive wedding industry is forever on the lookout for more innovative and individuated themes, formats, and aesthetics (Qianzhan Report 2014).

Bridal Photography as an Obligatory Ritual—Urban Professionals' Perspective

One day a few years ago, I noticed on my WeChat postings a group of photo images from Shan, my niece, who works as a bank teller in Nanjing. She was getting married, and her fiancé Zhao was a software programmer in a Japanese-owned company in the same city. The images show them in various settings including exotic and "sophisticated" backdrops featuring European-style and Art Deco furniture such as a chandelier, an antique desk, and bookshelves full of old books, as well as a more "natural" setting involving images of quiet cobblestone streets in an old town, serene gardens, and tranquil rivers.

The couple look extremely elegant in these pictures, and Shan, wearing a white wedding gown that suggests understated sexiness, looks impossibly glamorous. Although I could see the resemblance between the people in the photos and the couple I know, it is obvious that the images of both of them, and especially the bride, have been touched up: Shan has bigger eyes in the photos, fairer and smoother skin, slimmer arms, and a more slender body. After I expressed my amazement at the transformation, Shan replied, "The magic of software!" She also reminded me that hers was a common or garden package that was "nothing fancy": "It cost us only a few thousand *yuan*; we didn't want to spend a lot of money on it so we chose a deal in the low price range."

Seeing my niece's wedding photos made me realize that, although my main interest lies in asking young rural migrants how they partake in romantic consumption, it may also be instructive to talk to some young people from outside that cohort. This would afford a comparative perspective, hopefully shedding light on how education, socioeconomic circumstances, job security, and *hukou* status shape one's decision-making on romantic consumption. Guided by this question, I enlisted the help of my niece, who introduced me to a dozen of her friends in Beijing, Shanghai, and Nanjing. These individuals were from a similar socioeconomic background to Shan's—young, university-educated professionals in their twenties and thirties who enjoy considerable financial security, and have urban residency *hukou*. They are usually described in the popular media as the "young white-collar" (*xiao bailing*) class. Making every effort to get ahead professionally in the competitive job market, individuals in this cohort work hard to pay off their mortgages—although, with the help of their parents, some already own their home. Young white collars are therefore faring much better than individuals of the "ant tribe" (*yizu*), who, despite having a university education and a white-collar job, lack the requisite urban *hukou* status, and cannot afford to buy or rent a decent place of their own. As a result, they have to make do with substandard shared rental accommodation (Saunders 2015). Yet, in comparison with "gold collars" (*jinling*)—those in their forties and fifties who occupy managerial positions in the transnational corporate sector—the young white collars face more pressure and less security. Those still paying off their apartments often lament the high cost of living in the big cities, and dread the extra financial burden associated with bringing up a child one day in the future.

Almost everyone I interviewed—men and women, urban professionals, and rural migrants—thought that bridal photography was an essential part of the wedding ceremony these days. One particularly prominent reason, which was cited by individuals from both groups, was that having a formal wedding shoot is a key component of the ritual of getting married. Interviewees mentioned that the wedding is an occasion that families, relatives, friends, and colleagues all participate in, so even though they themselves see little practical use for a wedding shoot, sharing these pictures with or displaying them to members of one's circle performs an important social function. Another reason cited by young people from both groups was the sentimental value of a bridal portrait. Some said that they would like to have some visual evidence to remind themselves decades later of how young and attractive they once looked. Others mentioned that they wanted to give their children an opportunity to find out what their parents looked like when they were young. A saying that came up time and again in their justification was: "It [a wedding] is a ritual that happens only once in a lifetime, so of course we want to do it [have a photoshoot]." Some mentioned that parents and relatives love to keep these images on their mobile phones and show them around, and colleagues and friends also expect them to post them on social media.

All the young married couples working in professional jobs in Nanjing who agreed to talk to me had had their photos taken in Western-style bridal gowns, but a few donned a traditional red Chinese jacket after that for some photos, just to add some variety. While a few treated the photoshoot as an opportunity for self-expression, many others were content with whatever commercial deal was offered to them. Liu YY, in his early thirties, has a rural background, but his tertiary and postgraduate education paid off, and he landed himself a good job in Beijing. He is now a public servant in the Ministry of Hydraulics, is married with a young daughter, and is paying off the mortgage on an apartment he and his wife are buying. His photoshoot cost around 7,000 *yuan*, which, by his reckoning, was well below the median price range for Beijing wedding shoots. Most of Liu's friends also opted for a package below the median price as they did not see much point in spending a lot of money on something that usually ends up "at the bottom of the drawer." He and his wife booked their photoshoot as part of a group, which entitled them to a discounted price.

These professional couples are aware that they are merely participating in a commonplace consumption activity, and that there is nothing authentic and original about its form or content. Thus, my niece's husband Zhao mentioned that when he and a colleague shared their respective wedding photos on WeChat, they were not surprised to find that they had used the same studio, opted for the same package, and ended up with almost identical settings and backdrops. The lack of originality did not bother him or Shan, who believes that convenience is a justifiable trade-off for the loss of individuality:

> I have a colleague who is a music lover. She and her fiancé wanted to express their identity through music and wanted their wedding photos in the style of a music video, so instead of booking a commercial package, they asked a friend to photograph them. They booked their own gown, chose their own locations, and organized the whole thing themselves. I've seen their photos—she showed them to me on her phone—and they're really good, and it cost them only about 1,000 *yuan*, but it took them so much time and energy. Besides, the commercial studios have professional photographers, state-of-the-art equipment, and techniques for make-up, so, it's a one-stop shop. Very convenient. We're all already quite busy with life; who wants the extra hassle?

Zhang XW, a pre-primary school teacher in Nanjing in her mid-twenties, was yet to find a boyfriend, but she already saw the logic of going for a commercial package:

> Spending money will save you hassles. Doing it yourself means you need to spend lots of time putting on make-up. But you need someone to do that for you—someone who knows what they're doing. You'll have to rent costumes, arrange transport, and get someone to carry your gear. Even if your friends are willing to help, you can't prevail on them to do everything. You end up owing favors. You feel you need to treat them to dinner for their trouble. Too much hassle. Not worth it. You're much better off paying for it.

Although most young people in this cohort are happy to go along with the ritual, some seem to have a jaded view about its purported association with love and romance. Huang F, a reporter with a big newspaper in Shanghai, was about to marry her boyfriend of many years when she talked to me. She has thought a lot about the ritual of the wedding banquet and wedding photos:

> I personally think there's nothing romantic about wedding banquets and wedding photos. But I'll go along with all that because in China getting married is not just an individual matter between two people; it's about families. So, for the sake of parents and families, I'm prepared to be an actor once and appear in these photos as a puppet!

However, while owning a house/apartment and a car may be the most important—and most expensive—evidence of these individuals' achievements in life, the wedding shoot, having become widely affordable, is an eminently suitable consumption choice to mark a step along the way toward these bigger material goals. Nevertheless, the choice of a "suitable package" is likely to be made more on the principle of convenience and getting the "best value" than as a conspicuous display of their emerging consumption power.

You Have to Do It—Rural Migrants' Perspective

Although rural migrants work in the city, when they do marry, most prefer to have the wedding "back home." Most are likely to have celebrated their marriages with a wedding dinner attended by friends and family members in their hometown, which is also where their parents typically reside. Many first-generation migrant workers who married in the late 1990s may have marked the occasion of their marriage by having a simple photo taken in a photography studio in their home town. To this earlier generation, a wedding photoshoot in a professional studio, involving a wedding dress for the bride and a wedding suit for the groom, was either a luxury they could not afford, or an impractical form of consumption that was incompatible with their economic standards. At the same time, unattainable though it may have been, the professional wedding photo had become a sign that represented all that is urban, modern, and desirable.

Like their urban professional counterparts, younger-generation rural migrants also believe that commemorating their wedding in photographic terms is a meaningful thing to do, since marriage is supposed to happen "only once in a lifetime" and it is therefore important to mark it. In this sense, they are not dissimilar to their counterparts in Hong Kong, Taiwan, and Korea, who use bridal portraiture to document, witness, and authenticate an important ritual. At the same time, unlike their urban Chinese counterparts, young rural migrants more often than not view a professional wedding photoshoot as an aspirational consumption item, signifying a capacity to participate in the process of becoming urban and modern. Zhang YX, who works for Foxconn in Shenzhen, is yet to find a boyfriend, but she expects professional wedding photos to be an integral part of getting married—although she does not see the point of it, except as a once-in-a-lifetime excuse to indulge herself. Unlike the urban professional Huang F discussed earlier, who considers herself a reluctant "actor" and a "puppet" in these photoshoots, Zhang thinks this will be the only day in her life when she gets to be treated as special: "I know why we [rural migrant workers] want to do it. It's because we're poor, and there are not that many legitimate excuses to indulge ourselves, except for this." Zhang's desire to be treated as someone special just once in her life echoes the sentiment expressed by rural migrant brides in Taiwan in Adrian's (2006) study.

Second-generation rural migrants are more exposed to the urban lifestyle and consumerist values than their parents were, and—unsurprisingly—are more keen to participate in urban consumption practices (Chu 2013). Eager to tap into the market of young rural migrant couples, yet cognizant of their limited consumption capacity, some commercial bridal photography studios occasionally offer complimentary photoshoots to a limited number of rural migrants (see, e.g., Xu Jing and Zheng Y. 2012). These events are staged with the main purpose of creating new clientele, positioning rural migrants as the new class of desiring consumers. Would rural migrants be interested in taking advantage of these complimentary events? Before investigating this topic, I had imagined that some would say yes, as this would save them a huge sum of money, while others would say no, since not everyone wants to be the recipient of middle-class charity. While both speculations turned out to be true, the reasons workers gave for their decisions are complex. Li WJ, a Foxconn worker in her late twenties, is still looking for a boyfriend, but she is adamant that she will not be interested in a free wedding photoshoot:

> It's not that I don't like a gift, but a wedding is something that happens only once in a lifetime, and you have to think of what your parents, family, relatives, and friends would say. They may not accept it. What's more, nowadays the cost of a professional wedding photoshoot is not that high. A couple of thousand *yuan*. You could have a fairly good one with two months' salary. So, I may sign up for a free event such as this just for fun, but will still have a proper one as part of my wedding.

Thus, Li and her family/friends would seem to be happy to accept a commercial package at the low end of the market, as long as it is *not* free. To them, romantic practices such as this would not be legitimate unless they are purchased. And it is not just women who are subject to this social pressure. Cao ZL, a young man also working at Foxconn, echoed Li WJ's reservations, but was more explicit about why: "I'd lose face. My family would lose face. It would make my wedding look shabby. People would think we're cheapskates, wanting to save a bit of money on the most important event in our lives."

Qing ZB, another unattached Foxconn assembly-line worker in his late twenties, said that he would love to take advantage of a free photoshoot, but he is confident that most women would not go along with that. And, having dated quite a few women, he seemed fairly certain about what this imaginary "she" would say:

> She would say, "There's no such thing as a free lunch in this world; how can you prove to me that you love me without wanting to spend any money [on such an important event]?" She'd also say, "Am I worth nothing to you?"

Qing ZB echoes the sentiment of many rural migrant men who have their dream of romantic love dashed by the inferior financial circumstances they find themselves in. As Choi and Peng (2016) point out in their study of rural migrant men, rural-to-urban migrant men face inequalities on both fronts—they need to compete with more wealthy urbanites as well as their better-off rural counterparts.

It is obvious that both young urban professionals and young rural migrants embrace this ritual of romantic consumption, and both cite familial and social expectations as an important consideration. Individuals from both groups make it clear that they would be happy with a low-end package deal. But their reasons behind such a decision could not be more different. For young urban professionals, this consumption practice has more or less been de-coupled from connotations of power and social status. These packages are widely taken up by young and busy couples as a practical alternative to options that, while more individualistic, would be much more time- and energy-consuming. In the same way that they can outsource domestic work, they are also outsourcing the tedious work of having to organize the settings, costumes, equipment, etc. that are needed for producing images and memories of romance.

For cash-strapped rural migrants, on the other hand, the stakes are a lot higher if they forego the ritual in order to save a few thousand *yuan*. For them, this ritual of romantic consumption is not just a matter of choice; it is almost obligatory. They are paying for this service not so much to have valuable images and memories of romantic experience produced; they are paying for it in order to "keep up with the Joneses." For members of this community, like the working-class Koreans in Kendall's (2006) study, the act of consumption has become a highly recognizable means of "giving face" to themselves and families and gaining respectability and legitimacy within their own community. For many, the ritual of getting married is not legitimate unless and until it is mediated by the market.

Statements from several individuals I interviewed attest to Adrian's (2006) argument that, although people of different classes engage in the same ritual of romantic consumption, how and why they do so is significantly shaped by their socioeconomic status and occupational identity. Urban professional couples may choose to take a pragmatic, or ironic, or individualistic and non-commercial approach to the question of how to document a once-in-a-lifetime moment. For them, it is a matter of choice. In comparison with their urban professional counterparts, young rural migrants seem more susceptible to interpellation into the market ideology of romance. They are less critical of its formulaic nature, and are more likely to treat it as what Sara Ahmed (2010) calls "happy objects"—things "which become good, or acquire their value as goods insofar as they point towards happiness" (26). Since the question of legitimacy—in social and cultural terms—is key to aspirational consumption, and since this legitimacy is certifiable only through the act of consumption, many rural migrants' insistence on paying for a professional wedding photography service—even if a free one is available—is poignant but understandable. After all, thanks to the democratization of this service, the wedding shoot has become one aspect of modern urban life these workers can afford to participate in, and where they can exercise their agency as consumer-citizens.

The Semiotics of the Wedding Dress in Jia's Photo-Essay

Unlike the single rural migrants who definitely plan a professional wedding photoshoot, almost all the workers who appear in Jia's photo-essay were already long married. Since they had not had a proper photoshoot to commemorate their wedding, they were only too happy to make up for that lost opportunity by belatedly participating in the ritual of romantic consumption—free of charge.

Jia's idea of photographing brides and grooms against the background of the assembly line is artistically innovative, but it seems that he did not intend this juxtaposition to mean that the assembly line is a hotbed for love and romance. In fact, his choice of backdrop seems designed to point to the difficulty, or even impossibility, of a sustainable love when a worker's life trajectory is determined by the capitalist industrial regime in which individuals are treated as replaceable spare parts:

> Facing this group of young people, I can't be certain how happy they are with their marriages. But it's obvious they are very young and inexperienced, yet are already in the world of married life. Toughing it out away from home and leaving their children behind, I am sure there are problems. The road is long and tortuous. ... This special cohort of people, estimated to be around 8,487 million in total, are confronted with so many problems at once: love, marriage, family, employment, education, and housing. ... Their precarious situation is affecting their lives, and their prospect for a happy marriage is the first casualty. The assembly line has determined their fate.
>
> (Jia D. 2014)

If we read the narratives that accompany the images of each couple, it becomes clear that not all the individuals in the photos are newlyweds, and not all are happy or married. More importantly, the short biography attached to each couple makes it clear that their present reality is marked by "neediness, distress, and social problems," suggesting a context that is "antithetical to the glamour with which romance is usually associated" (Illouz 1997, 120). One couple confesses that theirs was a "shotgun wedding," under pressure from their parents. Another couple live apart even though both work in the same city, having left their two-year-old son behind in the village. Still another couple lost their baby son to pneumonia a few years ago, and the woman becomes tearful whenever she mentions him. Then there is a couple who have been dating for four years but the woman's parents object to the relationship because the two families live too far away from each other. To many of these individuals, having wedding photos taken was not so much about helping them relive and revisit the feelings of love and romance they experienced in the past. Rather, it was more about rewarding them for their faith in love and romance, despite the fact that they live in a time and context when these are scarce commodities. Seen in this light, the chance to wear nice make-up and wedding clothes and to have photos taken, all free of charge, seems like a form of moral accreditation offered to deserving recipients who have demonstrated their commitment, loyalty, and constancy—a reward for the hard work they have put in to making their relationships last.

While the white bridal dress symbolizes purity, and wearing one is usually intended to symbolize the intention of the newly wedded couple to enter into a committed and lifelong relationship, it can also be manipulated to become a consolation prize for individuals who maintain their faith in love, despite having been dealt that cruel fate of lovelessness. Jia's blog reveals that one young woman in the photoshoot was recently divorced and is the mother of a three-year-old child. The reason behind Zhang X's divorce was simple, according to her line manager on the shop floor: during a health check-up at work, she was found to have a growth of some kind, which the doctor diagnosed as a possible tumor. Not wanting to live with the possibility of his wife having a terminal illness, her husband insisted on a divorce. Sensing the young woman's disappointment, and her envy of the brides being photographed, Jia offered to take her photo too, complete with the "prettiest dress and make-up"; his promise brought a "sweet and heartfelt smile" to her face (Jia D. 2014). Jia's photo of this young woman is thus not meant to be a faithful expression of her current love life; it is a consolation prize given to an unfortunate young woman who has yet to experience—and perhaps may never experience—lasting love or romance. Dressed as a bride but photographed alone, this young woman's wedding gown is a signifier of absence. Abandoned by her husband, Zhang is quoted as saying that she hopes to walk away from the shadows, find love with someone, buy a property within three years, and start again.

The wedding dress would not become such a powerful signifier of modernity without the backdrop of the assembly line. The term "assembly line" refers to the industrial process of manufacturing. Each worker on the assembly line is assigned a specific task, which he or she performs repetitively, before passing the product on to the next worker. Usually credited as the invention of Henry Ford, the modern assembly line was adopted and lauded as a quick and efficient method of production, but it is also known to have an alienating and dehumanizing effect on the physical and psychological well-being of the worker. In China the much-publicized suicides of young workers in Foxconn, Shenzhen, from 2010 onwards, were attributed to long shifts on the assembly line, military-style dormitory life after work, and lack of socialization with the wider community (Pun and Chan 2012). These cases are a chilling and powerful testimony to the assembly line's devastating impact on workers (Pun 2005). As renowned rural migrant woman poet Zheng Xiaoqiong wrote of rural migrant women in the factory, "These people will be forgotten, completely and utterly digested out of existence in the stomach of the industrial machine of our age" (Zheng Xiaoqiong 2012, 156). To rural migrant poets and writers like Zheng, the assembly line is a dystopia for love, metonymic for the industrial regime, indifferent to sentiment, hostile to romance, and destructive of passion for life. The Chinese expression for "assembly line" here is *"liushuixian,"* literally meaning a "line of flowing water." In a play on this metaphor, Jia muses as follows in his journal: "A life that flows away, just like water. A love that flows away, just like water."

The Politics of Giving Love

The *Oriental Morning Post* explicitly promoted Jia's photography as a "love-giving" initiative, illustrating the familiar trope of cross-class care and compassion in public discourses. In this way, by sponsoring the photoshoots and publishing them, the *Oriental Morning Post* celebrated the love that exists among rural migrants, and at the same time was an example of "cross-class love" that showcased the generosity of the urban middle-class elites "giving love" to the rural migrant workers, one of several groups described as "weak and vulnerable communities" (*ruoshi qunti*), the usual recipients of such "donating love" initiatives. Charities targeting rural migrants often launch mediatized events featuring the grateful recipients and the generous givers, the latter being both privileged elite individuals and organizations. These individual acts of giving do not become known to the public without the participation of the media (Hassid and Jeffreys 2015). This process of mediatization is also one of moral exemplariness, whereby the generosity of the giver is put on display for others to emulate. Thus, the media, including both official CPC outlets and commercial mainstream media such as the *Oriental Morning Post*, play a central role in the discursive project of producing cross-class love.

With his free wedding photoshoots for these rural migrant workers, Jia was effectively making his photography an act of charity. At the same time, his act of "giving love" was different from and superior to the clichéd formula of handing out cash or goods. Instead, what he gave his selected few was a rare opportunity to participate in a self-expression of romance and love. By their mutual agreement to participate in his photoshoots, both the photographer and the photographed entered into a more complex politics of agency than the handover of cash. On the one hand, a number of rural migrant individuals enthusiastically participated in the event, and their voluntary appearance in these photos afforded them a rare opportunity to act out their desire for a modern, urban consumption practice. On the other hand, by agreeing to participate, rural migrants had to forfeit their right as consumers to choose the location, background, and style of the photographs; it was Jia, the (culturally elite) photographer, who made the significant decisions. He decided which scripts would be followed, which modern clichés of romance he would subvert, invert, or twist (Illouz 1997, 284), and indeed what would constitute the non-clichéd representation of love and romance. If we see rural migrants' participation as some kind of self-making activity, then it is clear that the circumstances and conditions in which these activities took place were both limiting and limited. As Illouz argues, romance is an unevenly distributed good, of a moral kind. In Jia's intervention, this unevenness manifested itself in the fact that the moral gift rural migrants received was chosen and packaged by the giver, whose needs and taste may have been much more unconventional and elitist than their own.

Unlike the simple act of giving money or things, Jia's initiative required a much higher level of reciprocity on the part of the recipients. In exchange for the free photoshoot, migrant couples had to be prepared to be cast in a certain role in a moral play whose political and ideological agendas were set by someone else, and over which they had little control. Perhaps unbeknownst to themselves, these migrant individuals were performing a particular kind of emotional labor, from which myriad types of symbolic value were extracted. Emotional labor is the process of managing one's feelings and expressions in order to fulfill the emotional requirements of a job (Grandey 2000). Unlike material value, symbolic value accrues in immaterial domains such as status, power, and prestige. Yet, like material value, symbolic value can also be exchanged, appropriated, and subjected to exploitation and capitalization (Bourdieu 1984; Veblen [1899] 2007).

Rural migrants' labor on the assembly line is systematically exploited to produce surplus value that is crucial to the accumulation of capital. Long used to being cast in this utilitarian role, rural migrants now assume another function: providing emotional labor in the production of symbolic surplus value. It is very clear that the individuals who participated in Jia's photoshoots could be regarded as "productive" on both accounts. Whether they looked sad, happy, contented, or unfulfilled for the camera, the participants were as much reacting to the camera's interpellation to "look the part" as they were expressing their inner selves. Their emotional labor was exploited on a number of levels to generate cultural, economic, social, and political capital on behalf of other, more powerful individuals and agencies. For instance, it gave substance to the creative impulse of Jia the photographer, who wanted to subvert and critique the visual clichés of commercial culture—a process that led to the enhancement of his professional and artistic prestige and recognition. It elevated the social standing of the *Oriental Morning Post*, as well as creating a business opportunity for the paper, which aimed to profit from the highly anticipated celebration of love and romance of Valentine's Day. Similarly, for middle-class elite spectators and artists in cultural and arts circles both inside and outside China, embracing Jia's artwork featuring China's subalterns affords them an occasion to demonstrate their compassion for members of the "disadvantaged communities," thus effectively absolving them from any moral imperative to address that disadvantage. Therefore, the question of who is actually doing the giving has come to acquire exceptional irony and poignancy. This "charity" initiative creates symbolic resources that lead to further capitalization for the middle class, and it does so, in part, by concealing the actual direction and magnitude of material benefit—from the rural migrant working class to the middle class.

To be sure, Jia's decision to feature the motif of the assembly line was not without criticism. As Jia himself has disclosed, some people have accused him of imposing his own artistic taste on the workers, thereby making the spectacle of suffering available for wider consumption. Why not photograph workers against the backdrop of something nice, such as "blue sky and white clouds," or "images of Shanghai's harbor"? Jia responded thus:

> As agreed with workers prior to shooting, the assembly line would be a more meaningful place to do these photoshoots. Imagine in ten years' time, they can show these images to their children and say, this is where your mum and dad once worked. These images will start their trip down memory lane. White clouds and blue sky will always be there, and so will the Bund in Shanghai. There's nothing special about them. But the past experience of having worked in this place, unless captured in a photo, will disappear forever. That's why it's worth capturing it.
>
> (Jia D. 2014)

"Your Art Is My Everyday Reality"

Jia received impressive accolades both within and outside China. As an American Public Broadcasting Service journalist wrote, "Ultimately, Dai Tengfei saw the factory as the perfect setting for lives that are 'like products on the assembly line'" (Fleischer 2013). The creative tension between the wedding dress and the assembly line has indeed paid off. Since publication, these photos have received numerous national and well as international accolades, and have featured in many international media outlets including *The Guardian*, PBS.com, the *World Post*, and the World Policy Institute. Later the same year, Jia, together with eleven other accomplished photographers from all over the world, were invited by the World Press Photo Foundation to a Joop Swart Masterclass in Amsterdam (World Press Photo Foundation 2017). Jia's original photos were also published in the final print edition of the US magazine *Newsweek*, as part of a special feature entitled "China's Great Dream," on social and economic transformation in China (M. Liu 2012). The images were used despite the fact that the *Newsweek* story was a compilation of interviews with political and cultural elites in China, and their interpretations of Xi Jinping's Great Dream.

It was not clear from Jia's own accounts, or from reports about him, how other rural migrant workers would respond to his images, and how they might interpret this charity event. Given these young workers' keenness to partake in the ritual of a professional wedding shoot, I wondered if Jia's photos, which had been taken and published a couple of years before my interviews with rural migrant workers, would strike a resonance with my research participants. I also realized that inviting them to comment on the photos could be a useful strategy for finding out if they related to the "conventional taxonomies of love," in the way that Jia the photographer had intended. I therefore showed my interviewees Jia's photos and asked them to tell me what came to mind. When I talked to JY he was not working, although he had worked at Foxconn for three years. He had an ongoing dispute with the management—he alleged that Foxconn had fired him on false pretenses and owed him wages, and he was seeking compensation with legal assistance from a local labor NGO. A native of Hubei Province, JY was in his late twenties and did not have a girlfriend. When I showed him Jia's photos on an iPad, he looked at them for a long time before saying anything. When I asked him to choose some words to describe how he felt, he first chose "cold," and then "sad," followed by "helpless" and "powerless." He said that the background was anything but warm and harmonious, which was what wedding photos should be. He said that he preferred somewhere "natural" and "outdoors." When I pointed out to him that it was precisely this tension between the coldness of the background and the warmth of the human relationship which made these photos prizeworthy, he responded by saying, "That may well be the case, but that's not what I would want for my own wedding photo." And then, lingering on these images a little longer, he added, "People don't feel happy unless they're comfortable with their environment. The people in these photos don't look happy to me."

After talking to JY, I asked the same questions of another twenty Foxconn workers—both men and women—and all of them, without exception, used similar words to describe their feelings when looking at the photos. They all told me that they preferred natural settings such as the beach, the garden, or the park as the ideal backdrop for their wedding photos. Among these respondents, a few workers—again both men and women—agreed that the factory shop floor may not be their preference, but they could see the significance of having a picture taken there: "After all, it would serve as a memento of the place we met, or where we spent our youth."

JY's response makes it clear that, while the creative tension between the cold, hard surfaces of the factory shop floor and the human fragility of the individuals in Jia's photos may have won him prizes, these artistic choices do not seem to resonate with workers themselves. Here, it is tempting to read this as the workers' failure to appreciate art and to interpret their preference for the clichés of romantic consumption—beaches and gardens—as evidence of their deficiency in visual literacy, artistic taste, or aesthetic sophistication. However, it is important to remember that the workers' response to the images of the industrial backdrop is visceral rather than intellectual, and that their relationship to the space of the factory shop floor is experiential and embodied rather than abstract and conceptual. In other words, while the middle class may find the creative tension artistically powerful, workers may find it alienating or too confronting—or just too mundane. It is not necessarily the case that they are unable to appreciate art; it is more likely that this art portrays a reality that is too close to their everyday lives.

WR, from Guangxi, also in his early twenties, has worked at Foxconn for two years. His parents were divorced and then formed new families. Unlike many of the single rural migrant men from Foxconn that I interviewed, WR has a girlfriend, who comes from Hunan. WR told me that his parents were putting a lot of pressure on him to get married, but that he was not in a hurry. He spent his spare time playing the guitar, but he told me that work on the assembly line consumed most of his life; he liked to do extra shifts at the end of the day, and often volunteered to work on Saturdays and Sundays. WR did not like days off because having days off meant spending money, and he had little money to spend. Even with all the extra shifts, his salary was still a bit shy of 4,000 *yuan* a month (less than US$600). This extended quote from WR may help us to appreciate why he would not want to associate the shop floor with any notion of romance, and why the art of extracting aesthetic value from the industrial machine may seem fanciful, or even cruel, from a worker's perspective:

> My job is on the assembly that produces webcams for Apple. On the line, my hands are moving quickly and repetitively, while my brain is completely disconnected from what my hands are doing. It's as if my hands have their own memory. It's boring beyond belief, as we are not allowed to talk to co-workers, certainly not while the supervisor is watching over your shoulder. I normally work twelve hours in a single shift, with only one hour for lunch, and then another hour for dinner if an extra shift is required. Every two hours, we are allowed five minutes' break, and during that time we take a nap sitting on the work bench; we're not allowed to leave the shop floor. When I first started there, they still allowed us to go to the factory kiosk to buy a snack or something, but then they changed their minds and we are no longer allowed to leave the building for these breaks. The only thing we're allowed to do during the break is to make a cup of tea in the tea room. There's a window in the tea room, and if you stand close to the window you can see the sky—although it's filtered through a safety net.[3] That's the only place and time I can catch a glimpse of the outside world. I stand there for as long as I can, looking out at the world and up at the sky. The place feels like a prison.

Jia the photographer may have successfully subverted, inverted, and twisted the modern clichés of romantic consumption, but this artistic intervention was achieved with the cooperation of worker individuals who, if asked to nominate their own preferences for a romantic place, are likely to have opted for the very clichés Jia sought to eschew. To rural migrant workers, there is nothing clichéd about the beach, the garden, and the park; they represent a life that most of them can never afford to live. The workers' responses indicate that Jia's photography is not an art that resonates with the very subjects it seeks to represent. Since Jia made a class-specific artistic decision, it is only logical that the appreciation of his artistic talent was also class-specific. An artist's cliché is a worker's paradise.

Conclusion

The transitional nature of social restructuring means that the formation of class relations through the consumption of luxury goods can sometimes take place in more uncertain and unpredictable ways. Individuals' thinking and decision-making processes, increasingly occurring in highly mediated visual genres, formats, and platforms, are indeed points of contact between objects and symbols, between commodities and desire, and between action and perception. These points of contact mediate individuals' aspirational desire for upward social mobility, as well as their anxiety about the possibility of downward mobility, and in doing so, they simultaneously highlight and obscure the boundary between classes.

My analysis was motivated by questions about the political economy of cultural production and interpretation, and by an interest in exploring what the processes of production and interpretation tell us about class division and the cultural politics of inequality in China. The discussion demonstrates unequivocally that consumption practices related to love and romance are far from "trivial," and that studying them is not a retreat into the private and personal. Instead, analysis of this topic promises to yield novel ways of conceptualizing inequality, and to provide reliable and new ways of getting at what Kleinman and his colleagues (2011) call "deep China." Resonating with Adrian's (2006) work, the discussion in this chapter suggests that the production of seemingly similar wedding photographs is enacted and invested toward different ends, and the implications of such differences can only become legible by exploring the relationship between visual images and the substance of the social lives through which these images emerge.

Equally significantly, this account of the production, circulation, and reception of Jia's photo-essay provides significant clues to class-specific ways of documenting emotional pains. As an artistic experiment combining aesthetic considerations with social commentary, Jia successfully brings together the tropes of cross-class compassion, moral accreditation, and aesthetic critique. His work is at once a critique of the capitalist ideology of romantic consumption and an enthusiastic endorsement of it. As a work of art, as I have already observed, it aims to subvert, invert, or twist the popular idiom of romantic consumption. As social commentary, it forces the public to reflect on the price of modernization and industrialization for marginalized individuals. The images have had a wide resonance among the social and cultural elites in and outside China. However, while his images reference a dystopia associated with industrialization and modernization, they also lend themselves to the state project of building social harmony. The political usefulness of his work is evidenced in both China Central Television's co-opting of his work (see the previous chapter) and the *Oriental Morning Post*'s enthusiastic support. This case study makes it clear that inequality works, in part, through cultural domination, which in turn is reproduced by extracting the surplus value generated by the "lower class" in the symbolic as well as the material domain.

This discussion about how the motifs of bridal dresses and wedding photography operate in different social cohorts points to the complex relationship between consumption and class identification. Consumption has long been considered an important class marker. Yet, the market also resorts to the language of consumerism to obscure class division. By being offered freely to a number of rural migrants who could not otherwise afford them, the wedding dress and professional photoshoot—essential icons in the ritual of romantic consumption—serve to obscure class division by actively interpellating rural migrants into the role of aspiring consumer subjects. And while Jia showed disdain for the clichés of romantic expression, his modus operandi spoke the consumerist language of desire, thereby exemplifying the middle class's attempt to hide class division through the "common language of consumerist solidarity" (Illouz 1997, 251). However, this language, deployed to "romance" the rural migrant worker, only obscures the reality of what Bourdieu (1984, 316) calls "cultural domination," whereby "dominated classes" recognize as legitimate those cultural practices that, in effect, exclude them.

Chapter 4

DARK INTIMACY AND ITS MORAL-ECONOMIC LOGIC

Professor Huang Yingying is a sociologist at the Chinese People's University in Beijing. She has been conducting research on sex workers in China for more than twenty years, but the public knew very little about her until July 2020, after she appeared on YiXi, China's equivalent of the TED Talk. In her talk, Huang related her experience of living among, interacting with, and befriending sex workers in Shenzhen. She ended by saying: "sex workers are human beings, too." She reminded the audience that "reality is complex and society is stratified, so please be careful when making moral judgments. Even though we live in a different world and have different lives, we still need to respect the life choices made by others who live differently from us. Life is hard for everyone, so live and let live" (Huang Y. 2020).

Reflecting on the enthusiastic public response to this "marginal" topic—according to Huang, the video online had received "quite a few million hits"—Professor Huang came to the conclusion that, although nothing of what she had said in the talk was new to herself, it still came across as a revelation to her audience. With the exception of a few grassroots NGOs providing assistance to sex workers, the general public still knew very little about this topic, and mostly saw commercial sex as transgressive, not only legally, but also morally (Huang Y. 2021).

Huang had been a student of Professor Pan Suiming, dubbed the "godfather of sexology research" in China. Following in Professor Pan's footsteps, Huang also achieved widespread recognition and respect because of her capacity to earn the trust of sex workers through sustained immersion in their work and lives, as is evidenced in the research she and her team undertook on this subject (Huang Y. 2017). Despite her exceptional success in obtaining first-hand ethnographic observations of the lives of sex workers, Huang is mindful of the fact that her findings need to be represented to the intended audience as a *text*:

> The text is important, but our interpretation of the text must be situated in concrete life and social reality. All the sociological data you gather, including interview material, eventually ends up as some form of text. When you read a novel or see a film, you may pay attention to aesthetic questions or emotional depth, but reading these sources as a sociologist, I would pay special attention to

what the text is trying to tell me and not tell me, how is the story related to the social background, what is the text deliberately avoiding, or what does it simply not know how to talk about.

(Huang Y. 2021)

Professor Huang's two insights—the value and difficulty of obtaining first-hand ethnographic material, and the inevitability and importance of conceiving texts as having potential sociological interpretations—resonate with some Western sociologists and anthropologists whose work I draw on. For instance, recognizing the difficulty of generating data about sexual intimacy, both anthropologists like Judith Farquhar (2002) and sociologists like Eva Illouz (2012) turn to fictional accounts and media texts. Farquhar, working in the Chinese context, considers works of literature to be "wonderful anthropological partners" (2002, 24) and believes that "self-health" publications in China offer considerable "ethnographic riches" (18).

While the CCTV love stories I discussed in Chapter 2 project positive figures who are motivated by and aspire to happy marriages, the warmth of family life, and spousal intimacy, and while the rural migrants' eager—and free—participation in romantic consumption discussed in Chapter 3 relies on a normative idea of love and romance, I am acutely aware that these rosy images are only one side of the coin. The other side, the "dark" side, is represented in the widely circulated public discourses about rural migrants' supposedly transgressive sex lives, including stories of migrant women selling sex and migrant men pursuing sex. As outlined in Chapter 1, the love lives and sexual practices of young migrants have frequently caused concern due to their perceived threat to public health, moral order, and social stability; they are therefore both alarming to the government and offensive to middle-class sensibilities. Although I was fortunate enough to have spent a lot of time interacting with my rural migrant research subjects, talking about "matters of the heart" and their feelings, and sometimes simply "hanging out" with them, I was confronted with a set of methodological problems. First, how could I—how should I—investigate someone else's love life, particularly when their heart is tired and broken? Second, how could I document intimacy, especially intimacy of the dark kind? Intimacy, by its very nature, usually takes place away from the gaze of the public, including that of the researcher doing fieldwork; and an understanding of dark intimacy—purchased, violent, injurious—is even harder, if not impossible, to obtain. Third, how should I go about writing about marginalized individuals who may have emerged from an intimate relationship feeling hurt, abandoned, sad, or angry, but who may not be willing or able to express these emotions verbally?

In this chapter, as a way of addressing these problems by "getting around" them, I take cues from Huang, Farquhar, and Illouz and the like, and turn to a range of texts: a novella, a novel, a cluster of news stories (from both commercial and state media), and a feature story in a popular "lowbrow" magazine in the genre of reportage. Juxtaposing these texts brings into sharp relief the possible contradictions, connections, and coalitions between several discursive positions, thereby helping to reveal the nuance and complexity of the cultural politics of inequality. These fictional and media texts are useful for at least two reasons. First, as Farquhar suggests, writers—both fictional and journalistic—are our potential research partners, in whose works we can mine ethnographic insights even though we know that the texts cannot substitute for ethnographic fieldwork data. Second, and perhaps more pertinent to the central concern of this chapter, these texts target audiences that are segmented along lines of class, gender, and the rural–urban divide; they are also published within various business models, and push diverse political-cultural agendas. In what follows, before I proceed to analyze these texts, I will first provide an account of my visit to "HL,"[1] a grassroots NGO that advocates for rural migrant sex workers. I will then set up the analytical and conceptual framework according to which I engage in the textual interpretation at the heart of this chapter.

Perspectives From a Grassroots NGO

On a warm day in November 2017, I left the workers' informal housing area where I normally lived and hung out, and took a day trip to downtown Shenzhen to meet BB, the director of HL, one of the NGOs that Huang Yingying mentioned in her talk. The organization's headquarters is an office in a high-rise building, just like any other company premises. BB and her colleagues provide practical and emotional support to *jiejie* (literally meaning "older sisters"—their respectful way of referring to rural migrant women who work as sex workers). *Jiejie* are spread around the city, ranging from high-end exclusive clubs to hair salons, massage parlors, and street corners. Because prostitution is illegal, the organization has trouble accessing sex workers—especially initially. BB told me that taxi drivers were valuable sources of information about their likely locations. Intriguingly, messages posted online by male clients warning about possible police raids also offered clues to where sex workers could be working. Although their intention is to help these women, BB's small team still has trouble gaining their trust. "When we approach them, they usually don't believe us at first, thinking that we're either touting for business on behalf of hotels or recruiting them for pyramid marketing. Some even suspect that we're working undercover for the police."[2]

HL also aims to destigmatize sex work, and the NGO advocates a more tolerant understanding of the decisions and choices made by these migrant workers. As BB and her colleagues made clear, *jiejie* are often mothers and daughters, wives, and girlfriends, and in most cases they opt to sell their sexual services in order to provide for their children and aging parents. Sometimes their husbands or boyfriends work as their pimps and protectors:

> A husband-and-wife team is not uncommon. I often come across women who come back to work as *jiejie* after a period of time back in the village. They go back, get married, have a baby, leave the baby behind, and come back. I know someone who returned to work as soon as her baby was one month old. She told me her family needed money quickly.

To BB and her colleagues, the "normalcy" of the *jiejie* phenomenon is evidenced by the fact that some of the *jiejie* they talk to still believe in love and romance. As one of BB's colleagues observed:

> Many of us dare not love once we are betrayed or cheated on, and one would imagine that *jiejie* are totally immune to falling in love, since many of them enter the trade following broken marriages, domestic violence, and sexual assaults. Sometimes they do fall in love, though, and some of them are incurably romantic. Others are still waiting to fall in love.

Another observation made by BB was that some *jiejie* have quite conservative and traditional ideas about sex:

> You may think that because selling sex is their job, they would be much more open and casual about discussing sex. We've been surprised that this is not always so. When we want to talk about sexual hygiene and contraception and so on, some get really shy and can't bring themselves to participate. Some even say things like "girls don't talk about this sort of thing."

BB believes that the migrant women she has encountered tend to fall into one of two categories: those who are very scared of being caught for their transgressive activities, are ashamed of their occupation, and feel very guilty; and those who believe that they are doing nothing wrong, since they are working to earn money— just like anyone else. BB and her colleagues were keen to stress that very few migrant women who work as *jiejie* regard selling sex as a permanent profession; many of them also work intermittently in factories:

> I've come across women who work day shifts in the factory but work as *jiejie* in the evening. I've also met women who start with factory work and then move on to sex work. And when business is slow in the sex trade due to police crackdowns or for other reasons, they may go back to factory work until business picks up.

HL regularly compiles in-house booklets, including stories written by sex workers themselves, so other sex workers can share experiences, provide tips and advice about self-protection, and give each other moral and emotional support. These are valuable ethnographic materials about a group of people whose work and lives are otherwise hidden. BB shared with me a series of fieldwork notes that either record her own conversations with *jiejie* or are transcripts of statements from *jiejie* themselves—statements that, once anonymized, were circulated via HL's WeChat subscription account.[3] One statement documents the story of a fifty-five-year-old rural migrant who had worked in the sex trade for twenty years. "Sister Li" was married with children, but her husband had no income and refused to share any household chores. "We were too poor. So, I had to get out and work." Sister Li worked at a number of odd jobs before deciding to "plunge into the sea" of sex work. Since then, she has experienced myriad misadventures, including being robbed, arrested by the police, intimidated by clients, and extorted by brothel owners. But she has no regrets:

> If I hadn't decided to take the plunge, I would never have been able to build a house for my son to get married, and pay for my social welfare insurance. Starting from next year, I'll be eligible for the pension. I'll be going home to enjoy my retirement.
>
> (BB's fieldwork notes 2018)

For this *jiejie*, her decision to become a sex worker was purely rational—there was nothing immoral or shameful about it. "Ah Mi," another sex worker, echoes this sentiment:

> Every decision I've made, I've made it for the sake of my family. I don't steal, rob, or swindle money from people. I make money just like every other business person. So, I hope I'll be treated the same way as everyone else. At least this way, I can provide for my daughter, and I'm doing my bit to ensure my financial security when I'm old …. I have no regrets.
>
> (BB's fieldwork notes 2018)

Both Sister Li and Ah Mi are painfully aware of the social stigma attached to their work, which exposes them to myriad forms of abuse, violence, and exploitation. A lack of legal status means they are unable to go to the police when they are robbed, beaten up, or conned by clients. Whether their clients are white-collar professionals in the central business district or migrant men in the cheap salons near factories, they have to have their wits about them in order to protect themselves.

Despite such challenges, these workers are adamant that they deserve just as much respect as any other person who is prepared to do honest work for honest pay. Like Sister Li, many other *jiejie* also work to ensure that their children are clothed, fed, and educated, and that when their sons grow up, they will have enough money to find a wife. Feeling that they should not be cast in a criminal light, they frame their work in terms of unconditional maternal love for their children and family, and stress that their willingness to make sacrifices on behalf of their children makes them as morally commendable as any other selfless mother.

Analytical Questions and Methodological Pathways

The sense of transgression and its likely consequences that *jiejie* have to reckon with points to the need to consider the cultural politics of this phenomenon. Understandings of sexual transgression are historically and culturally specific, and vary from one political/religious context to another. The basis on which behavior is determined to be sexually transgressive can be legal (legitimate/illicit), social (normal/deviant), moral (acceptable/objectionable), or political (conforming/not conforming to state authority). The concept of transgression has always been central to philosophers and scholars of other disciplines. While many philosophers have written on transgression in contexts such as religion, culture, or political power, it is Michel Foucault who sees sexual experience as a central domain in which boundary-crossing—a paradigm of transgressive behavior—occurs. Foucault sees subject formation as a process of "construction" and "deconstruction" through negotiating the boundary between "self" and "other." For him, transgression, defined as the repeated crossing of boundaries, leads to a destabilized subject that is neither unified nor rational. In terms of sexuality, this dualism would be defined in terms of normative (e.g., procreative) sexuality versus deviant sexuality (e.g., homosexuality) (Foucault 1977).

Drawing on Foucault, and in dialogue with Mikhail Bakhtin's work on the carnivalesque, Peter Stallybrass and Allon White (1986) identify four domains of transgression: place, body, social identity, and subjectivity. They suggest that ordering and sense-making in each of these domains is governed by "interrelating and dependent hierarchies of high and low" (2). The politics and poetics of transgression, they argue, is therefore not only about forming and maintaining these hierarchies, but also about the "processes through which the low troubles the high" (3). Finally, they argue that, since "what is socially peripheral may be symbolically central" (23), transgression has become an important concept for understanding how liminal or minority experiences help to form larger sociocultural boundaries.

A growing body of recent China-focused ethnography appears to embody this kind of intellectual endeavor, although not all of this work explicitly addresses the theme of transgression or intimacy. This includes Sandra Hyde's (2007) ethnography in Southwest China, where she examines the cultural politics of HIV/AIDS across boundaries of various kinds, and in the negotiations between corporeal, material, and discursive spheres. It includes ethnographic research on sex work (Pan 2006), queer voices (Bao 2018; Engebretsen 2014; Kam 2013; Kong 2011), and intimate services provided by rural migrant men (Jeffreys and Su 2018; T. Liu 2020; Tsang 2020), much of which explores the interface between the personal/individual and state power/socioeconomic forces in China.

Just as *jiejie* must reckon with the social stigma of transgression, so too must they reckon with what I call "dark intimacy." If intimacy is an "intrinsic good" that involves "mutual trust" and "caring attention," and "typically evokes ... intense, warm feelings" (Zelizer 2005), dark intimacy, as I define it, refers to those sexual relationships that (1) are intrinsically structured around an imbalance in power, either within the relationship or between the couple and their context; and that, as a result, (2) operate in ways that may lead to injury or threaten to diminish trust, respect, and dignity for one or both individuals. This power imbalance may derive from differences in gender, socioeconomic status, and urban versus rural origin, or personal attributes such as beauty, personality, or sex appeal. The imbalance can effectively restructure intimacy to produce feelings of shame, humiliation, anger, and low self-esteem for those who are exploited in the relationship. Tiantian Zheng's (2022) recent ethnography about intimate partner violence in China is a powerful case study of such dark intimacy. I have chosen the term "dark intimacy" to highlight both its similarities to and differences from Illouz's (2007) notion of "cold intimacy," and the kinds of intimacy Zelizer (2005) characterizes as "warm."

Cold intimacy can also follow the same logic of economic relations and exchange as dark intimacy, but as Illouz defines it, it is practiced mostly by the middle classes and uses the language and techniques of therapy and other market repertoires. Central to this understanding of intimacy is the technique of communication, and the concept and practice of communication is seen as an essential aspect of the self. Rather than allowing a relationship to take its "natural" course, cold intimacy subjects the relationship to a range of calculated and strategic interventions. Cold and warm intimacy share the goal of creating trust and security, whereas dark intimacy involves exploitation and the abuse of power in unequal relationships, or potentially risky but mutually accepted transactional exchanges driven more by socioeconomic and other external factors than by the desire to create a trusting and secure relationship. Dark intimacy may thus involve two consenting individuals and may sometimes possess the strategic nature of cold intimacy, but it rarely involves pursuing an enduring and mutually respectful relationship, which is the overriding concern of both cold and warm intimacy.

In exchanges involving dark intimacy, one or both individuals can often expect to experience a high level of humiliation, shame, anger, and despair: intimate encounters colored by a power imbalance bring with them the risk of injury, pain, and damage. But there are connections as well as differences between these conceptions of intimacy, and they exist on a continuum rather than as binary opposites. Furthermore, just as warm intimacy, considered to be an intrinsic good, is unevenly distributed, so too is dark intimacy, considered an "intrinsic bad," differentially distributed, usually based on social markers such as race, gender, and class (Illouz 1997). Studying the commercialization of intimacy, Arlie Hochschild (2003) observes that people occupying different socioeconomic positions have different emotional experiences, inhabit different emotional worlds, and may even have different emotional ontologies. Given this, it is worthwhile studying how gender and class affect not only one's chances of enjoying warm intimacy, but also one's capacity to avoid dark intimacy.

The statements of the *jiejie* in the previous section reinforce these sociologists' observation that intrinsic goods such as warm intimacy are distributed unevenly across class and gender, but they further remind us that the discursive resources available to construct the meanings of intimacy are also unevenly distributed. While there is little public understanding of the socioeconomic circumstances that propel rural migrant women into the sex industry, there is an abundance of widely circulated public narratives about rural migrants' sex lives, including migrant men pursuing sex and migrant women providing it, with both activities occurring in the gray zone of illicitness.

The account given by HL and the statements from the *jiejie* that HL supports give us a rare glimpse into how poor or socioeconomically marginalized individuals make decisions about their bodies and their sexual capital. But how are their decisions represented in public discourses, and how is their sexual intimacy constructed by someone other than themselves? What moral, cultural, and political frameworks do they use to make sense of their sexual choices, and to what extent do these frameworks resonate with the *jiejie*'s own perspectives? Answering these questions may yield important clues about the cultural politics of inequality, given that socioeconomic inequality goes hand in hand with the unequal distribution of discursive resources (W. Sun 2013), and that any intellectual critique of inequality must address both the material and symbolic dimensions of these two forms of inequality, as well as the interplay between them.

Below, I first discuss how state and commercial media responded to the controversy of some Foxconn factory workers who were moonlighting as sex workers. This is followed by a section that pits *jiejie* in Shenzhen against a rural woman whose experience was reported in the popular Chinese magazine *Soulmate* (*Zhiyin*). Then, shifting to the perspective of migrant men, I explore how the sexual economy in China's industrial zone reshapes the masculinity of men at the bottom of the social hierarchy, taking as my starting point two key literary texts: "The Sound of a Cleaver Being Sharpened in a Rented Room" ("*Chuzu wu li de modao sheng*"; hereafter "The Sound") and *Loach* (*Niqiu*). What connects and gives coherence to these cases is their capacity, when analyzed in conjunction with one another, to reveal traces of "the proliferation of distinctions, practices, stories, and moral injunctions concerning the interplay of economic transactions and intimacy" (Zelizer 2005, 20). Through the prism of these discrete cases, echoing Professor Huang's advice on how to read a text sociologically, I aim to address some key questions raised earlier: What are the practical, material, and economic circumstances in which rural migrants make decisions about sexual intimacy? What moral-economic grammar propels their decision-making? What perspectives and discursive positions are used to construct narratives about them? And what are the relationships and connections between these various discursive positions?

Foxconn, "Factory Girls," and State–Capital Complicity

The *Economic Weekly* (*Caijing tianxia*) is one of China's most influential and widely read publications, focusing on economic and business matters. Since its inception in 2012, it has enjoyed credibility in the business sector as well as among ordinary readers. On September 13, 2013, the magazine featured a leading story entitled "Foxconn's Night Life" (Sina Technology 2013b). Appearing without a byline, the eight-thousand-word article claimed to be an honest account of what life was like for Foxconn workers away from the factory shop floor, in the commercial and recreational spaces outside the industrial complexes in Shenzhen and Zhengzhou.

Drawing on interviews with individual workers, one section of the article landed the *Economic Weekly* in controversy. Subtitled "Factory Workers as Part-Time Sex Workers," this section began: "In a place where tens of thousands of people in their early twenties concentrate, love and sex are unavoidable subjects." According to the story, the budget hotels near the Foxconn industrial precinct do a roaring trade, especially on weekends, with lovers seeking some much-anticipated intimacy. Night clubs and disco dance halls are also portrayed as good places to meet someone for sex. Workers interviewed by the unnamed journalist seemed blasé about casual sex. Based on this journalist's observations, gynecological clinics are located next to night clubs—clinics of dubious credibility advertising "abortions without pain." Equally noticeable are myriad brothels camouflaged as "ten-bob massage parlors" and beauty salons.

While none of this would come as a surprise to most people, the story nevertheless made a claim that captured the public's imagination: that some women factory workers also sell sex for additional income. A young Shenzhen factory worker and part-time sex worker disclosed to the journalist that she knew a "considerable number of women in her factory" who were part-time sex workers, explaining that "when you put more than 100,000 single men and women together, sex is bound to happen. Since it's bound to happen, you might as well tap into this need and make some money. It all comes down to money." According to this young woman, some women end up quitting factory work to become full-time sex workers. When asked whether she regretted having taken this step, one woman answered, "My only regret is that I hadn't thought of doing it earlier." She felt that she should have taken advantage of her youth and made more money so she could go back home and start a small business sooner.

The *Economic Weekly*'s exposé of the sex trade among Foxconn workers was immediately reposted as many as 300 times. In order to attract attention, some websites reframed the article with a more sensational title, such as "Foxconn's Part-Time Sex Workers: Their Only Regret Is Not Having Done It Sooner"; "Sex Services Provided by Foxconn Workers: Their Own Account"; and "Foxconn Workers Sell Sex for 300 Each Time."

On the same day as the *Economic Weekly* article was published, the Foxconn Workers' Union issued a public protest via its microblog (Dagong bao 2013). The union described the article as "dark, and in poor taste," and called its use of "dirty and denigrating" language an insult to the 400,000 women workers at Foxconn, who were "hard-working, dedicated, and have made a contribution to China's manufacturing sector." They demanded that the magazine withdraw the article and issue a public apology to Foxconn workers. The union also published a longer blog further interrogating the *Economic Weekly*'s credibility, highlighting the story's failure to include the perspective of Foxconn management, criticizing the fact that the story was written by a cadet journalist, and castigating the *Weekly* for its "erroneous" apportioning of blame to Foxconn for the structural social problems that had arisen from China's rapid social transformation. Far from apologizing, however, the *Weekly* issued a statement on September 17, four days after the initial story, reasserting the truth of the article (Sina Technology 2013a).

A week after the controversy had erupted, on September 25, *China Women's News* (*Zhongguo funü bao*), the official newspaper of the All-China Women's Federation (*Zhonghua quanguo funü lianhehui*, hereafter the Women's Federation), weighed in on the debate by publishing a by-lined commentary entitled "It Is Worth Paying More Attention to Women Workers' Inner World." The article pointed out that, although a small number of Foxconn workers did engage in "illegal activities," it was wrong to regard all women workers at Foxconn through a tainted lens: "Behind this war of words are the real lives of many *dagong* [migrant workers; literally, 'working for a boss']—individuals who live with uncertainty and a sense of loss of purpose." Adopting a seemingly non-partisan stance, *China Women's News* apportioned blame to both sides. It criticized the *Economic Weekly*—as well as many websites that reposted the article with more sensational titles—for pandering to "voyeurism" and for irresponsibly catering to "low tastes." It clearly did not agree with the *Weekly*'s argument that some migrant women were simply making an economically rationalist decision by shifting from assembly-line work to sex work. And while it acknowledged the Foxconn Workers' Union for defending the workers, it pointed out that protesting in words was not enough, arguing that the union should take concrete action to give dignity to its workers. It also gave Foxconn's management a good dressing down for its failure to "own up to its responsibilities, urging the organization to upgrade its production structure and improve working conditions for its workers" (Yao 2013, A02).

To anyone untutored in labor politics in China, the Workers' Union appears to be the most logical advocate for Foxconn's workers. But research by labor sociologists such as Pun Ngai, Mark Selden, and their colleagues (2014) makes it clear that that is not so. The union has consistently remained silent on a wide range of crucial issues, including workers' wages, compensation for work-related injuries, suicides, working conditions, and living standards. The Foxconn Workers' Union consistently sides with management, and its role in the controversy concerning sex workers is at best ineffectual, at worst hypocritical.

If the *China Women's News* article gives the impression that the party-state, as represented by the Women's Federation and its official publication, is critical of transnational capital, a longer feature article in the *China Women's News* more than a month later confirms that there are actually considerable complicities and moral coalitions between the Women's Federation and Foxconn. In contrast to the "dark" and voyeuristic tone of the *Economic Weekly*, this second *China Women's News* feature, about the lives of Foxconn women workers in Zhengzhou, is full of optimism. Certainly, life is hard and work on the assembly line is "repetitive," but workers "face the challenges head on, and are rewarded with warmth and happiness." They forge friendships with and lend support to each other, and learn to get along with co-workers on the assembly lines and in the dormitories, with "understanding and mutual respect." The article suggests that Foxconn is also the birthplace of many love stories, with many couples having found a "harbor where they can rest and nurture their hearts." Both the local government (through the local Women's Federation branch) and Foxconn's management are reported as playing a caring and enabling role. Equally notably, Foxconn is depicted as a place of hope, where workers learn new skills, acquire useful knowledge and experience, and, for those who apply themselves, have opportunities for promotion. Everyone dreams of making enough money to buy a house and start a family. Workers exemplifying "positive" attitudes are quoted as saying that they were deeply hurt by the denigrating reporting on Foxconn women. While a small number of people "could not resist temptation and had gone down the wrong path," the majority of Foxconn's women workers were becoming "mature" and were as "hardy and resilient as the plum flowers blossoming in winter" (Yan D. and Su 2013).

This second story in the *China Women's News* clarifies the moral and political boundaries separating the legal from the illicit, the desirable from the objectionable, and implies that those who correctly observe these boundaries are morally superior. The article concurs with the Foxconn Workers' Union in saying that the *Economic Weekly* article was demeaning to Foxconn's women workers because it implied that it is shameful and morally unacceptable to sell sex to alleviate poverty. However, there is also an important divergence. The union wanted to gloss over the imperfections and defend all Foxconn women workers, whereas the *China Women's News* story acknowledges the existence of a "minority of women" who engage in "illegal practices" and who have "gone down the wrong path" due to their moral weakness. In other words, the Women's Federation, and the government it represents, wants to endorse the moral virtue of the majority of workers, while aiming to "separate the wheat from the chaff" by dividing them into "the good" and "the bad."

Despite their divergences, both Foxconn and the Women's Federation adopt a legal and moral framework that is based on a dichotomy of transgressive versus normative—a framework that is focused on governing and control. Sometimes at odds, but often complicit, the state, the market, and cultural/moral forces generally all shape public understandings of what is (un)desirable, (il)legitimate, and (un)acceptable in the sphere of sex and intimacy. These narratives, while differing in perspective, all insist on the binary division between the "good girl" (who works on the assembly line despite longer hours and less pay than sex work) and the "bad girl" (who transgresses moral boundaries, has no shame, and opts to sell sex for more and faster money). None of these narratives acknowledges the fact that, whether working on the assembly line or selling sex, migrant women's decisions are partly shaped by extrinsic forces that include state control, capital exploitation, and patriarchal practices. The war of words between Foxconn and the Women's Federation overlooks, or perhaps strategically ignores, the elephant in the room: transnational capital. Over a period of four decades, this force has securely installed a regime of industrial production and a way of life, both of which are dictated by and geared toward the logic of capital accumulation. This logic ensures that human interactions, including those involving sex, love, and desire, have no alternative but to unfold in the capitalist nexus between power and money. While being a moral and ideological bedfellow of both the Foxconn Workers' Union and the organization's management, the party-state is at the same time a stakeholder in the regime of transnational capital and, as a result, can only construct narratives that justify and normalize the logic of capital, rather than questioning or critiquing it.

Soulmate: *The Moral Grammar of a Popular Magazine*

Founded in 1985 with the humble sum of 30,000 *yuan* by the Women's Federation's branch in Hubei Province, *Soulmate* (*Zhiyin*) is a biweekly magazine. Its Chinese title means "kindred spirits," "soulmates," or "bosom friends." The magazine, specializing in long-form journalism on soft news topics such as family, friendships, and relationships, was an instant success, quickly reaching a circulation of 400,000.

According to a 2014 figure, *Soulmate* boasts a circulation of six million, second only to *Reader* (*Duzhe*), and is now ranked fifth globally in terms of circulation (Tao 2014). It is very likely that some of the *jiejie* discussed earlier have at some stage been readers of *Soulmate*.

Soulmate publishes only true stories, even though they are told in a long-form narrative style, and its winning combination of sensational news content, fictional narrative formula, and melodramatic style has even given birth to a "*Soulmate* genre." *Soulmate*'s recurring narratives revolve around individuals being thrown into life-changing situations, such as dire poverty, life-threatening illness, and debilitating accidents. A disproportionately highly percentage of the human dramas that feature in the magazine revolve around individuals' acts of selflessness and sacrifice, when someone in the family suddenly needs an expensive operation or a kidney transplant. Unfolding against this background of life-changing situations are the perennial dramas that reveal humans' capacity for compassion, selflessness, and sacrifice, with themes of love lost, found, regained, or betrayed being played out in the retelling of these dramas.

It is clear that the misfortunes commonly experienced by people in the *Soulmate* stories are often symptomatic of China's "compressed modernity" and the consequent widening of socioeconomic inequality. For instance, the diagnosis of a terminal disease may plunge an ordinary family into debt, due to the withdrawal of state-provided health care for all citizens. Manslaughter could be the result of a jealous woman's discovery that her husband, having become rich overnight, has taken on mistresses. Thus, whether they are portrayed as embodying moral virtue or moral depravity, the characters in *Soulmate* are individuals who are caught up in, flounder, and in some cases are dumped hard by the whirlwind of China's hurried and bumpy journey toward modernity. However, the readers of *Soulmate* are led to believe that fortunes and misfortunes in both money and love are a matter of luck, and that to keep misfortunes at bay they should learn a moral lesson from these stories, as a result of which they will ultimately be rewarded for being a "good" person.

To some cultural elites, the phenomenal and sustained popularity of *Soulmate* is a cause for concern. To them, the magazine is proof that, by catering to the taste and sensibility of the lowest common denominator, commercial popular culture has monopolized the cultural field (Zhang N. 2013). Despite such criticisms, *Soulmate* has a strong pedagogic agenda. Each issue features three leading stories, prominently labeled "recommended reading" in the table of contents; many of the stories are bookended with editorial comments urging readers to emulate the loyal, trustworthy, and selfless lovers, to learn a lesson from the mistakes and follies of those who have gone astray, and to condemn those who choose violent, unlawful, or immoral methods to resolve emotional conflicts. The magazine warrants careful analysis in that it is a mixture of positions: it outlines the socioeconomic circumstances that propel a woman to make certain choices about her intimate life, but it is still couched within a moral framework of the good versus the bad man/woman. The boundaries of transgression remain intact, while the motivations behind each story's protagonists are simultaneously traditional and neoliberal.

4. Dark Intimacy and its Moral-Economic Logic

We now look more closely at the pedagogic agenda of the *Soulmate* genre, through a December 2014 story in the magazine. The article is intriguingly entitled "A Legend about a 'Marriage for Sale': Fast Track to Money While Love Awaits." In April 2014, the story tells us, a twenty-five-year-old woman named Zuo Xiaofang places a notice in the personal column of a local paper, offering to marry anyone for a fee of 100,000 *yuan*—a sum equivalent to the customary local marriage dowry. Xiaofang's offer is motivated by her desire to save her brother, who suffers from leukemia and is in urgent need of money for a bone marrow transplant. While the advertisement is met with widespread derision, a twenty-six-year-old man named Liu Zhi from the same township answers it. He has heard that Xiaofang is a kind-hearted woman, that she had lost her father at an early age and left home early to work as a *dagongmei* (rural migrant woman) in order to support her mother. He has also heard that she has never had a boyfriend, but that she takes matters of the heart seriously.

Liu is moved by Xiaofang's devotion to her brother, and offers her the money in exchange for an opportunity to spend time with her and her family. Liu is not a wealthy man. He has saved a little but has to borrow the rest. He says that his only expectation is to get to know her. He promises he will not force Xiaofang to marry him, and is prepared to wait until both he and she feel certain that marriage is what they want. Writing from the perspective of an omniscient third person, the reporter says:

> Xiaofang is deeply grateful, but she does not know what else to do except to make herself fall in love with Liu Zhi. She knows that the only way to repay his kindness is for them to fall in love with each other within the shortest possible time.
>
> (Aying 2014, 36–8)

And fall in love they do, marrying soon after, and Xiaofang's brother, having survived chemotherapy and a bone barrow transplant, is soon discharged from hospital. The reporter is at pains to assure readers that the marriage is based on mutual understanding and admiration:

> Liu could have insisted on getting married straight away, asserting his conjugal right as a husband-to-be [based on Xiaofang's offer], but he doesn't. Instead, he waits patiently, looking after Xiaofang and her brother in hospital, in the hope that by doing so she will get to know him and appreciate him, and will eventually, of her own volition, fall in love with him.
>
> (37)

Are we to read this as a romantic story, or does this couple embody the very antithesis of romance? More importantly, in what ways—if any—do Xiaofang and Liu Zhu embody exemplary moral virtues? After all, Xiaofang's offer of marriage in exchange for money seems downright mercenary to her fellow townsfolk, not to mention foolhardy. And Liu Zhu's decision to purchase an opportunity to win Xiaofang's heart seems an equally risky investment. One could be forgiven for a cynical response: Xiaofang may be a dutiful daughter and sister, and she apparently places more value on family than her own happiness; having very low expectations of marriage, she may not be concerned about forfeiting her chances of finding love, as long as she can make a difference to her own family. Similarly, Liu Zhi wants a wife and has the money to "purchase" one, so why not embrace the offer when it arises?

Xiaofang's marriage-for-sale offer and Liu Zhi's willingness to go along with it may contravene modern ideas about love, in which free choice, equality, intimacy, and emotional fulfillment are foundational. Yet in this story it would be too simplistic to read the couple's actions as examples of feudalism and patriarchy. Faced with poverty and a terminal illness in the family, Xiaofang does not expect a handout from the government or the community, nor does she blame the system for having failed her and her family. Even when she feels she is at the end of her tether, she does not resort to illegal means of acquiring wealth, such as prostitution. Instead, she maintains hope and actively seeks to change her own and her family's lives for the better. She is simultaneously an exemplar of the virtuous, self-sacrificing daughter promoted within the old feudal moral code, and—quite consistent with the contemporary ethos of neoliberal governmentality—a self-managing, self-enterprising subject, an individual who is able and willing to overcome her family crisis through her own devices. However, unlike her society's elites, who have more resources at their disposal, her capacity to be self-reliant and enterprising is very limited; she must achieve her goal by sacrificing her freedom to choose whom she marries and falls in love with.

Why should such a story be considered newsworthy? Why should Xiaofang's and Liu Zhi's choices receive any kind of validation? There is at least one clear take-home message from the story. If a woman in a socioeconomically marginal position decides to marry for economic rather than romantic reasons, she should not be chastised for being pragmatic or not modern enough. While a few people in the highest echelons of Chinese society may base their love options on ideals of individual choice, freedom, and a high level of warm intimacy, the majority still cannot afford such "luxury goods." Just as class privilege is reflected in differentiated levels of consumption, so too does such privilege manifest itself as stratified access to love as a "moral good" (Illouz 1997). Indeed, Xiaofang's marriage as an economic transaction, made morally acceptable to her by her status as a part-feudal, part-neoliberal consumer subject, is one of the few options individuals from the underclasses can afford. Given that genuine Cinderella-meets-Prince stories are the stuff of fiction, myriad self-arranged poverty-alleviation strategies through marriage may well be many women's only realistic option.

Also worth asking is why a purely pragmatic marriage arrangement is narrated here as a love story. Xiaofang and Liu Zhi could have "married first, and waited for love to grow" (*xian jiehun, hou lianai*), through familiarization, just as older generations did. But instead of adopting this non-romantic but more plausible framework, which nevertheless involves some kind of "love," the story wants readers to believe in the possibility of romantic love, even though Xiaofang and

Liu Zhi's agreement comes across to many as the very antithesis of romantic love. To imagine Xiaofang and Liu Zhi getting to know each other reasonably well and ending up liking each other enough to want to marry is one thing. But to convince readers that Xiaofang succeeds in "falling in love" with a person not of her own choice within the required time is quite another. Can falling in love be construed as a form of emotional labor, requiring, as Hochschild (1983) observes, such "deep acting" that the self comes to believe in it?

Readers are told emphatically that Liu Zhu will not want to consummate their marriage unless Xiaofang falls in love with him, and that Xiaofang wills herself to fall in love as soon as possible. However, nowhere does the reporter acknowledge that, as the modern ideology of romance has us believe, love is spontaneous and individualistic, that it cannot be bought, rushed, forced to happen, or derived from gratitude. By insisting that marriage-for-sale and genuine love can go hand in hand, *Soulmate* does not aim to produce a fantasy of social mobility; nevertheless, its ideological agenda is no less ambitious. The magazine wants readers to contemplate adopting a more practical and instrumental approach to love as a way of coping with life's difficulties and challenges; but it also wants readers to believe that the pursuit of this instrumental approach to love can be just as romantic.

"The Sound of a Cleaver Being Sharpened in a Rented Room"

A fine-grained portrayal of dark intimacy and rural migrants is not complete unless it also discusses migrant men's sexuality. When the topic of sexual loneliness among rural migrant men is mentioned in policy discourses, it is often couched within the framework of social order and stability. The emotional experience of a large number of single, sexually repressed men is seldom available in public discourses outside the framework of criminality and transgression. The following story, written by migrant worker turned professional writer Wang Shiyue (also known as Wang Shixiao), offers us a rare glimpse of this experience.

Wang Shiyue has published numerous prize-winning novels, but it was the publication of "The Sound" (Wang S. 2001) that established him as one of the earliest and most promising *dagong* writers in South China. Wang adopts a first-person narrative to tell the story of Tianyou, a rural migrant worker in a Taiwanese-owned factory in Shenzhen. Like many co-workers, Tianyou is content with having a bed in the company-provided dormitory, sharing the room with eleven other people, until he starts dating He Li, a worker from another factory. Tianyou then rents a room far from the city, at a fraction of the cost of the dormitory, and for a brief period each weekend the lovers ensconce themselves in blissful intimacy, oblivious of the man who rents the room next door. Tianyou and his girlfriend want to be together, alone, in a space of their own, without being bothered by or bothering anyone else—a privilege taken for granted by most middle-class people. Their desire is desperate and intense precisely because this is not something they can enjoy on a routine basis. Many circumstances conspire against them, including a precarious living environment, job insecurity, bad labor conditions, and insufficient money for decent, convenient accommodation. While most middle-class individuals take their right to intimacy—either warm or cold—as a given, the precarity of rural migrants' existence makes their right to intimacy at best contingent, conditional, and vulnerable to violation and exploitation.

The couple gradually realize, with mounting fear and horror, that the man next door sharpens his cleaver whenever they make love. Their appetite for intimacy evaporates, and Tianyou is suddenly plagued with impotence. They are unable to afford a rental room elsewhere, so the girlfriend leaves Tianyou, saying, "I went out with you because I wanted to feel safe and secure. But that place gives me the creeps and I now feel terrified."

Abandoned by his girlfriend, Tianyou becomes depressed and distracted at work. One day he loses four fingers while operating a lathe. His boss accuses him of carelessness and refuses him compensation. Tianyou is enraged. Alone in his rented room, he is greeted by Hong, the woman who lives with his cleaver-sharpening neighbor. Tianyou flies into a rage at her: "Now my girlfriend has left me, my body is deformed, and I've lost my job, all because of your stupid man!" Sensing Tianyou's seething resentment and feeling empathy toward him, Hong visits one day and gives him a chance to "get even." "Have me," she says, "if that makes you feel better." It is an offer that both surprises and placates Tianyou, and the scene ends with Tianyou taking up her offer, thereby releasing—albeit temporarily—his sexual frustrations onto the body of the cleaver sharpener's wife.

Still, Tianyou cannot fully appease his anger. One day, consumed with blind rage, he bursts into the room next door, wildly wielding his own cleaver, and before he knows what he is doing, he cuts the man numerous times. Instead of fighting back, the man tells Tianyou his story. Apparently, he and Hong had been childhood lovers. Unable to gain their parents' approval, they left the village to work in the southern factories so they could be together. For years they stuck together, going through numerous abortions as they could not afford to have a child. Hong's luck then took a turn for the worse. She was sacked from her job, became an escort, and one day she was raped by her boss. Hong and her lover agreed, against their better judgment, that she would work as a prostitute for one year, then they would leave to start a new life elsewhere. But the man was tormented by the thought of his woman being with other men. The noises of the lovers next door made it even harder for him to dispel the demons in his head. But he was not a violent man, so to control his violent urges—toward his own wife, her boss, her clients, the world in general—he would shut himself in his room, sharpening his cleaver. The "repetitive movement of sharpening the cleaver becomes an integral part of his life, and with this he is able to enter a state of non-existence." Readers are also told that "the knife-sharpening man and Hong eventually leave the rental room and move on. Nobody knows where they have gone." Yet each night, the sound of a cleaver being sharpened can still be heard, except that "now, it is Tianyou who is sharpening the knife." Having experienced both warm and dark intimacy, and by turns victim and perpetrator, Tianyou is, in Foucault's (1977) words, a "destabilized subject" who cannot achieve stability, rationality, and internal unity.

In contrast to the relatively comfortable lives of contemporary middle-class Chinese men, rural migrant men's existence is dominated by their inferior class position as unskilled laborers engaged in precarious work, as well as by their concomitant inability to provide a stable, secure home for their family, should they be fortunate enough to find a partner. For the two men in this story, capital is seen to have injured their male pride and rendered them impotent—both physically and metaphorically. If the cleaver-sharpening husband's sexual identity is threatened by the market, which purchases his wife's body, Tianyou's masculinity is also questioned because his position in the lowly, precarious, and cheap labor system gives him little bargaining power in the market. The humiliation felt by these two men is a stark reminder that, as Chinese sociologist of gender Du Ping (2017) points out, while men are the beneficiaries of a patriarchal system, some are also oppressed by the social pressures and expectations that are shaped by class, the rural–urban divide, and persistent gender inequality.

Hong, the migrant woman in this story, is a complex character who deserves careful analysis. Her decisions about what to do with her body regarding different men suggest that she is capable of both positive intimacy and transactional sex. The story's ending is indeed poignant. Like many young rural migrant women, Hong becomes a prostitute because, rather than give her body to capital by working in a factory, she wants to "appropriate" her "own surplus value" (Cartier 2001, 200). As a young woman she yearns for love and is willing to defy parental authority to pursue intimacy with her lover, but she soon realizes she cannot survive on love alone. A victim of sexual assault and violence, she nevertheless uses sex for a range of purposes, including making a living, and offering it as a moral compensation to her neighbor. Hong's moral-economic grammar revolves around utilizing her own body as a site of exchange and conflict resolution, rented out to mediate inequalities that are structured by class, gender, and the rural–urban divide. Hong emerges from the story as a victim of socioeconomic exploitation and patriarchal oppression, but in the eyes of its author, her myriad sexually "transgressive" decisions are not only morally blameless but also demonstrate a strong survival instinct and exemplary resilience—moral courage, if not superiority. Adopting a moral-economic grammar that highlights structural inequality, Wang's narrative of rural migrants' sexual decisions seems to depart from the judgmental discourse of transgression, and instead compels readers to appreciate their own socioeconomic circumstances. This is an important counterpoint to the dominant discourse of transgression—an indispensable piece in the jigsaw puzzle of the complex cultural politics of inequality in contemporary China.

Loach

While ample fictional accounts exist of rural migrant women as sex workers (see, e.g., W. Sun 2014), there is little insight—fictional, journalistic, or scholarly—into the roles that rural migrant men play in the intimacy market, although recent scholars have begun to study this (see Jeffreys and Su 2018; T. Liu 2020; and

Tan and Xu 2020; see also Tsang 2020). In this context, You Fengwei's (2002) *Loach*, one of the earliest novel-length works focusing on the sexuality of rural migrant men as well as women, warrants closer examination. Narrating the virginity, chastity, lust, and sexual decisions of a group of rural migrant workers, the novel centers on the sexual adventures of Gui, a young rural man who now works as a removalist, casual laborer, kitchen hand, cleaner, and construction worker. Poor and humble as his status is, Gui—like the gamekeeper in *Lady Chatterley's Lover*—has one advantage: he is young and very good-looking. Readers learn that he resembles a younger version of Chow Yun-fat (a successful Hong Kong movie star). Gui's girlfriend from his village comes to join him in the city; however, constrained by traditional rural values of chastity and female modesty, she refuses to have sex with Gui, whom she loves, until they marry—no matter how much they may want each other.

Meanwhile, through the intervention of a friend, Gui becomes the housekeeper of a middle-aged woman, Gong Yu. Gong's husband is rich and powerful, with close connections to the city's government officials. He lives apart from his wife, and surrounds himself with younger and prettier women. As a trade-off, he provides well for his wife, giving her an extremely luxurious home to live in. Gong accepts this arrangement and lives a materially privileged but emotionally empty life. When Gui takes the job as Gong's housekeeper, he has no idea that his role is going to extend to that of "lover boy"—he is hoping to lose his virginity with his girlfriend on their wedding night. Now, living in a secluded mansion with lots of money at his disposal, Gui is grateful to his employer. He also finds her attractive, despite their age difference. After repeated attempts by Gong, the two eventually become lovers.

In many ways, *Loach* reverses the mainstream narrative of migrant male sexuality, which equates the male migrant body with criminality, and instead turns it into a site of desire and eroticism. At the same time, the novel does not simply represent Gui's body as a passive object. Despite the stark inequality between them in terms of age and class, Gui is made to feel like an equal sexual partner. However, their blissful life as "love birds" comes to an abrupt end when Gong's husband's scheming lands Gui in police custody and then prison for a crime he has not committed: he plants incriminating evidence on Gui for a crime he himself has committed, then flees town. Gong tries to argue for Gui's innocence, but in vain. The fantasy of their intimacy transcending social and economic differences dies, pointing to the tragedy—the impossibility—of negotiating an equal sexual relationship in the face of extreme socioeconomic inequality. Any illusions of equality Gui and Gong may have entertained are instantly dashed when Gui's wrists are handcuffed. Meanwhile, Gui's former girlfriend, being unable to fend off sexual prowlers in the city, becomes distraught and ends up going mad.

This is a vivid example of how patriarchy joins forces with class domination to produce a domino effect: the rich city man leaves his wife for younger women; his rich wife makes a younger rural migrant man the object of her desire; the rural migrant man betrays his rural girlfriend, leaving her to a tragic end. Gong is "ambiguously placed" (McClintock 1995, 6) in this narrative, like white women in the heyday of colonialism, who were "not the hapless onlookers of empire" but were "complicit both as colonizers and colonized, privileged and restricted, acted upon and acting" (6). Measured against the criteria of traditional patriarchal expectations regarding marriage, fidelity, and female chastity—expectations that are shared by the Women's Federation—both Gui and his middle-class lover in *Loach* are morally transgressive in more than one sense. Gui's rural migrant girlfriend is the only one who is bound by traditional sexual morality and refuses to have sex before marriage, yet she is punished by her descent into madness, rather than being rewarded for her chastity and constancy. To You Fengwei, this is a cautionary tale about cross-class, and therefore transgressive, intimacy. Such boundary-crossing intimacy is not only illusory, but the illusion can lead to disastrous consequences for both parties. This is where the novel departs from the moral narrative framework of transgression we have seen in the public statement from Foxconn's management, as well as in the *China Women's News* and *Soulmate* stories. The author wants us to think that the characters in the novel are morally blameless, and that the choices they make about when to have sex and whom to sleep with are either constrained or enabled by the dynamic interplay of gender, class, and political and socioeconomic power. Readers are likely to finish the novel feeling that the only morally reprehensible person in the story is the rich woman's husband.

From a Moral to a Socioeconomic Framework

I have chosen examples from the media and popular culture for analysis, because I see them as jigsaw puzzle pieces that, when put together, conjure up a nuanced and complex—though not necessarily comprehensive—picture of the cultural politics of inequality. By asking how these narratives help to explain rural migrants' motivations and choices in entering into intimate transactions, we can see that transgression is a central theme circulating across a wide range of state-sponsored media narratives and statements from transnational capital. The Women's Federation's and Foxconn management's responses to rural migrant women workers selling sex adopt a normative perspective within which to criticize and condemn these individuals' sexual choices. Both organizations maintain a dichotomy between the docile body and the transgressive body, as well as a binarism between love and sex. This framework aims both to govern and to provide moral guidance. Others—such as the authors of "The Sound" and *Loach*—reveal both the inadequacy and political expediency of the framework, thereby initiating moral interventions within that framework. When juxtaposed, these narratives—both fictional and journalistic, both state-endorsed and market-driven—reveal the moral fault lines in the public discourse of sexuality.

This discussion points to an increasingly complex cultural field whereby the state, the market, and other social and political forces all shape public discourses of what is morally (un)desirable, (il)legitimate, and (un)acceptable. There is a coalition between state and capital that further reinforces the "triple oppressions"

(Pun 2005, 4) of migrant workers. A further complication is the ambiguous role of the government-sponsored commercial media, which sometimes challenge the government and transnational capital, but at other times are either complicit in their strategies of governing or exploit dark intimacy for the purpose of generating profits. The Women's Federation's response to the "Foxconn factory girl" debate suggests that the state's position toward rural migrant women sex workers is founded on a moral boundary between the morally commendable *dagongmei* seeking love and the morally questionable woman who trades dignity and self-respect for quick and easy money. The position of the Women's Federation is couched in patriarchal values that, while criticizing women on moral grounds, nevertheless do not concern themselves with sexual exploitation, or with the use of sex as a site of economic exchange within marriage.

This discussion reveals the fraught nature of the *dagongmei*'s intimate sexual practices. Most of the rural migrant women in these stories have, in various ways, done away with the vigilantly maintained dichotomy between the good and the morally transgressive. Whether it be the Foxconn assembly-line worker who sells sex to male workers, the woman who marries a stranger to raise money for her brother's medical costs (in *Soulmate*), or the *jiejie* who insist on pressing their claim for dignity and respect, these narratives invariably point to the complex and contradictory nature of these women's agency—an agency marked by a refusal to succumb to the state, patriarchy, and capitalist logic, and a capacity to enter the market as a calculative agent. However, a confluence of political, social, economic, and cultural forces is likely to drive them into various forms of dark intimacy that produce mostly negative feelings such as shame, anger, and injured dignity. Their actions and decisions on intimate matters make it necessary for all parties—the government, capital, subaltern writers, and feminist NGOs—to regroup and adjust, forming a new dynamics of political and ideological alignments and contestations.

The cases analyzed in this chapter also reveal the complexity that marks rural migrant men's masculinity. These fictionalized yet rich and ethnographically significant accounts of men "at the bottom" remind us that no man exists outside the power dynamics that result when class, gender, and rural–urban inequality intersect (Du 2017). The emotional pain and humiliation that are acutely familiar to both Gui in *Loach* and the knife-sharpener in "The Sound" demonstrate how patriarchy negotiates with political power and social structure to reshape rural migrant men's gender-based self-identification. Struggling at such an inhospitable nexus, migrant men also experience gender- and class-specific shame and humiliation.

By analyzing these representations, I have demonstrated the political usefulness of an alternative strategy for seeking to explain subaltern sexual practices in China. I suggest that a critical socioeconomic framework, rather than a normative framework of transgression, may get us closer to understanding the emotional consequences of inequality. Such an approach is necessary because (1) a normative moral discourse of transgression sets up a dichotomy between love and money and sees intimacy and economic transactions as mutually exclusive or, at worst, mutually contaminating; and (2) the connection between sexual intimacy and economic transactions is natural and rational (Zelizer 2005), as the experiences of migrant men and women in the stories suggest. Further, as the various cases discussed here show, it is socioeconomic inequality, rather than a normative notion of moral competence, that shapes individuals' capacity to achieve dignity and respect and to enjoy those "intense, warm feelings" that are typically expected from sexual intimacy. Finally, the framework of transgression, which often evokes law and order, stigmatizes and punishes migrant women who pursue sex to support their families. The actions of sex workers may be unlawful, yet the *jiejie* argue that if honest work for honest pay can confer dignity, then they deserve as much dignity and respect as every other working person. Conversely, as in the *Soulmate* story, the rural migrant woman's decision to marry the first man who is willing to pay her brother's medical bills, while falling within the moral boundaries of marriage, nevertheless raises questions about whether the institution of marriage itself can function at its best in the contemporary world when it is a site of unequal socioeconomic exchange.

This discussion also advances a methodological argument pertaining to the empirical status of ethnography, and asks what we should do in the absence of "first-hand" data on dark intimacy. It is only with the help of "second-hand ethnography" that I have been able to sketch the landscape of dark intimacy. Much of the ethnographic material presented here was produced by my "surrogate ethnographers"[4]—writers, journalists, NGOs. Given that some of these narratives are fictional, I have presented them as unreliable yet crucially useful "data." I argue that, although some may doubt their empirical reliability, and although they certainly cannot replace fieldwork research data, they nevertheless add value of another kind to our intellectual inquiry, by revealing the contestation and complicity that exists between various storytellers. Thus, if we juxtapose, compare, and contrast these stories, and trace their differences/connections methodically in terms of perspective, frame, and discursive position, we may be able to "get at" the cultural politics of inequality and its intimate consequences—an intellectual opportunity that exclusively fieldwork-based research does not usually offer.

Part III

Doing Intimacy

Chapter 5

MAKING CHOICES OR MAKING COMPROMISES: WOMEN AND THE ONUS OF INTIMACY WORK

In October 2017, I spent two weeks in Guangzhou, mainly to meet and talk with worker-poet Zheng Xiaoqiong. While there, I also visited Huazhen (Flower town), China's first and largest marriage and relationship counseling service. Set up in 2008, and featuring nationally renowned internet celebrity "love and relationship experts" such as "Leng ai" ("Cold Love," male) and "Anyawawa" (female), the center offers myriad services advising mostly female clients wishing to improve their love life, manage relationships, or find Mr. Right. Having read the regular blogs of Mr. Cold Love and Ms. Anyawawa through their public subscription account on WeChat, I was keen to see their center in action.

The main office occupies an entire floor of a building in downtown Guangzhou. The operational heart of the center is a large open-plan office with about seventy individual cubicles, each equipped with a computer station and a phone headset, with consultants taking calls from clients. Operating on an almost industrial scale, it is akin to a large commercial call center. This open space is flanked by smaller offices and seminar rooms. I sat in one of the rooms where around twenty-five people, mostly young women, were in the middle of a four-week training course—they were hoping to become professional relationship consultants one day. During the break, I got chatting with some trainees. One of them, a well-dressed woman in her early thirties, told me that she was "between jobs," and that she had signed up for the course for three reasons: she thought she could do with some knowledge about how to manage her own relationship; she believed the training course would also be a chance for general self-development; and counseling was a booming profession, and she may want to be part of it.

I found out from Huazhen's website that this training course cost around 6,000 *yuan*—twice the monthly wages of the Foxconn workers I talked to. Most of the participants came from outside Guangzhou, so they would also have needed to factor in the cost of traveling and accommodation for four weeks. And this is despite the fact that Huazhen does not provide participants with a degree, or any sort of professional certificate that is recognized by the government. A big banner was prominently displayed on the back wall in the seminar room: "Our Plan Is to Produce the Best Relationship Counselors." The teacher that afternoon was a Ms. Shang Cuijun, who identified herself as a disciple of Mr. Cold Love.

Quoting theories from international experts and also drawing on her experience of managing her own love interests, she freely shared tactics and strategies for handling relationships, including, for instance, what to do to free yourself from a bad relationship, and what to say and do to get the man who does not seem to reciprocate your interest.

It was remarkably appropriate that the most revered expert in this center calls himself Cold Love. The knowledge and advice he imparts—and the overall raison d'être of the training center—is intended to produce what Illouz (2007) calls "cold intimacy," which operates according to the logic of the "economy of personhood" within late capitalism (Skeggs 2009, 632), whereby individuals are encouraged to develop the emotional skills needed to manage relationships as if they were a capital investment. The take-home message of Ms. Shang's talk that day was that knowing how to communicate is key to a successful relationship.

Sitting in on the training course on communication skills, my mind frequently drifted back to a workshop I had been asked to conduct with migrant workers in Guangzhou two years earlier. The workshop was part of the regular activities organized by a local labor NGO as part of its initiative to reach out to workers and provide support and services. Knowing that I was conducting research on intimacy, the NGO staff asked me if I would be willing to offer some advice to workers on how to improve intimate relationships through communication. The organization advertised to workers that the event was a talk on "communication skills in intimate relationships."

It was a very warm day in November, and I was surprised to see at least thirty migrant men and women, married and single, crowding into a small room. I started by introducing some key dimensions of "intimacy" as anthropologists and sociologists understand it (e.g., Giddens 1991). Taking cues from Nicole Constable (2009), I suggested that, in intimate relations, two people are expected to be physically and/or emotionally close, personal, sexually intimate, private, caring, and loving. To further elaborate, and following Viviana Zelizer's (2005) lead, I suggested that two people in an intimate relationship have their own shared secrets, private languages and rituals, and exclusive knowledge about each other's body, mind, and vulnerabilities. Workers seemed somewhat surprised to realize that the definition of intimacy I offered and the examples I gave were much broader than just what couples do between the sheets.

I then outlined some aspects of what I see as the key ingredients of effective communication, and illustrated this with examples from everyday life that were chosen to resonate with the workers. They seemed convinced by my argument that communication was crucial to achieving intimacy, and were genuinely interested in my tips on how to communicate better. But the conversations following my talk made me realize that, while communication is indeed crucial to intimacy, it requires a willingness to engage in the process, as well as the emotional know-how to follow it through. One married woman said, "The moment I try to say something to him [her husband], he'll say, 'There you go again, nagging.'" Another woman concurred: "More than once I've said I wanted to talk, but he'd say, 'Can't be bothered,' and would then walk off." For both educated urban professionals and rural migrants, it seems that the burden of learning about and initiating communication—the stuff of "intimacy work"—rests with women. This is consistent with the fact that most of the trainees in Huazhen's seminar were women, and that the training was mostly about how to communicate with men.

The migrant men who attended my presentation admitted they themselves had been guilty of such responses to their wives or girlfriends, but they had excuses. A single man said, "What's the point? Without money, nobody wants to go out with you, no matter how well you communicate." A married man said, "I am usually so tired when I get home from work. All I want is some peace and quiet." Some workers say the only time they talk is when they quarrel. Other workers in the room interjected with comments such as, "At least you're living together and get to quarrel. My wife and I are in different places so I don't even have that privilege." This was echoed by a female worker, who said that she and her husband lived together in a rented room, but since he worked night shifts and she worked days, they hardly got to see each other, let alone communicate.

It is clear that the material reality of living apart, long work hours, fatigue, stress, little leisure time, and the lack of opportunities to participate in the "ritual of romantic consumption" make it much harder for rural migrants to engage in intimacy. In other words, inequality in material terms is closely bound up with, and often seriously restricts, one's capacity to enjoy intimacy.

This chapter, foregrounding four women individuals, aims to paint a fine-grained and longitudinal picture of how rural migrants pursue intimacy against the backdrop of the structural socioeconomic disadvantage they face. I situate these migrant women comparatively with some educated urban women, on the one hand, and with some rural migrant men, on the other. Here I use the term "intimacy work" to mean four things. First, it includes making efforts to overcome obstacles—both socioeconomic and cultural/moral—that impede one's chances of achieving a certain level of intimacy. Second, it refers to what Boris and Parreñas (2010) call "intimate labor," defined as the need to forge, sustain, nurture, maintain, and manage interpersonal ties, as well as the work of tending to the sexual, bodily, health, hygiene, and care needs of individuals. Third, it refers to the need to manage the pain, disappointment, and other emotional hardships that arise when efforts at intimacy fail to deliver expected outcome. And fourth, it extends to the performance of mental and emotional labor in negotiating conflicts and disagreements with people outside the spousal relationships—parents, sibling, children. While my concept of "intimacy work" is much broader than "intimate labor," it is also "customized" to suit a narrower context of conjugal relationships.

The "Deinstitutionalization" of Intimate Life in Urban China

Until the beginning of the twentieth century, interpersonal relationships in Chinese society—between the sexes, between parent and child, and between self and family—were predominantly shaped by traditional cultural forces. These forces include Confucianism and other religious/philosophical traditions—what

Francis Hsu (1948) calls the "ancestors' shadow." Under the ancestors' shadow, the individual's practices in matters of intimacy were largely shaped by age-old cultural values including patriarchy, filial piety, and duty. Similarly, the purpose, function, and cultural practices of marriage were largely informed by traditional ideas that prioritize ancestry, family, and kinship. However, at different historical junctures in the last century or so, Chinese individuals have found themselves walking out of the ancestors' shadow. Socialism, by replacing the authority of the ancestors with that of the party-state, went some way toward dis-embedding the individual from the rich composite set of traditional cultural values and norms. This process resulted in what Yunxiang Yan (2009, 494) describes as a "partial and collective type of individualization." In the case of socialist China, this process shifted the individual from the individual–family axis to the individual–state axis, thereby significantly reducing parental control over individuals' choice of marriage partners (Davis and Friedman 2014).

In the decades of the Revolution, young people were encouraged to engage in courting practices based on the modern notion of romantic love (Cai X. 2010). Young people in the new socialist China were told that matchmaking, arranged marriage by parents, obligatory dowries, and betrothal gifts were "feudal" and "backward" cultural practices, and the new Marriage Laws issued by the CPC in the early 1950s in fact banned such practices. Yunxiang Yan's (2009) longitudinal ethnographic work on rural youths in China indicates that in the socialist era, following the promulgation of the Marriage Law, young people in rural China started to pursue romantic love and enjoyed a considerable degree of autonomy in arranging their own marriages.

Sociological studies of how educated urban Chinese people conduct intimate relationships points to reduced state oversight of sexual relationships and the "deinstitutionalization" of marriage and intimate life in the reform era (Davis and Friedman 2014). Divorce rates had increased, and while there is a high level of anxiety and insecurity associated with the possibility of spousal relationships not working, it has become much easier for urban residents, especially in big cities (Farrer 2014), to get a divorce (Davis and Friedman 2014). Furthermore, there has been a tendency to delink sex from reproduction and marriage, and to some extent sex for reproduction has given way to sex for pleasure (S. Pan 2006). For some people, sexual pleasure is no longer even necessarily tied with romantic love (E. Zhang 2011). This process has afforded young people more freedom than ever before to "script their lives" (Davis and Friedman 2014, 3). New means of expressing and achieving sexual intimacy have emerged, which in turn pose challenges to the residual normative, traditional modes of sexuality.

How these changes affect the intimate lives of young people in urban China has been carefully documented. In April 2018, the *People's Daily*, the official newspaper of the CPC, published an article encouraging tolerance toward gay people, resulting in China's main microblogging platform, Sina Weibo, reversing its ban on homosexual content (Shepherd 2018). While homosexuality is still not widely accepted, anthropological work has confirmed an increased level of "affective individualism" (Donner and Santos 2016) in navigating heterosexual marital relationships, especially in big cities. For instance, individuals in Shanghai are putting more emphasis on "personal choice and self-fulfillment" (Y. Cai and W. Feng 2014, 114). Among educated youths in Shanghai, pre-marital sex has become increasingly acceptable, as long as commitment and intimacy are present in the relationship. Young people in the city nowadays have the option of marrying late (Y. Cai and W. Feng 2014) or not marrying at all (Davis and Friedman 2014). Marriages between individuals from different provinces and regions are increasingly common due to increased geographic mobility (Zhou T. and Qiu 2005), as are inter-racial and cross-border marriages (P. Wang 2015). Young people also have more chances to "enter and exit relationships," and now have more relationship models available to them (Farrer 2014, 90–1). The notion of intimacy has to some extent replaced marriage as a worthy goal in relationships, and educated urban youths are increasingly aware of the need for "constant communication" as a way of achieving and maintaining intimacy in an "emotional terrain of increasing ambiguity, risk and fluidity in intimate relationships." It is now widely understood that increased levels of mobility are linked to a more relaxed sexual culture (Farrer 2014, 91).

In their efforts to minimize risk and cope with new anxieties and uncertainties thrown up by a more open and mobile life, growing numbers of Chinese middle-class consumers turn to professional advice given in the form of psychoanalysis and psychotherapy (J. Yang 2015; L. Zhang 2014, 2017). They are also actively seeking advice from talk shows on radio, reality shows on television, and expert advice regularly delivered to subscription accounts on social media (W. Sun and Lei 2017). The success of Huazhen—the marriage and relationship counseling service described earlier—is an integral part of this new social practice.

The proliferation of multiple sexual subcultures documented in the existing literature takes place mostly in large Chinese cities, which provide the anonymous social backdrop for urban life. However, this is not to suggest that educated urban young men and women no longer face social pressures to conform to traditional gender roles, or that they are now free from all parental pressure to get married. So called "leftover women" (*shengnü*), referring to single urban women professionals (Fincher 2014), are also having to deal with expectations from their parents—and from society in general—that they will get married and have children (J. Zhang and P. Sun 2014). However, in comparison with rural migrant women, these urban professionals have more economic resources and social capital to assert their independence from parents. In comparison with their rural migrant women counterparts, city-educated women are choosing not to marry or to marry late, much to the frustration of their parents. A few years ago, a group of young women professionals placed an advertisement in Beijing's subways, appealing to parents and society to give them "no more pressure, please!" Describing themselves as members of the "marriage-phobic tribe" (*kong hun zu*), these women resorted to crowd-sourcing to raise money for the subway advertisements (Zhang X. 2016). Unable to persuade their children to go on blind dates, parents of these young professionals in Chinese cities regularly go to the matchmaking corner (*xiangqin jiao*) in public parks, a regular and self-organized event whereby parents display the credentials and attributes of their children in the hope of finding a perfect match for them. In most cases, these parental attempts are futile, due to a lack of cooperation of their children (P. Sun 2012).

The proliferation of multiple sexual subcultures documented in the existing literature takes place mostly in large Chinese cities, which provide the anonymous social backdrop for urban life. However, as James Farrer (2014) observes, while Shanghai affords educated urban youths a plethora of new and alternative relationship scripts, small-town youths might find less social support for such scripts. Everett Zhang (2011) also reminds us of the need to heed the uneven distribution of romantic love and access to sexual intimacy.

Some empirical work suggests that rural-to-urban migration, which started in the second half of the economic reform era (i.e., from the early 1990s onwards), has to some extent liberated rural individuals from traditional rural practices and facilitated their progress toward becoming modern individuals. Many studies of rural migrant women (e.g., Gaetano 2015; Jacka 2006; Murphy 2004) have found that, although migration puts more stress on family and spousal relationships for migrant women, it has also created more opportunities for women to exercise a greater level of agency over decisions related to marriage and family. Young migrant women are found to have embraced an urban, consumerist, and modern outlook, and are keen to pursue love and intimacy away from the control and surveillance of their parental, kinship, and rural networks. Similarly, migrant women returning to the village are found to have experienced an improved status in marital dynamics due to their increased earning capacity (Murphy 2004), and even those women remaining in the city are now expecting their partners to make "masculine compromises" due to their own increased earning capacity (Choi and Peng 2016). At the same time, Judd (2010) found that decisions around mobility in rural households are part of "family strategies," and rural migrant women have to negotiate uneven power relations within the family. Shannon May's (2010) ethnography of a rural village in China found that, while parents wish to see their daughters marry up, they also expect rural migrant women to return to the countryside to get married when such attempts to marry up fail.

The four rural migrant women factory workers—two single and two married—to be discussed below were all employees of Foxconn in Shenzhen at the time of their interviews, and living either in the dormitory provided by Foxconn or in rental rooms in the "village in the city" near the factory. I have chosen to focus on their stories, not because they embody the "problematic" trends and "deviant" practices highlighted in government discourses (which I discuss in the next chapter). On the contrary, I argue that precisely because their experiences of mobility are so ordinary and subterranean—and therefore mostly left out of policy research and sociological investigations—they provide an effective prism through which we can explore the myriad forces that impede individuals' capacity to achieve satisfactory levels of intimacy.

WJ, Caili, and a Possible "Naked Wedding"

WJ, a clerical employee at Foxconn, comes from a rural village in Xin Yang County, Henan Province, one of the biggest labor-force-sending counties in Henan. When I sat down with her in August 2015, she was twenty-seven years old, and had been away from home for more than ten years. WJ's mother was a first-generation rural migrant worker, having worked in a garment factory in Dongguan, Guangdong Province. Several years of long hours and night shifts finally took their toll, and WJ's mother returned home, nursing a chronic high blood pressure condition. WJ's only brother had just gotten married and was expecting a baby, so he was living at home for the moment. At the age of sixteen, and having just finished middle-school, WJ decided to "go out" (*chu qu*—i.e., leave her hometown), since there was nothing to do in the village, and there was no work. The small piece of farming land available to the family brought in little income.

WJ exemplifies the dilemma of being caught between parental opinions and her own desires. Born in 1988, she is aware that time is not on her side. Many women of her age are already married with children. WJ has a romantic interest in someone she met on QQ, a Chinese social media platform commonly used by rural migrants, but she is not sure how to proceed, as "his material circumstances are not so good." In the eyes of her mother, this potential marriage partner has three strikes against him: he owns no property; he has two younger, unmarried brothers (hence he may need to support them in the future); and his mother is not interested in helping with childcare. And to add the final straw, he may not be able to afford a betrothal gift, even though the expected betrothal "fee" in WJ's hometown is not high. WJ is obviously keen on the man, but the attitude of her mother and neighbors is impossible to ignore: "My mother keeps saying that he combines all the undesirable attributes in one person." She said that she admired Xiao Qing's courage to marry Xiao Han (see Chapter 2), but she does not have that courage. She feels stuck. In the meantime, the clock continues to tick while she works on Foxconn's clerical team, and the pressure to end her single status continues to mount.

Compared with other Foxconn workers on the assembly line, WJ enjoys two days off on weekends. The only thing is that her wages are lower than for those who worked on the assembly line. And she has been there for several years. When I first saw her, she was living in a dormitory room inside the Foxconn compound. She was shy and softly spoken, and was not optimistic about the prospects of finding love. She said she was not sure whether she "technically" had a boyfriend. WJ had met Shao (she referred to him as Xiao Shao—"little Shao") through a "friend of a friend," and found that he came from a county near her own hometown in Henan Province.

The fact that Shao is one year older than WJ, has a university degree, and now works in a company in Shenzhen, normally should have stood him in good stead: like many rural migrant women, WJ hopes to find someone who is better educated or is financially better off than she is. This traditional preference to "marry up" on the part of female rural migrants explains why, despite the disproportionate percentage of male workers in Foxconn—up to 70 percent of their workforce is male—women still report difficulty in finding "suitable partners." Even though WJ did not think Shao was very "handsome," she felt that what he lacked in looks was compensated for by his superior education.

While WJ was keen on Shao, her mother disapproved. Shao's mother was mentally ill, and there was not a marital house for the would-be couple. Furthermore, Shao's family could not afford to pay betrothal money—an amount of about 100,000 *yuan* in WJ's hometown. The practice of giving "betrothal money" (*caili*) to the bride's family has survived in China from a much earlier era. Traditionally, as in many societies, marriage in China was seen as little more than a kind of property transaction (Ebrey 1991), and vestiges of this remain in many parts of the country. Since a new bride becomes a member of the groom's family according to this tradition, the groom's family is expected to give betrothal gifts. WJ was aware that paying a betrothal fee to the bride's family was a bad "feudal" custom, but it has been done for generations and her family felt that it should be followed:

> Personally, I don't care if he has no *caili*, but I know my family would be embarrassed. What would our neighbors think of us? Everybody else follows the tradition, and who are we to break it? People may say that your daughter is so cheap she's prepared to go without any betrothal money.

WJ's mother put pressure on her to consider a young man who now had a small local business, and whose family was keen to cement the marriage with a handsome amount of betrothal money as well as an engagement ring. WJ was not in the least interested in that man—"we have nothing in common"—but she was worried that her open defiance might further upset her mother's health. So, while her mother went ahead and accepted the betrothal money and ring from the other suitor, WJ secretly continued seeing Shao.

WJ understood her mother's position, but she was less concerned about these materialistic considerations. She said that she loved Shao, and implied that as long as he was prepared to work hard and save money, she would stick with him. She was desperate for some sort of declaration of love from him, a sign of his commitment and his intention to "give it a go," and in this sense she shared similar views to the other migrant women I discussed in Chapter 2—about the need for men to at least be prepared to work hard, even though they do not have "the goods" for the time being. But such a declaration was not forthcoming. Instead, Shao back-flipped.

When I spoke with WJ the following year (2016), her boyfriend had stopped talking about getting married. In fact, he had told WJ more than once that if someone suitable came along, she should just go ahead and marry him. When I asked her if she wanted to tell him that she loved him and wanted to be with him no matter what, she said, "Well, I have effectively implied this, but at the end of the day, I can't be too pushy about it, can I? After all, I am a girl." Like some of the other migrant men I discussed earlier in the book, Shao seemed reluctant to make a promise to "provide," to "protect," and assume "responsibility" for supporting the family and upholding the "moral codes" that are essential to the "dignity of working men" (Lamont 2000), despite the fact that he had better education than many other rural migrants.

Six months after my second interview with WJ, I noticed her posting a few images of herself on WeChat, visiting Shaoguan, Guangdong Province, as a tourist. I asked her via WeChat if the pictures had been taken by her boyfriend. She said yes. Keen to get an update, I rang her and we had a phone conversation. WJ told me that there was still no talk of marriage, but she sounded more positive about her relationship with Shao. She had left Foxconn and now had another job in sales in Shenzhen. The job also offered her dormitory accommodation. She had returned the engagement ring and the betrothal money to the other man. Although she and Shao lived separately, they now managed to get together on the weekends, and occasionally, they took a short holiday out of Shenzhen. She implied that they were sexually intimate. As for the future, she was sure they would not be able to afford to buy a place in Shenzhen, so they might settle in Zhengzhou, the provincial capital of Henan, but it was too early to tell. WJ's mother had softened a bit, probably because neighbors and friends persuaded her to respect WJ's own choice. "She probably also realizes that I'm getting old and my clock is ticking."

I caught up with WJ once more toward the end of my fieldwork in 2017, to get another update on her love life. Sitting in a bubble tea shop in downtown Shenzhen, she looked much happier, more confident, and more outgoing. She smiled a lot, and was quite talkative. She told me that she had moved in with Shao, and that they were living together in a rented room. Although they were yet to marry, she let me in on one of her secrets: she calls him "husband" (*lao gong*), and he calls her "wife" (*lao po*). I made her promise me to tell me about the wedding—a promise she was only too happy to make.

Prompted by her WeChat postings in February 2018, I got in touch with WJ to wish her a happy Chinese New Year. She was back in her hometown visiting her parents, while her boyfriend stayed on in Shenzhen. She told me that they may go to the marriage bureau to apply for a marriage certificate later that year, and that the wedding might take place in the following year. Then she wrote, on WeChat, "It's mostly likely going to be a 'naked' wedding; no apartment, no cars, no nothing." When I replied by saying, "Sure, love comes first, right?" she responded, "Well, he did save up 200,000 *yuan* and we were going to use that money for our wedding, but he lost it all after making an investment mistake." After signing off on our WeChat conversation, I wondered what WJ's mother would think of her daughter's choice now, when she realized that a sizable betrothal fee, which had been so close to hand, had just evaporated.

During the period of Covid-19 (2019–2021), travel to China was impossible, so I was limited to staying in touch with workers via WeChat. I seldom saw any postings from WJ, but based on our last conversation, I had assumed that she would have been married and possibly now had a child, or was pregnant. I got in touch with her to wish her a Happy New Year in February 2022, only to find that she was no longer with Shao, her boyfriend of several years. Indeed, she had just come back from home, and was now betrothed to another man—the two families had exchanged betrothal gifts, which, according to local custom, was tantamount to engagement. WJ told me that her fiancé was from a village not far from her own (something that was very important to WJ's mother), and although he couldn't match her previous boyfriend in terms of education, he was nevertheless an automation engineer in the city of Luoyang in Henan Province, where he was already paying off an apartment.

I sensed that, after a few years of waiting but eventually being disappointed, WJ was now more realistic: "Life's not a fairytale; it's the day-to-day decisions about 'kindling wood, rice, cooking oil, salt'" (*cai mi you yan*). When I asked her if she was hurt by her earlier boyfriend's decision not to marry her despite all his promises, she was surprisingly forgiving: "It wasn't easy for him, either. He wants to succeed in his career first before starting a family, but as my mum says, I'm not getting younger."

XM, Xiangqin, and the Price of Love

I first met XM in 2015, when she was working as a volunteer for a local labor NGO. Born in 1994 and, like WJ, a native of Xin Yang County in Henan Province, XM was fair in complexion and slender-bodied. Wearing a pair of glasses, she looked more like a university student. In fact, she told me that she was hoping to go to university, but her entrance examination score was a few marks shy. Reluctant to be a financial burden on her parents—she has two young sisters—XM decided to come to Shenzhen.

Like WJ, XM worked in a clerical job at Foxconn. The pay was exactly the same as for assembly line workers, but she believed her job was harder. "If anything goes wrong, they blame us, whereas if you are on the assembly line, you just follow orders." The only advantage was that she did not have to do night shifts. She had worked on the assembly line before and had found it mentally less challenging, but she preferred her current job, as she did not have to wear an anti-shock metal ring around her ankle, as those on the assembly line have to do. "It's harmful to the skin," she told me.

Like WJ, XM also lived in a dormitory provided by Foxconn, and found the living experience there alienating. There were many people living in each room and her roommates changed frequently, so she hardly had a chance to get to know any of them. Her room was adjacent to a communal shower and bathroom, so she heard the flip-flop of people's slippers all the time. The room was damp and moldy. Everyone had a lock-up cabinet, but any decent-looking clothing items risked being stolen if left on the clothesline. She said that she had lost a pair of really ordinary pants that way.

Sitting in a room in the NGO office, I learned from my first conversation with XM in 2015 that she still did not have a boyfriend, and at that stage had had no romantic experience. A co-worker was keen on her and had declared his intentions, but she was not interested. Her mother had arranged a few blind dates (*xiangqin*), but she did not meet anyone she found appealing. She agreed to consider one of them, someone who was one year younger than she was. But she decided very soon that his motives were "wrong." All he wanted was to get married. His mother wanted to see him married as soon as possible and have children. But XM, then twenty-one, said that they were too young to rush into marriage, and in any case, she did not want to get married within the next three years. That put him off, and they ended the relationship before it had a chance to get started. XM was deeply averse to parental matchmaking in the village. "That wouldn't work. They all just want to get married straight away. I can't marry someone I don't know well." She said that her father was more understanding, but her stubbornness greatly frustrated her mother, who wanted to see her married as soon as possible. XM's aversion to parental matchmaking resonated with most of the workers I talked to: what is suitable from the point of view of parents for the sake of the family may not be suitable for young individuals in search for love.

In my second conversation with XM that year (2015), I asked her to imagine for me her ideal married life. I still remember the vivid details with which she conjured up this scenario:

> We both have our own jobs during the day, but when we go home in the evening, we talk and we read books. He won't be just looking at his mobile phone or playing computer games. He has to be interested in life, not boring. On weekends, we go out and have some recreational fun (*wanwan*). I'm not saying he has to be the romantic type, but it would be nice to have a small surprise from time to time.

Would owning an apartment or a car be essential to this ideal scenario? XM said that she would be happy just living like that, in a rented place. Her ideal life does not include ownership of significant property, but given the array of socioeconomic and familial forces she is up against, it seems that her aspirations in terms of spousal intimacy, which are remarkably resonant with the educated urban women trainees in the seminar of Huazhen, may be harder to obtain than an apartment.

WJ's worry about *caili* and XM's frustration with *xiangqin* point to the emotional pressure facing young rural migrant women. These practices dominate the journeys of these women in their search for intimacy, even though they more often than not impede rather than facilitate their search. *Caili* is the "hallmark" of marriage property exchange between the groom's and the bride's families (Watson 1991, 354). Similarly, in *xiangqin*, parents' expectations often trump their children's own choices in deciding what is a suitable marriage (Sun P. 2012). This emphasis on family considerations has become all the more pronounced in the post-socialist era, when the state has withdrawn from providing most social goods and services, and individuals are more and more dependent on their family rather than their workplaces (W. Sun and Lei 2017).

The tradition of continuing the family lineage is strong, and most rural parents would consider it their biggest failure in life if their sons could not find a wife. There are two dimensions to the increasingly competitive marriage culture in the typical Chinese village. Parents are anxious that their children will be left on the shelf if they do not act early enough to secure a marriage partner; and such failure would be a major source of shame and loss of face in the eyes of the neighborhood (Guo J. 2016).

Young workers, both men and women, feel the pressure from this competitive marriage culture in the village even though they now live in the city and are still only in their late teens and early twenties. They are constantly requested by their parents to come home and meet someone, and told that if they wait any longer, there will not be any "good catches" left. While quite cynical about the process, most workers say that they nevertheless go along with these arrangements, especially when they are visiting home for a week or so for Chinese New Year. It is not uncommon for them to see half a dozen marriage prospects lined up by their parents during these brief breaks.

When I saw XM in October the following year (2016), her parents' gentle pressure had turned into persistent haranguing. They would call her incessantly, telling her to quit her job and come home. Her mother had been the one to make the calls in the past, but now her father also joined in. This made XM realize that she could no longer live in denial. Every phone call ended up in a fight, and her mother was so upset that she started to have trouble sleeping. And XM's father accused her of being selfish.

Finally, having failed to get her back from Shenzhen to meet the man of their choice, XM's parents changed tactics. Through an introduction, they met a young man who would be a good match for their daughter: he was a university graduate, and now worked as a technician in Suzhou, Jiangsu Province. His home was in a nearby county, he had a married brother, and the family had no trouble paying betrothal fees. XM's parents even visited his home, and were very impressed with what they saw. XM was adamant that she did not want to come home just for another round of matchmaking. But this time, she agreed to a compromise: she would be prepared to speak to him on the phone.

When I spoke to XM in 2016, she had just received a picture of him via social media. She said that she was not fussy about appearance but she did not want to risk getting involved with a very "ugly" person, so she demanded a photo. XM showed me the picture on her phone, and when I asked her what she thought, she said, "Average looks and average height." But it was clear that XM was prepared to give this man a chance. Six months after my last face-to-face conversation with her, XM told me via WeChat that she may go to Suzhou to see the man, now that he had visited her in Shenzhen. "I've become more realistic now, and I know I have to make a few compromises."

When I returned to Shenzhen in November 2017, the biggest news waiting for me was that Xiao Li—now her boyfriend—had quit his job in Suzhou and had come to Shenzhen. When I met the bespectacled young man, I noticed that he was indeed of "average looks and average height," as XM had described him to me earlier. But it was clear that the relationship had progressed and they were obviously very happy in each other's company—even though mutual friends intimated to me that XM, being very traditional, still lived separately from him. I was so pleased to see both of them, and was eager to find out if a wedding was being planned. But when I sat down to have a one-to-one chat with XM, I realized that a lot had changed, and all was not well. A tragedy in Xiao Li's family has cast new doubt on their developing relationship. Xiao Li was one of two children in his family, and his elder brother, also a rural migrant worker, had jumped from a building and killed himself after a bitter fight with his wife, leaving her and two children, aged six and eight, behind. Xiao Li's mother believed that the wife would eventually remarry, but that her second husband would not be prepared to share his home with another man's children. Her mother therefore preferred to keep the children under her care. This meant that Xiao Li now faced a future where his mother might expect him to step up to the paternal role in relation to his two nephews. Concerned for her daughter's prospect of marrying a man with two dependent children in tow, XM's parents, who had urged her to date Xiao Li in the first place, were now putting pressure on her to reconsider. But XM refused to reconsider—she had fallen in love with Xiao Li:

> Things were tense again with my parents. I had a huge row with them during my last visit. I was so upset. My mum and dad were also angry with me; they couldn't understand why I had to be so disobedient (*bu ting hua*). Now they keep telling me, "You'll regret it soon enough. Remember, you'll be the one who'll eat all this bitterness."

Hearing what she had just told me, I tried to imagine the amount of pain this slender-shouldered and soft-spoken young woman must have had to live with. While she finally seemed to have found someone she felt was the love of her life, she also had to face the uncertainty of her own future security, and the bitter disappointment her parents were now experiencing. This was a constant source of emotional anguish for her.

Despite these circumstances, XM married Xiao Li, and they are now living in Dongguan, an industrial city a few hours from Shenzhen. Xiao Li was a technician in a big factory, and when I contacted her during the Spring Festival period in 2022, she told me that she was in the middle of job hunting, preferably for one that came with social security benefits. She said that they couldn't see themselves ever being able to afford to buy an apartment in Dongguan. Her mother desperately wanted her to have a baby, but XM said that "she was not ready."

MB and Her Futile Attempts to Communicate

MB, born in 1984 in a village in Shanxi Province, first came to Shenzhen as a single woman. At the age of twenty-four, she returned home to meet a man her parents had arranged for her to consider as a possible husband. The young man, who was one year younger than her and a migrant worker in Dongguan, came from an adjacent county. After she had met him for the first time, her parents asked her what she thought of him. MB agreed to see him again. After a couple more meetings, the parents from both families got together and agreed on a date for the wedding. At twenty-four, MB was still completely inexperienced with romance of any kind. When I talked to her in 2015, she repeatedly described herself as being "unable to speak well," "clumsy with words," "totally clueless," "in the dark," and utterly lacking in any understanding of what she wanted in a man, or how to talk to them. She deferred to her parents, who liked the man because he seemed "nice," and he was "tall" (MB's father was short, so he was keen to find a tall man for his daughter). The pattern described by MB—parents arranging matchmaking, the couple getting married after a few meetings, the relationship falling apart soon after marriage—was fairly common among the workers who talked to me.

After their daughter was born, the couple left home again, this time both working for Foxconn in Shenzhen. Their daughter, four years old at the time I met MB for our first interview in 2015, was being cared for by MB's mother-in-law back in the village. At that meeting, MB told me that she had not seen her daughter for a couple of years. She could only get leave during the Chinese New Year period, but she could not secure a train ticket because of the high demand during peak seasons. Once, she got up at 4:00 a.m. and queued for three hours, only to find that the tickets for her train home had sold out. Her girlfriends tried to help her by "ticket grabbing"[1] online, but with no luck. Also, in order to save money, MB always tried to buy hard seats, which would have been extremely uncomfortable, given that it took more than two days to get home from Shenzhen.

Social media platforms such as QQ and WeChat were useful to connect with her daughter, but only to a limited extent. Her mother-in-law did not know how to use QQ—she did not even have QQ on her phone—so MB could only see her daughter on QQ when her mother-in-law visited relatives. On average, she saw her daughter once every two or three months. Despite the ubiquitous use of QQ among rural migrants, MB more often than not resorted to talking to her daughter on the phone.

As if it was not challenging enough that MB could not enjoy having her daughter in her everyday life, she was also now equally estranged from her husband. She lived in Foxconn's dormitory, whereas her husband lived in a small rented room near the factory. They seldom saw each other in the factory—it was a huge complex and they worked in different departments. MB went to visit him on Sundays when they both had a day off. She told me that she would help him tidy up his room, wash his clothes, and cook a meal. My first guess about their decision to live separately was that it was a way of saving costs. But it was not until I met MB for a second face-to-face interview in the following year that she became more open about her conjugal problems.

In that meeting, MB told me that her husband may end up going to Zhengzhou in northern China, where Foxconn had opened another plant. She said that if that were to happen, she would not go with him, as she would like to stay on in Shenzhen. MB did not regret marrying him, as she clearly remembered growing very fond of him after they got married, but she has become less and less sure if there was anything left in her marriage now. According to MB, her husband did not want to live with her, because her "nagging" annoyed him. They fought all the time, and could not agree on anything, even though she was quite sure there was no other woman in his life. They also had separate lives financially:

> So I said to him, if you want a divorce, that's fine with me. Let's find a time to go back home to do the paperwork. Initially, he agreed to the plan, but every time I asked him to arrange the trip, he wouldn't engage with me on this topic. I don't think he wants a divorce now, but I'm not sure what he thinks of "us."

MB's penchant for "nagging" was in fact an incessant attempt on her part to reach out to her husband. For the past couple of years, MB has tried to engineer opportunities for her to talk with her husband. But he did not see any need for communication, and he found MB's attempts to communicate annoying. Sometimes, he would say to MB, "You've been talking non-stop, but I have no clue what you're talking about." Other times, he would say, "There's no need for you to say anything. I know exactly what you're going to say."

The tension between the couple was not just due to an incompatibility of personalities. They also disagreed about the future. MB believed that they should work as hard as possible while they were still young, and save enough money so that they would not have to work so hard when they eventually went back home. For her, this meant staying in Shenzhen for as long as possible, and continuing to pay for welfare benefit insurance (*shebao*) in Shenzhen. At this stage of her life she also preferred to be living in the city, and did not want to go back home. In comparison, her husband was less enthusiastic about city living, and would not mind going back home.

> His rental room is small—only big enough for a bed—dark and stuffy, so [one time] I suggested we go out for a walk. So, we went for a walk, and I sensed he was in a much better mood, and for the first time, he talked about some things from his childhood. After that, whenever we had another fight, I'd suggest we get out of his room and go for a walk. But he wouldn't do that anymore. He said, "That's just your trick of getting me out so you can discuss our relationship."

MB knows in theory that she needs to "communicate," but she said in practice, she does not know how to do so. Nor does she know how you can effectively communicate with someone who refuses to engage in communication. Here, MB echoed the sentiments of quite a few migrant women, who were eager to talk to their husbands but did not know how to get through to them. An expression that came up frequently in my conversations with migrant women about their partners was "cold violence" (*lengbaoli*), referring to the absence of physical violence but the presence of aggressive and hostile refusals to engage—in effect, emotional abuse.

My last meeting with MB took place a year later, in late 2017. We had arranged to meet at the western gate of the Foxconn plant around 8:00 p.m., after she had finished her shift. Over a bowl of noodles, MB told me that the arrangement with her husband remained more or less the same—she lived in the company dormitory and he in a rented room near the plant. They managed to spend some time together on weekends, and as before she used this time to tidy up his room and wash his clothes.

The main point of contention between them had now shifted to whether they should purchase an apartment in the township near their respective home villages. MB felt a lot of pressure to buy an apartment now, because her daughter had started primary school and was not adjusting well to boarding with her aunt and uncle. She was also showing signs of behavioral problems. MB believed that if they had an apartment near their home village, her daughter could live there, possibly with her grandmother. But her husband disagreed. To him, it would be unrealistic to save enough money on their wages or to take on a big mortgage. He did not want to be more "enslaved" than he already was. MB said that she wanted to take on as many extra shifts as possible so she could save enough money to buy an apartment. "I don't want my daughter to end up like me. I think she should at least go to university."

A core disagreement was whether to go or stay. Her husband constantly thought of quitting his job and going back home, but she wanted to stay. "I like Shenzhen." I remember that she had paid social security insurance for six years, in the hope that once she had paid it for fifteen years, she would be able to receive a pension from the Shenzhen government. If she stopped now, she would forfeit all the money she had paid. However, I heard from another worker that the Shenzhen government had recently changed its mind, requiring people to pay for twenty years, five years longer than originally stated.

But my biggest surprise came just we were saying goodbye. She mentioned that she was thirty-six years old and she might want to have a second child before she was too old. "I haven't been a good mum for my daughter, and I'd like to try again." She hoped that, should she be successful, her mother would help with looking after the second child while she was still working in Shenzhen.

To stay or go home, to buy an apartment or not, to stay together or get a divorce, to have another child or not—these are weighty dilemmas facing XB. And all the while, she continued to work on the assembly line twelve hours a day, six days a week, as well as picking up extra shifts on Sundays whenever she could.

A few years after I last saw her, I heard from another worker that MB was now divorced. I re-established contact with her on WeChat toward the end of 2021, and while having an audio chat with her, she told me that her ex-husband was now back in the village and that he had custody of their eleven-year-old daughter, although the girl was living with her grandmother. I said that she must have missed her daughter very much. MB told me that she tried to speak to her on the phone as often as she could, but very often, the girl did not want to speak to her. Then she said, "Sorry I have to go. It's time for me to go in." She was still working at Foxconn, and her night shift was about to start.

PC and Her Decision to Pick Her Fight

PC was born in 1982 and had only gone as far as middle-school, but she was the most vivacious and humorous of the women I talked to. Being a natural storyteller, she was always the life of the party, with her wisecracks and witty observations.

She met her husband through an introduction by family relatives. He hailed from another village in the same county as PC in Henan Province, and soon after meeting, they got married. After a failed attempt to start a farm raising ducks, the couple decided to "get out," initially going to Beijing and a few other places, and they ended up working for Foxconn in Shenzhen. We first talked in 2015, over a bowl of rice and some dishes in a Hunan restaurant in the industrial quarter outside Foxconn. She and her husband lived in a small rented room nearby—their teenage daughter living with her paternal grandparents, their son living with his maternal grandparents. "One family, three places," she told me.

PC was the longest-serving Foxconn employee I talked to. When I commented that she was a "veteran worker," she said in a self-mocking tone:

> Well, that's because I have two weaknesses. One is that I'm outspoken and I complain a lot, and supervisors don't like me. The other is that I'm not good-looking. In Foxconn, if you're pretty, your supervisor tends to be nicer to you. You either end up as his mistress, or at least you get transferred to a better job. I've seen quite a few women getting a transfer from the assembly line to the supervisors' office. Who wouldn't want to see pretty girls all the time? I've been here for nearly a decade and I'm still on the assembly line.

The biggest problem PC had with her husband was his gambling habit, a tendency shared by many migrant men, and a constant source of conflict within couples (Choi and Peng 2016). It was also a trigger for his occasionally violent behavior toward her. PC recalled a period in Beijing a decade ago when he was earning only about 900 *yuan* a month—which he gambled away. Frustrated and angry, PC warned her husband that if she ever caught him gambling again, she would storm into the room and upturn the gambling table. And this was exactly what she did one day. Having his masculine pride hurt in the presence of his male friends, her husband dragged her out of the room and threw her to the ground. Tears welled up when PC recalled this incident from a decade ago:

> That day, I sat on a park bench alone for the whole night. As it got dark, the park became deserted. I sat there crying, heartbroken. He didn't bother to come out and look for me. I felt that human feelings are so cold and skin-deep, like a piece of paper. Yet, before I'd got married, like other young women, I imagined romantic love and a warm home, and I imagined being in love with a boy who would protect me and make me feel safe. The next day, I started to pack up—I wanted to go home. Seeing this, he knelt down in front me and asked for forgiveness. He said that if he ever did it again, I could chop off his hand. So I forgave him.

According to PC, that was a promise her husband kept breaking, although since then it happened much less frequently, and he usually "begged" PC to let him have a "play" at the gambling table, just to "chill out." PC told me that although she was heartbroken, she still felt it was worth sticking it out in her marriage, for the sake of her family and children. And she believed that, deep down inside, despite his weaknesses, he was a "good person." PC once got sick with a high fever, and her husband borrowed a three-wheeled cart and took her to the nearest hospital, even though she did not want to go. "He cried and begged me to go, so I agreed. On the way, it started to rain, so he took off his coat and shirt to keep me dry, and pedaled all the way to the hospital."

In addition to a couple of sit-down interviews, I also talked with PC at length on numerous occasions in 2015, often over a meal in the local café in the industrial complex, and in various self-organized get-togethers of workers. She said that her husband, despite his occasional relapses, admired her strength and resilience. This perception is borne out by other workers who know PC and her husband. They all agree that she is a "fighter," and that she had "reformed" her husband to some extent—that she is the one "wearing the trousers" in the house. Being a few years older than most other workers, she is usually seen as more experienced in life— the image of a "big sister"—and is always ready to help out when other workers are in trouble of some kind. PC is actively involved in the activities organized by the local labor NGO in its efforts to raise awareness about domestic violence. She is outspoken about her own experience, and offers support to other women in similar circumstances. She told me at length how a good friend of hers struggled in the hands of her abusive and controlling husband, and how at different times she had attempted to get her friend away from her violent partner. PC can also be quite clear-eyed about the sexual politics between married couples. Once, in a casual conversation, she mentioned that her husband was cooking chicken soup that night, which was her favorite comfort food. When I commented, "What a sweet husband he's being," PC responded with a chuckle. "But what you don't know is that he only ever does that when he wants to have his biological needs met!"

When I returned to Shenzhen in the following year, a couple of things had changed in PC's life. Her husband had left Foxconn in Shenzhen and now worked as a cook in a service station near their hometown—his job in Foxconn had been going badly, and his wages had dropped by 1,000 *yuan*. PC was in her eighth year with Foxconn and was already beginning to think of returning home, but she was not sure what she could do. Her daughter was in high school, and she felt that without parental supervision, her academic performance was slipping. "Now, it's one family, four places," she kept saying. PC was still outspoken and active—for example, I went to see her taking part in a number of rehearsals and performances in the local community center during a week against domestic violence.

PC's ultimate goal is to save up enough money to buy a three-bedroom apartment in the township nearby their hometown in Henan Province. For this, they needed 700,000 *yuan*, and so far, they have saved around 400,000 *yuan*. Her dream is to buy an apartment where she, her husband, and their two children can all live together. However, when she had enough money to put down a deposit, she started to wonder if it would be wise to put her whole life's savings—earned with blood, sweat, and tears, and at the price of living separately from her children and now her husband—into an apartment. She was also less sure about her feelings for her husband. According to PC, he had done two things in the past year that "chilled her heart" somewhat. Toward the end of 2016, her husband took more than 10,000 *yuan* from their savings and gave it to his nephew, a gambler, who had gotten into debt and was in trouble with the law. PC was furious, and incredulous that her husband would give away half a year's wages for no good cause, and that he would not think of discussing it with her in the first place; after all, they had their finances in joint names. Another incident involved an argument between PC and her husband over a family reunion dinner during the Chinese New Year, which resulted in her husband hitting her, in the presence of their children. When I asked what her plans were in relation to her family, her future, and her husband, she said, "I don't think. I'm very torn. All I can feel about my relationship with him is despair, and I've told him so. But he said I was not 'generous enough,'" referring to the grudge PC was holding against him for lending money to his irresponsible nephew.

Like many other migrant men, PC's husband puts a lot of emphasis on homosocial connections, and his gambling habit and his unilateral decision to lend money to his nephew were at odds with PC's pragmatism and frugality. PC exercised her agency by confronting and to some extent managing her husband's behavior, but her actions hurt her husband's masculine pride, which in turn translated into violent behavior toward PC. As we saw earlier, XB and her husband could not agree about whether to stay or return, so XB had had to resign herself to living a separate life—both physically, financially, and emotionally. In contrast, PC and her husband went from one rough patch to the next, yet they were both prepared to compromise for the sake of the family.

Prior to my last visit to Shenzhen in November 2017, PC told me that she had had a very eventful year, but preferred to tell me all about it when we met. Again, as with MB, I met up with PC at the gate of Foxconn after she had finished her shift, and then we walked back to her place—a room in a rented apartment in the middle of a village in the city, about fifteen minutes' walk from work. Her apartment had three bedrooms, and she and the other woman she shared her room with were lucky enough to have their own toilet facility, whereas the other two bedrooms, sleeping a couple of men in each—had to share a toilet. Most of PC's room was taken up with two beds. It was hot and stuffy, and loud music from the shops downstairs blared right into her window.

My main aim was to get an update about PC's personal life—how was she getting on with her husband, and was she still coping with being separated from her children? But PC was keener to talk to me about her ongoing fight with various levels of management at Foxconn. Being a good storyteller, she related, in vivid detail and with unfailing eloquence, how her line manager, workshop floor managers, and the Foxconn Workers' Union had ganged up on her. In their eyes, PC talked a lot and complained too much. So, she claimed, they tried to pick on her and punish her—more work and less pay—for daring to talk back and speak up. Most offensively to PC, they humiliated her in front of her co-workers. The company tried various strategies, including appeasement and intimidation, and when these failed, attempted to sack her. Being a strong woman, PC was not going to take these challenges lying down. She wanted moral redress, demanding that the wrongs be righted and that her supervisors apologize to her in front of her co-workers. With the advice and legal support of the labor NGO, she escalated her complaints all the way up to Foxconn's senior management, while also documenting, in detail, her battle with the company. PC's writings were widely distributed via WeChat and promoted by the NGO's subscription account—another irritant to her employer's management. Before I said goodbye, PC thrust a big pile of paper in my hand. "Here, read this. I've written it all down." When I asked her about her family, she only replied briefly: "The same as before. Four people in four places." But she told me that her husband was very supportive in her fight with Foxconn, and that she spent a lot of time talking to him on the phone, strategizing and planning her next moves. She had not yet bought an apartment, since she was still trying to decide whether it was worth it.

In early 2018, three months after my last face-to-face meeting with PC, I wrote her a WeChat message wishing her a happy new year. PC replied instantly, saying that she was now back in her home province. "Foxconn sacked me. I'm on their blacklist now. But I settled with a small amount of compensation from them."

PC was now working as a cook alongside her husband in a highway service station, but was still separated from her children. On the eve of the Chinese New Year, she was all alone, her husband having gone back to the village to see their children. "Someone has to take the New Year's Eve shift, and I have no choice but to stay and work." But in a message of strength that was characteristic of her, PC wrote, "As long as I'm willing to work hard, I don't believe I'll go starving." The next morning, checking my WeChat postings, I noticed an animated emoji posted under PC's WeChat ID ("Life imitates drama, drama reflects life"), showing her jumping with joy, with a word-balloon saying, "It's pay day today!"

PC had been fighting gender-based battles with her husband in the first two years after I met her, but after taking on Foxconn, with her husband rallying behind her in the last year, she had had to reckon with the brutal strength of transnational capital, her intimate troubles receding into the background. Not surprisingly, she lost in this David-versus-Goliath battle, but the fight had brought her a bit closer to her husband than before. By February 2019, on the train to Shenzhen from her hometown, PC texted me to say that she had finally purchased an apartment in a township near her home village and had bought a car on a loan. "Finally, we have a home we can call our own. My husband and two children can all live under the same roof with me, and we're finding work locally to pay off the mortgage." She sounded upbeat, and was looking forward to a new phase in her life.

But I should have realized that this situation was not final. By late 2019, PC and her husband had rented out the apartment back at home, and were back in Shenzhen and working in another factory. Her husband was also working in the same factory, but the couple stayed in their respective dormitories provided by the factory, as it was "much cheaper"—they needed to save money to pay off debts. What happened to the idea of living together under one roof? I asked her. Interestingly, she told me that she was only a few years shy of having met the minimum period of paying social security insurance, and she didn't want to let go of that—she had a similar idea to MB about this. But it was only after she came back to work in Shenzhen and made further inquiries that she realized that the Shenzhen local government had changed its pension insurance requirements yet again, making it difficult, if not impossible, for outsiders to enjoy a retirement pension similar to residents with Shenzhen *hukou*, regardless of how many years they had been paying for it. She found that she would have to keep paying till she was fifty-five. "If the government wants to muck you around, what can you do? Policies keep changing. I don't want to think about this anymore. The more I think about it, the more I feel trapped by it. It depresses me. I try to put it out of my mind and take each day as it comes."

But at least PC and her husband were no longer living apart. They had decided to rent a place and were now living together, and while her daughter was still back home living with her grandmother, her son was now working in another factory in Shenzhen and living separately from his parents. She continued to write about her experiences, and the last article she sent me, in early 2022, was about all the seemingly impossible hurdles she had had to jump in order to go back home during the Spring Festival—endless Covid-19 tests, permissions from authorities to travel from one location to another, and approval from management of her request for leave, at a time when the factory was short-staffed.

Discussion

The stories of the migrant women discussed in this chapter provide compelling testimony to the argument that inequality necessarily translates into a stratified "capacity to achieve socially and historically situated forms of happiness and well-being" (Illouz 2007, 73). In the case of reform-era China, the experience of rural migrant women has to be explored against a backdrop of the state, the market, and traditional culture—what Chinese sociologist Wu Xiaoying (2010, 150) calls "the three fundamental elements constructing gender discourse," or the "triple oppression" (Pun 2005, 4) of global capitalism, state socialism, and familial patriarchy. The cheap labor of migrant women is sought by capital, which prefers their docile female laboring body with its nimble fingers. But in addition to the feminization of the labor force at the structural level, the "alliance of market discourse with traditional discourse" (Xiaoying Wu 2010, 150) is putting pressure on rural women to continue a range of patriarchal practices at the personal level. These practices range from patrilocal marriage patterns to measuring a woman's worth by the size of her betrothal wealth. The former denies a woman's opportunity to have the same level of emotional, economic, and social-relational continuity as her husband (Watson 1991). The latter—*caili*—was practiced in the past on the assumption that marriage was a market and women were men's property (Ebrey 1991). It has been undergoing a revival in rural China in the decades of market economy as a means of improving the economic circumstances of the bride's family, and, as we saw in the case of WJ, as a strategy for defraying risk and uncertainty within the current state-endorsed neoliberal economic order. Furthermore, if WJ were to have a "naked wedding," her family might "lose face" and be perceived to have married off their daughter "cheaply," whereas the groom's family might feel lucky to have gained a daughter-in-law without having to spend much. While, as discussed in Chapters 3 and 4, the inability to find a wife is source of frustration for migrant men, migrant women have to face more moral and social stigma if they fail to get married by a certain age, or if they get married without a decent-sized bridal dowry.

The two single migrant women discussed here—WJ and XM—both consider romantic love to be the most important criterion in choosing a partner, but their view is at odds with that of their parents, who consider material gains through marriage to be crucial ways of shoring up future security for both their daughters and themselves. Although they now live and work in the city, these women are expected to plan their future intimate relationships to suit their parents' economic and practical considerations.

Negotiating between the expectations of parents and their own desires is a difficult and fraught process for most migrant women. This is because, even if they do not intend to return home and live with their parents, they see their parents as their most reliable source of practical, financial, and emotional support, especially if their marriages do not work. Having less bargaining power than their educated urban women counterparts, they try to assert their own preferences to the best of their ability, while being painfully aware of the conflicting expectations of their parents. But they cannot simply reject their parents' preferences in relation to the rituals of *caili* and *xiangqin*, or ignore their insistence on property ownership as an important goal. For the same reason that educated urban young people turn to counseling and expert advice to minimize risk and uncertainty in intimate relationships, rural young people consider making compromises with their parents as a way of maximizing emotional and material security in their future lives. Going against their parents' advice may enable them to pursue the love of their lives; however, they then have to live with the uncertain and risky consequences of having bitterly disappointed their parents.

WJ and XM started dating after they left home and became part of the industrial labor force in Shenzhen. Unlike them, MB and PC married in their villages, had children, and then came to Shenzhen, leaving their children behind to be cared for by their grandparents. In comparison with educated urban professional women, both single and married migrant women have more limited access to "alternative relationship scripts" (Farrer 2014). While the delinking of marriage from sexual intimacy affords young urban professionals more freedom to pursue a variety of options in conducting intimate relationships according to the principle of individual autonomy and fulfillment, marriage remains one of the few socially legitimate and morally respectable bases on which rural migrant women can access intimacy.

But there is further differentiation between these two sub-cohorts. In comparison to their married counterparts, single migrant women like WJ and XM—mostly born in the 1990s—seem to demonstrate more "capacity to aspire" (Appadurai 2004, 59) for a relationship with a higher level of intimacy. They can also aspire to marry a man with somewhat better education and a white-collar job, although he may still have a rural background and be in poor financial circumstances. In contrast, married women—mostly born in the 1980s—have these options already closed off for them. Instead, they have transferred their aspirations onto the next generation. Married migrant women such as MB and PC have to do more intimacy work to maintain spousal relationships, including absorbing the emotional backwash following incidents of physical abuse or "cold violence," including being sexually available to their husbands despite a lack of emotional intimacy. Since divorce brings more stigma to the individual and family for rural migrant women than for their urban counterparts, and since they are much less likely to be able to remarry than migrant men (especially when children are involved), some, like MB, may feel stuck in a spousal relationship that lacks intimacy.

In February 2018, I noticed that MB had posted a short video entitled "How I Yearn to Have This Kind of Love" on her WeChat. The video turned out to be a series of animated pictures showing a young couple being tactile while doing mundane housework, including hugging each other over the kitchen sink, and cuddling up together while watching television. Seeing the video and knowing the lack of intimacy in her marriage, I could sense the aching sense of lack that MB must have been experiencing. I also wondered what her husband, also on WeChat, thought of her post. However, within the same week, MB posted a link to another video entitled, "Do You Still Dare to Get a Divorce after Seeing This?" In this dramatized scene, a girl is treated cruelly by her stepmother while her father is away on business. In the context of this investigation, we could read this video as saying that, while single women like WJ and XM may have to live with emotional pain in relation to their parents, married women like MB and PC must deal with emotional anguish in relation to their children. For MB, the video may have triggered fears for the safety of her own daughter, now that the child was in her husband's custody.

In addition to the fear that children will suffer from divorce, the child factor also inhibits migrant women's desire for independence in other ways. With their children "left behind" and being brought up by their grandparents, both MB and PC felt guilty for not "being there" to see them grow, and sad to realize that, after years of slogging on the assembly line for the benefit of their children's future, the children were increasingly estranged from them, and no longer wanted to talk to their mothers on the phone. As their primary carers when their babies were first born, MB and PC would most probably feel more emotional pain as absent parents than their husbands.

Yet, in comparison with rural women who were still in the village, both MB and PC demonstrated a greater capacity to negotiate with their husbands on a range of domestic decisions, including whether to return home or stay in the city, and whether to build or buy a house in the village or in the township near their hometown. But as we saw with both women, and especially PC, their raised status and greater assertiveness may sometimes have also been a source of spousal tensions, including suffering domestic violence—especially given that some migrant men, with their masculine power in the household challenged or threatened, are not so good at adjusting to the raised status of their wives and at making masculine compromises.

Ultimately, despite her husband's tendency to give her the cold shoulder, MB's decision to stay in the relationship as long as she did before finally divorcing, and, even more so, PC's decision to stick with her husband despite his history of domestic violence, reminds us that these women make decisions on intimate matters against a constellation of structural and social inequalities. Although they have both demonstrated unequivocally what Sherry Ortner (2001) calls the "agency of intentions," what seems more remarkable is their resilience when having to live with the "agency of power." MB lamented that her husband hated it when she tried to talk to him. Her difficulties with her husband make it clear that access to the "technology of communication" (Illouz 1997, 151) is stratified and uneven. "Communication," Illouz (2007, 19) points out, is a "technology of self-management" that relies on language and on the proper management of emotions. In the same way that willingness to communicate is a gender- and class-specific attitude, communication itself, a kind of speech act that aims to maintain or improve intimacy, is also gender- and class-specific.

Despite much work pointing to the individualization of intimate relationships in contemporary China, J. Liu, Bell, and Zhang (2017, 283) argue that "cultural practices and values of patrilineal family organization, together with material circumstances, continue to influence marital relations in China" across the social spectrum. The experiences of the four women discussed here certainly support this view. Even though migrant women and educated urban professional women alike aspire to spousal intimacy, they may, as Hochschild (2003) suggests, end up having different emotional experiences and inhabit different emotional worlds in their pursuits, simply because they occupy different positions in the socioeconomic and gender hierarchies. Rural migrant women, both single and married, are more constrained than their urban counterparts by their rural *hukou* status, their gender, and their inferior socioeconomic status, and because of these factors, their intimacy work is more often than not about making compromises rather than making choices. Furthermore, in negotiating their relationships with their spouses and future husbands, migrant women—both single and married—seem to perform the lion's share of intimacy work in establishing and sustaining those relationships. This does not mean, however, that the experience of emotional hardships that are caused by socioeconomic disadvantage is unique to migrant women. As the next chapter shows, many migrant men are also confronted by social pressures and gender-specific expectations.

Chapter 6

LEFTOVER MEN AND THEIR MASCULINE GRIEVANCE: MAKING SENSE OF RURAL MIGRANT MEN'S EMOTIONAL HARDSHIPS

Introduction

Early one morning in May 2017, I woke up, checked my WeChat feeds, and noticed that I had received a message from "ZB." I had returned home to Sydney, Australia, some months earlier, after an extended period of fieldwork in China, and ZB was one of the rural migrant workers at Foxconn's Shenzhen factory whose life I had been following in my longitudinal study. ZB's message was succinct: "*Laoshi* [teacher], I just got married," he said, and signed off with a smile emoji. Along with his message was a photo of a red marriage certificate issued by the local government.

Born in a village in Hubei Province in 1987, ZB was one of the 80s cohort ("*balinghou*"). He was on the short side, of solid build with a relatively dark complexion, but he had beautiful, animated eyes. He was also a keen amateur actor, and the most active volunteer for a theater group organized by a labor NGO that provided me with vital assistance in my research. My first interview with ZB, in 2015, was about the difficulties he was having in finding a wife. He told me that he had been on quite a few blind dates arranged by his parents and relatives back home, but none of them bore any fruit. In fact, most of the dates did not go beyond the first meeting. He grew "sick and tired" of these staged meetings, but the pressure from his parents was relentless: "My parents are so worried that their hair has turned white," he told me. With one of the women he had met in this way, ZB managed to persuade her to exchange QQ numbers, and they talked on QQ a few times. ZB was feeling hopeful, but then the matchmaker said that the girl's parents wanted 200,000 *yuan* as a betrothal gift, or a deposit on an apartment in the township nearby. Either way, that meant that ZB's parents would have needed to go into debt—a prospect ZB did not want to contemplate. He had a younger brother who would also need to buy or build a home and raise a betrothal gift in order to get married, and he did not want to ruin his younger brother's chances, so he broke off with the woman, went to Shenzhen, and joined Foxconn as an assembly line worker. On quite a few occasions of such matchmaking, the woman's family was upfront about a house or a car as a prerequisite on the first date, and

ZB's experience is typical of many Foxconn workers I talked to. But despite his experience, he did not blame the women: "They were also under a lot of pressure. If they agreed to go out with someone whose family couldn't afford a new home or betrothal gift, they'd be looked down upon by others in the village. They compete with one another. Girls don't want to look like losers."

On that trip to China in 2015, I heard on the grapevine that ZB was sweet on a young migrant woman who was a fellow Foxconn worker, but she—who also became one of my longitudinal research participants—was apparently not keen on him. When I caught up with ZB in the autumn of 2016 for a second interview, he had managed to find a girlfriend. He filled me in on the journey of his courtship, the smile on his face imbued with happiness and contentment. ZB promised me in 2016 that he would let me know if he was getting married.

It turned out that ZB met his future wife on one of the activity tours that had been organized by the labor NGO. As a veteran volunteer of the organization, ZB was fortunate enough to be paired up with another volunteer, a young woman from rural Guangdong Province who worked as a carer in a kindergarten. ZB said that his girlfriend was very "enlightened" and had "progressive views." She did not mind the fact that ZB did not have an apartment or a car to his name. But ZB considered himself exceptionally "lucky," for a number of reasons. First, he attributed his good fortune to his association with the labor NGO. He believed that it was through his involvement with the organization that he had managed to meet a like-minded woman, and it was through volunteering for the organization that he had acquired the social and communication skills that he believed many of his migrant worker peers desperately lacked. Second, rural families with daughters in coastal Guangdong do not expect a high betrothal gift—unlike families in most Chinese provinces in the hinterland. ZB's family managed a betrothal gift of 38,000 *yuan*—a fraction of the size of the betrothal gifts expected in many other parts of the country.

Delighted to hear news of ZB's wedding on WeChat, I dashed off a quick message of congratulations to him, followed by a request for him to accept a *hongbao* (red packet) via WeChat. A *hongbao* is a red envelope containing a small amount of cash—a traditional gift from friends or family that is suitable for weddings and other occasions—which, thanks to WeChat, has become possible as an electronic transfer. Later in 2017, about six months after ZB's exciting announcement, he and I met again on my next visit to China, and when I made the observation that he looked a bit "chubbier" than I remembered, his friends chimed in, not without envy, "Of course, he's got a wife to take care of him now. He looks like a contented married man." To add to his happiness, ZB was going to be a dad soon.

My delight with ZB's news was also due to the fact that, among the dozen or so 80s-cohort male rural migrants whose love lives I had been following closely, he was the first—and so far only—one to finally "make it" in the marriage stakes. In February 2022, I took the opportunity of the Chinese New Year to get an update from the other three single men in the 80s cohort in my longitudinal project. Sadly, but not completely surprisingly, they were all still single.

Despite considerable work in labor sociology on the Chinese rural migrant, and public debates about the marital difficulties of this cohort,[1] how these men make sense of their emotional experiences and what this tells us about their masculine identity construction has received much less attention. This is despite the fact that, in recent years, there has been a growing body of scholarship on Chinese masculinity (Louie 2002, 2016). Choi and Peng's (2016) study, which draws on interviews with around two hundred rural migrants in the industrial zone of the south, goes a long way toward addressing the absence of rural migrant men's experience of romance and conjugal intimacy from previous scholarly investigations (Guilmoto 2012; X. Yang et al. 2017). Approaching migrant men as husbands, lovers, boyfriends, sons, and fathers, Choi and Peng develop a feminist concept of "masculine compromise" that accounts for the ways in which migrant men (re)negotiate gender practices and identity in response to mobility and social change. While their study interviews migrant men from a wide range of sectors, it does not explicitly differentiate between the 80s and 90s cohorts, even though the men they interview come from both. Furthermore, while focusing on how migrant men negotiate their relationships as husbands and lovers, the subjective experience of the figure of the "leftover man"—the single man who has not yet been able to find a marriage partner—is largely absent from their study. Additionally, the question of how some traditional practices, such as *xiangqin* (parentally arranged blind dates) and *caili* (the giving of betrothal gifts), shape migrant men's marriage prospects is also mostly unexplored in their book.

Departing from existing sociological work on the phenomenon of the leftover man, I want to take a cultural-anthropological approach, and ask how rural migrant men feel and talk about their "leftover" status, with a view to exploring the connection between socioeconomic inequality and gender identity formation. More specifically, by concerning myself with their subjective views and sentiments, I aim to shed further light on the complex ways in which socioeconomic inequality shapes emotional experience. In particular, is there a distinct emotional experience shared by many of the mostly unmarried 80s cohort—an experience that the concept of "masculine compromise" may not fully capture? How do these leftover men maintain their self-image of masculinity, despite their repeated failure to secure a marriage partner? How do they use their comments about migrant women—as well as about men from their own peer cohort and migrant men from the 90s cohort—to manage symbolic boundaries in terms of gender and generation, and how do they carve out a particular form of masculine identity while living a marginalized existence?

The Phenomenon of Leftover Men

In early 2022, a journalist conducted a quantitative survey of the academic journal articles that had been published over the previous two decades on the topic of leftover men, and the resulting report for the *Shanghai Observer* produced some telling statistics (He S. 2022). For instance, the term "leftover men" (*sheng nan*) began to appear in 2006, but in the first few years it was mostly in an urban context, and in specific comparison with "leftover women" (*sheng nü*), a distinct social phenomenon that had already captured the public imagination both inside and outside China. However, in recent years, especially since 2011, the expression "leftover men" has begun to be discussed mostly in a rural context. As a part of her research, the journalist also posed a question on the Zhihu website—China's equivalent of Quora—asking, "Why is it difficult for young rural males to find a marriage partner?" Among the more than eight hundred responses, she found that the word that was mentioned most frequently was *caili* (betrothal gift), and the expressions that were most frequently associated with *caili* were "exorbitant amount," "how much?," "dramatic increase," and "houses/apartments."

Some sociologists account for rural migrant men's difficulties in finding a wife as a consequence of the historically derived imbalance in the sex ratio, and the subsequent "marriage squeeze" phenomenon. The imbalance in the sex ratio is a result of a number of factors, including a culturally conditioned preference for boys over girls, the adoption of a family-planning policy that was initially focused on one-child households, and the prevalent practice of sex selection in rural China. As a result of such factors, the prominent sociologist Jing Tiankui predicted a decade ago that by 2020 there would be thirty million more men than women in the twenty-four to forty age bracket (Inner Mongolia Morning Post 2012). Similarly, a report in *Banyue Tan* (China comment), a fortnightly news and current affairs magazine published jointly by the Department of Propaganda and Xinhua News Agency, claimed that there were nearly thirty-four million more men than women at the end of 2014, with the male–female ratio among unmarried individuals born in or after the 1980s sitting at 136:100 (Li L. 2016).

Another often cited and significant factor is that the marriage market in China operates on the logic of hypergamy, whereby the woman desires to "marry up"—what is widely referred to as the A-*nan*, B-*nü* (A-male, B-female) marriage formula. According to this formula, individuals are divided into four groups—A, B, C, and D—based on their wealth and social position. Since women aspire to marry up, it makes sense that a B-female would want to marry an A-male, a C-female to marry (at least) a B-male, and a D-female to marry a C-male or above, leaving A-females and D-males "on the shelf." Again, as sociologist Jing Tiankui observes, while A-females are on the shelf by choice, D-males are there through no choice of their own. "The problem of leftover women is not a real problem. The problem of leftover men is a really big problem" (Inner Mongolia Morning Post 2012).

The processes of urbanization, modernization, and transnational/translocal migration in post-socialist China have led to new ways in which gender, class, and race impact on the meanings of Chinese masculinity. Research has documented these new gendered formations in the sphere of the transnational (Hird 2016; Hird and G. Song 2018; G. Song 2019), as well as among middle-class and white-collar individuals in China (Hird 2016; E. Zhang 2011). Additionally, in the decades of economic reforms, the transformation of family structure and changing expectations and practices surrounding courtship, marriage, and conjugal intimacy

(Y. Cai and W. Feng 2014; Farrer 2014; Wu Xiaoying 2012, 2017; J. Zhang and P. Sun 2014) have presented great challenges to the patriarchal system (Harrell and Santos 2017). In many parts of rural China, the changing role of sons—from carers for aging parents to financial burdens—has led to a certain level of empowerment for women (Lihong Shi 2017). Recent work also identifies new patterns of gender collaboration within some rural households that are intended to enhance their son's marriage prospects (Driessen and Sier 2019).

Academic research on China's rural migrant men has also started to emerge. These works demonstrate rural migrant men's attempts to negotiate their "dislocated identities" at the nexus between rural and urban life (X. Lin 2013, 2014), between their online and offline realities (T. Liu 2020), and in those service sectors—such as taxi driving—that require male workers (Choi 2018).

Differences Between the 80s and 90s Cohorts

While both the 80s and 90s cohorts and their families back home may face similar levels of precarity in terms of employment, financial security, and rural poverty, the two cohorts are often believed to be different in many respects. These widely perceived differences are the outcome of a two-pronged and possibly mutually constitutive discursive process. The first prong takes the form of scholarly commentary presented in journalistic accounts. For instance, drawing on surveys conducted by local governments in Liaoning and Anhui Provinces, an article published on the *People's Daily* website finds that rural migrants in the 90s cohort differ not only from their parents' generation, but also from those born in the 1980s and 1970s. In comparison with these older cohorts, members of the 90s cohort feel less pressured by their families to send money back home, tending to prefer spending all they earn rather than save it in preparation for marriage. They are keener on consumption activities such as going to the cinema, visiting internet cafés, eating out, and shopping. In terms of employment options, the 90s generation are less willing to take on dirty, manual jobs, and instead are more interested in pursuing skills-based occupations (Zheng Xupeng and Zheng Wenxi 2013).

Public commentators also often observe that the 90s cohort tend to take a less cautious approach to marriage than the 80s cohort. For instance, a 2012 article drawing on interviews with a number of scholars that appeared in *Zhejiang ribao* (*Zhejiang Daily*), the daily newspaper owned by the provincial government of Zhejiang, observed that members of the 90s cohort take a much more casual approach to sex, and are less concerned with the myriad undesirable consequences of a hasty marriage, such as divorce and unwanted children. The article comments:

> While the 80s cohort are enslaved by the pressure of having to make money in the hope of realizing the pipe dream of owning an apartment or a car, the 90s cohort are already married and having children. They are mostly financially dependent on their parents, emotionally unstable, and psychologically immature. These

post-90s families are a source of social instability, and warrant attention from all parties concerned.

(Zhang L., Zhou Z., and Zhang Y. 2012)

The second prong in the discursive process, as I hope my ethnographic accounts of individual rural migrant men below will make clear, takes the form of self-description by rural migrant men themselves, especially those of the 80s cohort. But all of these perceived differences between the two cohorts—whether they be self-ascribed, mutually ascribed by the cohorts, or ascribed by others—interest me. This is not because I believe that the differences are necessarily borne out by the evidence, but because I want to understand how their ascription has become an essential aspect of the emotional subjectivity of both cohorts. Furthermore, viewing the distinction between the two cohorts as constructed rather than as self-evident may have the additional value of allowing us to understand the complex relationship between the subjective experience of rural migrant men individuals, on the one hand, and those public, often state-sponsored, narratives that seek to construct them in a particular way, on the other.

"I'm the Lucky One"

ZB had told me that he felt exceptionally lucky to have found a woman who valued him for who he was, not for what he had, and he also felt that his active involvement as a volunteer in the NGO-organized theater group had given him the opportunity to meet his wife, not to mention the confidence to court her in spite of his family's humble means. He was acutely aware that other men in similar circumstances hadn't had much luck even in finding a girlfriend, let alone getting married. When I asked him how he mustered up the courage to ask his girlfriend out and declare his intentions, he laughed and said, "I had to be bold, but I was sweating with nervousness."

ZB believed that, despite his own good luck, the odds were against migrant men like him "getting girls":

> People like us come from the countryside, and we don't own a house or car, and many of us can't afford the cost of getting married, including *caili*. ... If you're poor but good-looking, you may have a chance. But then again, if you are that good-looking, you wouldn't be a worker at Foxconn, would you? Also, girls like boys who have glib tongues and pay them a lot of attention and shower them with gifts, even though these boys may not have serious intentions. ... Younger people, those born in the 1990s, tend to have a more casual approach when it comes to girls. Older ones [like me] who were born in the 1980s are more serious. I've seen too many boys who are honest and want to do the honorable thing by girls, but they're shy and don't know how to talk to them. That may not be a problem if you're loaded with money; your money can talk on your behalf. But what chance do you have if you have no money, you look ordinary, and you don't know how to talk to girls? Most of the men you see here fit that

description, especially those born in the 1980s. And let's face it, girls like men who are confident and can sweet talk them, even though they may not be as dependable as the honest, quiet ones. That's why you see so many lonely souls here—starving for love, sexually frustrated, and feeling lost.

ZB seemed to reinforce the distinction between his cohort and those born in the 1990s—also a widely accepted view among scholars. Some of the *gudu de linghun* (lonely souls)[2] ZB is referring to resort to purchasing sex. As he told me, "If you're in certain QQ groups, you always have people bragging about their sexual adventures, such as, 'I had lots of fun in Dongguan over the weekend,' or, 'I slept with half a dozen girls.'" But, he hastened to add, "My advice to you is don't believe those who brag to you about it. The reality is that those who do it usually don't tell; those who tell don't necessarily do it."

When I touched base with ZB at the end of 2019, I found that the labor NGO had closed, and ZB was still living in the same area in Shenzhen, but in a rental flat with his wife and one-year-old son. His mother was also in Shenzhen to help with childcare. No longer a Foxconn worker and labor advocate, he now sold insurance for a living. He said that his income was often better than his wages at Foxconn, but since he was paid on commission, he had no financial security. Settling in Shenzhen remained a pipe dream, since they could not afford to purchase an apartment—a prerequisite to obtaining a local *hukou*[3] and becoming a permanent Shenzhen resident. Nevertheless, ZB was content to live in a rental property in the industrial areas where rent was cheap, and was thankful that he had a wife, a son, and his mother, all living together as a family, under one roof. He was acutely aware that he was the object of envy for most of the rural migrant men he knew who shared his socioeconomic circumstances. "I'm the lucky one," he said to me, more than once.

"Men Like Him Used to Be Exemplars of Fine Character"

Compared with ZB, YY has been very unlucky. He was born in 1988 in Hubei Province, and is like any one of the thousands of other Foxconn workers I see in the course of my fieldwork—ordinary looking, perhaps a little on the short and small side, and plainly dressed, but he has a nice smile, and is quietly spoken. When I talked to YY he was not working, although he had worked at Foxconn for seven years. Several weeks earlier, he had had a dispute with management—he had alleged that Foxconn had fired him on false pretenses and owed him wages—and he was now seeking compensation with legal assistance from a local labor NGO. YY's older brother and sister had had to quit school and find work when they became too much of a "financial burden" on the family. Being the only one in the family to have completed high school, YY was encouraged to sit for the university entrance exam. Although he was the most promising one in the family in an academic sense, he was also the least robust in terms of physical health and mental strength. Weighed down by too many family expectations, YY failed the entrance exam. "I wasn't feeling well and got so nervous that my nose started to bleed. My exam papers were soaked with blood." There was a discussion in the family about YY repeating the exam in the following year, but he decided against it, considering that his father was getting old, and his mother had died a long time ago.

YY first came to Shenzhen to join his brother and sister-in-law, who were running a shop. But their relationship soon soured when YY realized that his brother and sister-in-law were treating him poorly—they encouraged him to come and work for them, but exploited him by refusing to pay him a proper wage. "My sister-in-law gave me the cold shoulder, as if I was a free loader, and when I asked my brother to pay me as an employee, he said I should be content with having free food and free accommodation." Unwilling to be exploited in this way—least of all by his own brother—YY left the business and went to work for Foxconn.

YY seemed to me to get along easily with women, and this observation was confirmed by his friends, who joked that he was every girl's best friend but nobody's boyfriend. YY thinks that women who work at Foxconn tend to have unrealistic goals in their choice of a boyfriend.

> I know this girl. She's plain-looking and quite ordinary, but more than once she's said she wouldn't date anyone who was shorter than 1.8 meters, older than twenty, unable to afford an apartment and a car, or had savings of less than half a million *yuan*. Her male colleagues on the shop floor laughed at her, and told her to get a mirror and look at herself.

Even so, YY was acutely aware that, as a *zuoye yuan* (ordinary worker) on the assembly line, he invited contempt. His job was the "lowest of the low" in terms of workplace hierarchy.

Clearly, it was hard for an ordinary male assembly-line worker to feel confident about courting a girl. As YY said to me:

> I think I'm a shy person. I tend to be low-key. Many people just assume I'm already married. Even if I like the look of some girl, once I get rejected I'll leave her alone. I respect her decision. I'm not like some men, who wouldn't stop till they get the girl, and who are prepared to use all sorts of tricks. I can't do that.

It turned out that YY was not just exploited by his brother, and then Foxconn. He also had an exploitative experience with his one and only girlfriend to date. He had met her online and asked her out—both of them were Foxconn workers, and both came from the same area in Hubei Province. But the relationship didn't last long; it turned out that the women had turned to YY only for emotional support and comfort, neglecting to tell him that she actually loved a migrant man from Xinjiang Province. "The night she finally told me the truth, I cried the whole night, and for three days after that. It was the first time I'd ever cried." Even though her parents disapproved of her boyfriend, who came from such a far-flung province, she eventually left YY to get married to the Xinjiang man. She had a child with him, only to realize that the marriage wasn't working. She then returned to Shenzhen, hoping that he would take her back. YY was willing to do this as he still had feelings for her, but his father resolutely opposed the relationship. She eventually found someone else from Hubei Province, but all the while, YY was still there as her emotional crutch.

YY eventually found work in a factory near Shenzhen airport in 2016. When I saw him again in Shenzhen in early 2017, he still hadn't had a proper girlfriend, and his father had died. Still estranged from his brother and sister-in-law, he was now alone in Shenzhen.

When I talked with ZB (discussed earlier) about YY's lack of luck in finding a girlfriend, ZB put it down to YY's lack of *qingshang* (emotional intelligence):

> I've had quite a few chats with him about it. It's funny that we can see what his problems are, but he can't. He comes from a poor family, his brother has abandoned him, he has a house back in the village, but a house in the village is worth nothing. He doesn't know how to attract a girl, nor does he seem to have a clue whether a girl is genuinely interested in him or just using him. He's kind, honest, dependable, and a good shoulder to cry on when girls are hurt and are in need of a confidant. He never thinks of taking advantage of them. These are good qualities. Men like him used to be exemplars of fine character, but no girls want men like that anymore.

But ZB acknowledged that, in order to get lucky with girls, socioeconomically marginalized rural migrant men would usually need to have at least one outstanding quality, be it good looks, a winning personality, supreme self-confidence, or exceptional emotional intelligence. "But look around Foxconn. Do you see many good-looking men? No. And why not? Because if they're tall and good-looking, they would be doing something else, like working as a sales person or in a nice hotel."

Since 2018, YY had been mostly back living in his village home, doing some repair and renovation work to his house to make it more livable. From time to time, he would "go out"—he went to Chongqing for a couple of months, just to "look around"—and then went back to Shenzhen and worked for a metallurgy factory for another couple of months, before deciding to go back home again. Since Covid-19 started, he has not left home, and remains without a girlfriend or wife.

"It's Hard to Have Courage Without Money"

In addition to YY, one of the other leftover men I followed in my longitudinal study was JH. Born in 1986, JH grew up in a mountain village in rural Jiangxi Province, in the southeast of China. He dropped out of school to help his parents with farm work, but soon realized that there was no money to be made in the village, so he left for Shenzhen to try his luck. When I first met him in 2015 in Shenzhen, he was working twelve hours a day, six days a week at a Foxconn plant in Shenzhen, assembling iPhones. He noticed my iPad and said, "That's one of the iPads we produce."

With no tertiary education or secure employment, and being qualified to work only in low-skilled jobs, JH had to work long hours for low pay, which made the practicalities of dating daunting for him. By the time I visited China in the third year of my fieldwork, he had left Shenzhen for a job in a furniture factory in Foshan, an hour's drive from Guangzhou. He told me that the pay there was better than at Foxconn. Eager to hear his latest news, I traveled to Foshan to catch up with him in September 2017, where we met in a cheap restaurant close to a four-star hotel. It turned out that he had chosen this place to meet because, since arriving in Foshan, he had changed jobs again, and was now working as a security guard in the nearby hotel: while the furniture factory work had paid better, the hours were too long and crushingly hard on his body. I also learned at this meeting that JH's family back in the village had just received a subsidy from the local government to repair their house, by virtue of being a "poverty-afflicted household." Other than that, the financial circumstances of his family had hardly improved. Nevertheless, in order to live, he had to keep going, from job to job. After that meeting, JH changed jobs three more times, one of which was going back to his old job of furniture-making. However, by August 2019, he was back in Foshan, this time as a security guard in a hotel. When I asked him why he had left his old "trade" of furniture-making, he told me that the company had to lay off many people because of China's trade war with the United States, and his company faced too much competition from inland factories in Chengdu and Jiangsu, so he had to work more for less pay. He could no longer make enough to support himself.

Clearly, JH has been extremely mobile in his job, but his mobility has always been horizontal—moving from one job to another with no improvement in status, pay, or skill-level—rather than upward. When I communicated with him via WeChat late in 2019, he was working as a security guard in a holiday resort in Foshan. This high level of horizontal mobility is not motivated by the prospect of the accumulation of social, economic, and professional capital. In fact, such mobility leads to the gradual attrition of these goods. His decisions have been propelled by precarity and a lack of security. After all these years of job hopping, he remains a source of disposable cheap labor, earning enough money to survive on, but having nothing left to save, and certainly not acquiring any certified professional skills. He seems to be the perfect specimen of Guy Standing's description of the precariat: "the precariat also has no ladders of mobility to climb," and knows that what it does is not for its own purposes; "it is simply done for others, at their behest" (Standing 2011, 20).

JH is tall and dark, with a well-chiseled face—my assessment of his good looks was shared by other workers, both male and female. But he had had no luck in finding a girlfriend. In my meetings with him he was quiet, softly spoken, and shy. He found it difficult to strike up a conversation with a stranger. But other migrants who knew him well all commented on his loyalty as a friend. Unlike those glib-tongued men who "get girls easily," JH would not ask a girl out even if he was attracted to her because he feared rejection, and because of this, he lived with a constant sense of failure. Furthermore, he did not believe in wasting time on frivolous affairs:

> If I like a girl and want to go out with her, I want to make sure she knows I'm serious. I don't want to waste her time, or my time. Also, I want to behave responsibly toward the girl. I don't want to take advantage of her, only to leave her later. I also don't want to say and do nice things—such as buying her gifts—just to please her and get close to her, with no intention of marrying her. It's not the right thing to do. I know I'm old-fashioned.

JH was referring here to some younger rural migrant workers in their twenties, some even as young as their late teens, who "get girls" easily, but have no intention of staying in a relationship with them or getting married. He echoed the view often found in public commentary—as discussed earlier—that members of the younger, post-90s generation take a casual approach to marriage, and for some, sexual intimacy does not necessarily lead to marriage.

A member of the 80s generation, JH thinks he is different from the 90s generation, as he does not want, nor can he afford, "fast-food" love. But his ethics of dating—informed by traditional values—has not served him well. This, coupled with a feeling of inferiority and low self-esteem, makes his attempts to "get girls" incredibly challenging.

In addition to his loneliness, JH's sense of failure is exacerbated by a feeling of guilt for letting his parents down:

> They [his parents] sacrificed so much to bring me up, and all they want to see is that I'm married. But I'm not able to give them that. They try not to put too much pressure on me, but I know they're also under a lot of pressure from neighbors and relatives. I have two sisters and I'm their only son. So, they always try to set me up with a date when I go home. I feel I need to go along with these meetings, but nothing ever comes of them.

Having no girlfriend, but with time on his hands after his shifts, JH is often active on social media, and his WeChat posts are mostly self-motivational messages aimed at cheering himself up, despite being single and lonely. He also updates his WeChat ID image frequently, replacing the existing photo with yet another younger-looking, fairer version of himself (courtesy of his phone's digital image enhancement capabilities). He has not given up yet, but he is becoming somewhat despondent. He blames his lack of romantic success on his low social status and lack of money. He is also scathing about the myth that true love exists despite poverty: "When a man has money, every woman falls in love with him," he told me wryly via WeChat. "But would you muster up the courage to ask a girl out if you met someone you liked?" I asked him. JH replied with a crying emoji, saying, "It's not about whether I have the courage. It's about whether I have the money. It's hard to have courage without money." In the past, JH had believed that, as long as he was prepared to work hard, he might have been able to change his circumstances. Now, he was adamant that "you never get ahead by working hard." But his motto was still focused on money as the key enabler—*xian tuopin hou tuodan* (first get out of poverty and then get out of singlehood)—because, as he put it, "In this day and age, without the capacity to provide material comfort, you can't expect a girl to stick with you through thick and thin." JH's sentiments, and the vicious and self-reinforcing circle of "no self-esteem and no girlfriends" that they embody, chime with those of many of the other rural migrant men I talked to.

Given how frequently he changed his jobs, I was a bit surprised that when I was in contact with him in early 2022, JH was still doing the same job as a security guard in a holiday resort in Foshan. The only change I noticed was his WeChat name. He now called himself "*Leng Xin*" (cold heart). Also, knowing that he felt bad about not being able to pass on the family name, it seems possible that his heart was feeling not only cold but also guilty. In answer to my question about whether he was planning to go home to see his family for the Chinese New Year, he wrote back, "I can tell my parents are getting old. They're at the age when they expect to be grandparents, but they're still just parents." He signed off with an emoji of helplessness at the end of his message.

"My Deadline Is When I Turn Thirty"

The decades of ceaseless social transformation and economic reform in China have given rise to an unprecedentedly high level of mobility and translocal household practices. Mobility has seriously challenged traditional notions of family structure and familial relationships, and significantly undermined intergenerational expectations, unleashing a process whereby the family is rendered increasingly fragile, unstable, and fragmented (Wu Xiaoying 2017), requiring, more than ever, resilience in migrant families, particularly with regard to intergenerational relationships (Y. Yan 2016). In this sense, members of the Chinese precariat can be characterized in terms of their relatively poor capacity to cope with these processes.

Like JH, BH is another Foxconn employee who also has had to live with the danger of becoming a leftover man. However, this is not due to a lack of attractive qualities on his part. Born in 1989 in Chaozhou, in a rural part of Guangdong Province, BH is a technician at Foxconn. But rather than working on the assembly line, he is in charge of repairing machines and equipment on the shop floor. Because of this, he is granted considerable flexibility of movement, and he is allowed to bring his mobile phone to work. BH has taught himself some technical skills, and is now enrolled in a technical training course which eventually will earn him a diploma of some kind. Being seen as the "smart one," he is very popular among workers, and is always available to help out when friends and workers ask him to fix their phones and other electronic gadgets.

In comparison with many other Foxconn workers, BH has had more luck dating girls, but so far, none of these dates have borne fruit, and he told me that he has stopped dating altogether since he turned twenty-five. He also said that he would wait until he turned thirty, and if he still hadn't found anyone really suitable, he would just give up and get married for the sake of it. "If you don't marry, people back at home will think there's something wrong with you, biologically or mentally."

One thing that has held him back from succeeding is his inability to reconcile his responsibilities as a son with his desire for a woman of his own choice. He had dated a few girls in the past, but as fate would have it, they were all northerners. He broke up with them mainly because he believed that *yidilian* (distant love)[4] would not work. His aversion to *yidilian* was both cultural and practical:

> Back in my hometown, people of my parents' and grandparents' generations tend to believe that girls from the north are dumb and simple, so they are against their children marrying an outsider [from that area]. Dialect is another problem, and we also have different habits and customs. Besides, marrying someone from outside my hometown isn't practical. My dad died a few years ago, and I'll need to take my share of responsibility for looking after my mum. My two brothers and I will also have to look after our grandparents on both sides of the family. I can't shirk my responsibilities and live somewhere else. So, for my first couple of years of dating, I ruled out girls from outside Guangdong.

BH told me that, apart from practicalities, there were a number of reasons why people in his hometown of Chaozhou looked down on brides from inland and northern provinces. BH had grown up hearing that the first arrivals of brides from outside his province were "purchased," in the sense that women from poor provinces expect a much higher betrothal gift from the groom's family than is usually accepted in Guangdong:

> In my hometown, not only do we not expect the groom's family to pay a betrothal fee, but brides from Guangdong also come up with their own dowry. This is a very different custom from other places.

It seems that public opinion—in the form of idle gossip and moral judgment from rural kinship, family members, relatives, neighbors, and acquaintances in the village—weighs heavily on BH in his decisions about whether to date or not to date someone, or whether to consider someone as a suitable marriage partner, even though he now lives far from home. This is not only because he and his family care what other people think of them, but it is also because he believes that public opinion often has a way of affecting the conjugal relationship itself:

> So, if an outside bride's family demanded, say, 200,000 *yuan* from the groom, this would practically put the groom's family in dire financial circumstances. Neighbors would say that the groom's family had practically purchased a wife, so, after their marriage, being aware of such public opinion, it would be very difficult for the family to feel kindly toward her. And if she was not treated well, she in turn wouldn't be that dutiful toward her parents-in-law. This makes it hard to ignore parental expectations and the judgments of your neighbors in the village back at home.

BH would also break up with a girl mainly, but not exclusively, because she was a single child, as he believed that single children had to shoulder the responsibility of looking after their parents and grandparents singlehandedly—something that, in his view, would not be practicable: "Just imagine that between the two of us, our wages are still below 10,000 *yuan* [per month]. How could we expect to be able to support my parents and grandparents as well as hers?" he asked.

But what if the woman—a single child—was happy to come and live with his family, and help take care of his family? BH replied, "If a girl wasn't even prepared to look after her own parents, I'm not sure I'd want to marry her." Having said that, he told me that his mother was now so anxious to see him married that she no longer insisted on any rules. She just wanted him to find someone and settle down. "So, I'll have to marry, eventually. Maybe when I turn thirty."

Before I met BH, he had gone on quite a few blind dates, but—in a now-familiar narrative—none of them had come to anything. "Either they didn't think I was good enough, or I wasn't prepared to *gui tian* (grovel; kneel down and lick their boots) just for the sake of getting a wife." He made it clear that he was not one of those unscrupulous men who prey on innocent women. BH told me that, in recent years, he had often heard stories of such scheming and conniving men. They would befriend trusting and inexperienced women from his hometown in Guangdong, as well as from rural Guangxi Province, promise them the world and make these women fall for them, and then get them pregnant. These women's families, fearing reputational damage to themselves and their daughters, were then left with no choice but to agree to marriage, no longer feeling entitled to demand a handsome betrothal gift. This strategy is called *fengzi chenghun* (marriage by having a child). "After marriage, these men then show their true colors."

While BH is disgusted by these conniving men, he is equally unforgiving of the women: "They have little schooling, don't know the first thing about sex, and become pregnant without knowing how. Many have to have an abortion in an illegal clinic." He then added, "I, for one, would not accept a woman who had already had an abortion." But he did admit that he was more conservative than those born in the 1990s, even though he was only a couple of years older than them. He believes that members of the 90s generation don't think about consequences, don't plan for the future, and don't care, and he has nothing in common with these "children."

When I last spoke to BH, in 2019, he was fast approaching the deadline he had set for himself—turning thirty—yet he still had not had much luck. "It's okay. I'd rather have no marriage than a bad marriage. It's not the end of the world if I end up being single." His view on marriage had not changed when I spoke to him on WeChat in 2022. He still did not have a girlfriend, and reiterated, "If you can't find someone that you can get along well with day in and day out for the rest of your life, why bother getting married?" He justified his position with the following argument:

> I've seen quite a few of my co-workers who got married after meeting someone following *xiangqin* [a blind date]. But there was no emotional closeness between the couple. [For example,] the man works in Shenzhen and the woman stays

back at home looking after kids and the elderly. Or both the man and woman are working in Shenzhen and sending money home to their parents and kids. They fight all the time, and some even shack up with someone else as a temporary arrangement. The only thing they've managed to achieve by getting married is to avoid the stigma of still being single. Nothing else. Is this really better than being single?

Despite his resistance to the idea of getting married for the sake of it, BH had gone through a few rounds of *xiangqin*, but almost all the women he met expected him to be able to purchase an apartment or to already own one, if not in the place of their current work, then at least in the town close to one of their village homes. But BH did not see the logic of buying an apartment while working somewhere else:

Once you go down this path of buying an apartment, you're chained to the monthly mortgage, which will be a huge drain on the couple's meager income. And if the couple ends up in divorce, it would be even harder to keep up with mortgage payments. But let's assume that all goes well with the marriage. Even then, you need to ask yourself, "What's the point of buying an apartment in the township near home if you don't plan to live there? We only go home to visit parents once in a while, so what are you going to do with the apartment?" Unlike in Shanghai, Beijing, or Shenzhen, it's not that easy to rent out apartments in small rural townships. And when you get too old to work in the city and decide to come back, wouldn't you prefer to live in a spacious house you build for yourself in the village, rather than in a small apartment building in the crowded town nearby?

Some fellow workers said that BH was still single because he might have expected too much from a marriage. But he insisted that the opposite was true: "I have no specific requirements about her looks or height. All I want is to find someone who shares similar values, and who doesn't insist on 'having face' through the possession of an apartment or a car, someone who is happy to settle down with me in the village, and is content to get around on a bike."

Masculine Grievance

Accounts of men on the bottom rung of the social ladder remind us that no man exists outside the power dynamics shaped by the intersection of class, gender, and rural–urban inequality (Du P. 2017). Wu Xiaoying (2017, 121) argues in her discussion of rural migrant men that inequality and hierarchical power relations exist as much between men as they do between men and women: "Men are not just beneficiaries of patriarchy; they are also oppressed and controlled by its gender structure and systems." This snapshot of the lives of four migrant men in the 80s cohort points to a specific kind of subjective experience that is characterized by emotional pain, quiet desperation, and low self-esteem. Given these suggestive and troubling findings, an important focus for future research could be the discursive constructions of gendered identities among rural migrant men in the 90s cohort, given that the attitudes and experiences of younger rural migrants are likely to be evolving rapidly under the impact of China's changing social and political policies.

To my 80s informants, purchasing sex or exercising sexual domination—commonly characterized as key ways of asserting a masculine identity (Illouz 2012)—are not only economically unviable but also morally unacceptable. For some migrant men in similar socioeconomic circumstances to theirs, sex may be one of the few activities available to them for experiencing some form of gender-based self-validation. It may well be for this reason that, as ZB told me, bragging about one's sexual conquests or one's capacity to purchase sex was common among rural migrant workers. While the individual leftover men I discuss in this chapter have less to brag about than their younger counterparts, they nevertheless assert their moral superiority by criticizing the braggarts alongside whom they work.

The experiences of these men demonstrate how patriarchy negotiates with political power and social structure to reshape rural migrant men's gender-based self-identification. Both migrant women and men are subject to the shaping forces of the "triple oppression" of state, capital, and patriarchy (N. Pun 2005), and their gender identities are shaped by "the three fundamental elements of gender discourse" (Xiaoying Wu 2010), albeit in different ways. While both state and public discourses express anxiety about migrant men's inability to find wives, such anxiety arises from a perspective that is focused on social order and stability, and also betrays a tacit assumption that it is more important to solve the problem of emotional loneliness and sexual frustration for migrant men than it is for migrant women (W. Sun 2017), even though migrant women have to face additional moral and social stigmatization if they fail to marry by a certain age.

Struggling at such an inhospitable nexus, some individual migrant men experience gender- and class-specific shame and humiliation. For instance, all four men discussed here, including the "lucky" ZB, complained to me about women's materialistic aspirations—their quest to find "a better catch"—and their inability to see beyond their own current and future economic circumstances. Similarly, they griped about the demands these women's families made for exorbitant betrothal gifts, and for their treatment of their own daughters as commodities in a transactional marriage. However, these men failed to acknowledge that, in making these demands, the women and their families were primarily seeking to defray the risk and uncertainty brought about by the prevailing state-endorsed, gendered economic order, and were not necessarily expressing a deeply held conviction that improving their economic circumstances was an intrinsically more valuable goal than finding loving husbands for their daughters.

All four of my 80s interviewees criticized younger men (from the 90s cohort) for their casual, irresponsible attitudes toward sex and intimacy in their courtships, and distanced themselves from those "morally questionable" men who either purchase sex and then brag about it, or who are prepared to do whatever it takes to get a wife without having to pay a betrothal gift. However, it is noteworthy that their more cautious, more "conservative," and less "modern" approach to women seems somewhat paradoxical. For example, these men want to treat women with honor and respect, but at the same time they are reluctant to extend such treatment to women who, through no fault of their own, have fallen victim to one of the less-than-honorable men my interviewees despise—as BH made clear when he told me that he would not choose a woman if she had had a pre-marital abortion, presumably even if she did this to avoid marrying an unscrupulous man who had sought to secure her through the strategy of *fengzi chenghun*, discussed earlier.

Their grievances make it clear that, while rural migrant men are beneficiaries of the patriarchal system—albeit in limited ways—they are also oppressed by social pressures and expectations that are shaped by class, the rural–urban divide, and gender inequality. My discussion seems to have uncovered a cohort of older rural migrant men within the new generations of migrant workers who have not necessarily "absorbed Western ideals of love and intimacy" (Choi and Peng 2016, 64), and who are in fact still caught up in traditional ideas regarding sexual morality and appropriate conduct in negotiating their relationships with women. Accordingly, we can interpret the assertion of their difference from—and even their moral superiority over—the younger cohort as a crucial means of making sense of their self-described failures in marital and intimate terms, as well as of their sexual frustration and emotional loneliness as a result of such failures. Furthermore, by commenting on the younger cohort's myriad moral "transgressions"—be it casual sex, prostitution, or irresponsible attitudes to marriage—and by declaring their refusal to follow suit, these men are able to claim a certain sense of moral superiority, and therefore self-esteem.

Finally, this ethnographic account of the emotional experience of some 80s men uncovers a complex relationship between rural migrant men's emotional subjectivity and public/state discourses about the experiences of this social group. On the one hand, my informants' experiences point to the hollowness of the officially declared commitment to reducing inequality and bringing about a people-centered, harmonious society, prosperity, and a "well-to-do" middle-class existence—the stuff of President Xi's *Zhongguo Meng* (Chinese Dream). The emotional lives of these migrant men are a sobering reminder that, while achieving success and prosperity may enhance masculinity for some men of certain classes, such a "dream" may have a deleterious impact on those who are structurally denied access to these goods. Furthermore, while policy discussions about the marital problems of rural migrant men are mostly concerned with the taken-for-granted link between marital unhappiness and social instability, my discussion here suggests that, despite their disillusion, disappointment, and, in some cases, even despair—all of which dominate the widespread discourses of masculine grievance—none of my 80s informants showed any inclination to engage in behavior that was socially disruptive or illicit.

On the other hand, there does seem to be a high level of agreement between what my 80s informants say about the 90s cohort, and what the public/state discourses say about that group. As this discussion shows, in accounting for their own failures to find a wife, my informants apparently find the widely accepted wisdom regarding their differences from the 90s generation discursively useful, as a result of which the distinction has become an integral trope in their "masculine grievance." Since my ethnography is more concerned with how unmarried rural migrant men talk and think about their failure to find a marriage partner than with how they actually negotiate gender relations with their wives, girlfriends, and lovers, I have found "masculine grievance" to be a useful analytic term. What seems to have emerged from this account is a persistent trope of grievance, characterized by a mixture of feelings of loneliness, bitterness, and dissatisfaction with the status quo of their lives, and a quiet yearning for the possibility—however remote—of "finding someone" in the future. Masculine grievance is also a self-narrative that expresses a "wounded" (T. Liu 2020) but dignified masculine identity, often articulated through these men's criticisms of migrant women and their families, of migrant men from younger generations, and of less-than-honorable migrant men who behave badly toward women. Finally, masculine grievance becomes a way of making sense of their own gender- and class-specific emotional hardships.

CONCLUSION

Two More Stories about Love

Xiaohe, married with a son and a daughter, is a live-in maid in a big household in Beijing. Her husband, Wang Daxue (an aspirational name indicating his parents' hopes for him, "daxue" meaning "university"), is a long-distance truck driver. So, when his truck passes by Beijing, he books a room in a budget hotel on the outskirts of town, planning to spend a night with his wife. The couple long for each other's company, as they have not seen each other for over half a year.

Xiaohe anticipates the meeting with quiet excitement. She wants to assure herself that her husband is still loyal to her—a nightmare a few days ago featuring him in bed with another woman is still bothering her. She washes herself carefully the night before, and sets out at dawn to traverse the city—first by bus and then by subway—and finally arrives at the hotel. Upon arriving, Xiaohe sees that her husband's buddy and co-worker is snoring in bed—they have been driving many hours and are both exhausted. Xiaohe does not feel comfortable being intimate with her husband in the presence of another person. And so, knowing that her husband has a bad back, she sits him down in a comfortable position, and they while away their time catching up on things.

When the co-worker wakes up, the three of them go out to have lunch. After lunch, the co-worker departs, leaving Xiaohe and her husband alone—finally. Then their daughter, currently studying at a Beijing university, visits, shares a quick meal with her parents, but then hurries away to "allow more time for her parents to be alone together." With a palpable sense of anticipation, and fantasizing that the day might come when their daughter lands a job in Beijing and gets a place of her own, the couple walk back to their hotel, only to be stopped by the woman at reception, who seems friendly but officious. She wants Xiaohe to produce her ID, saying that she cannot allow her to spend the night without proof of her identity and her relationship to Daxue. Begging her to be "understanding" is futile. The reception has a good reason for sticking to the rules. This is the week of the "two congresses," referring to the National People's Congress and Chinese People's Political Consultative Congress. And, as any Beijing resident would know, security is always tight during the time of national congresses. Police are expected to do random checks, and if guests fail to produce their ID, the hotel runs the risk of a fine or, even worse, losing their license. Not wanting to lose her job, the receptionist, though sympathetic to the couple, asks them to be "understanding" of her decision.

To show that she is flexible, the receptionist allows the couple to stay in the room until eleven o'clock that evening, but only in the presence of a hotel staff member. They go along with this proposal, since it is not practicable for Xiaohe to go back to fetch her ID (the journey would take more than two hours, and cost twelve *yuan*). So, the hotel employee turns on the television and tries to ignore the couple as much as she can, while they talk quietly to each other. Then it is eleven o'clock, and Xiaohe has to leave. Not wanting her to go yet, Daxue leaves the room with his wife so as to spend more time with her outside. The couple pace up and down the street till five o'clock the next morning, eyeing the bed longingly through the window of the still brightly lit hotel room. Then it is time for them both to depart. Xiaohe heads back to her employer's house—a new day's work awaits her—while her husband drives his truck out of town. They cannot tell how long it will be before they see each other again, since he has to go "wherever the goods have to go."

This is what unfolds in "*Chunfeng Ye*" ("Night of the Spring Breeze"), a short story written by Tie Ning (2010), one of China's best-known contemporary writers, and, since 2006, president of the China Writers' Association. It was published in *Beijing Wenxue* (Beijing Literature), a prestigious literary magazine, and its title is a coded phrase alluding to a night of sexual intimacy. But on this "night of the spring breeze," Xiaohe and her husband's wish to enjoy some well-deserved conjugal intimacy is repeatedly thwarted. Absurd as it may sound, the often futile experiences of socioeconomically underprivileged individuals running up against the inhuman face of politics and bureaucracy are very real and very common. Tie Ning is clearly compassionate toward the characters in her story, but her political and social critique is subtle and implicit. And perhaps the story is poignant precisely because of this gentle subtlety.

While Xiaohe's hope for a brief reunion with her husband ends in disappointment, the couple in an episode of a television series meet with a violent and more catastrophic outcome. Dazhuang works on a construction site; his wife Zhaodi works in a shoe factory. Although in the same city, they both have long work hours and live far apart, so the couple don't get to see each other much. Even when they do meet, they don't have a place to be alone—Dazhuang lives in a makeshift dorm on the construction site, while Zhaodi sleeps in the dorm room provided by her factory. As a newlywed ten days into his marriage, Dazhuang feels sexually frustrated. Initially, they resort to booking a room for an hour or so in a karaoke bar equipped with booths. Though their activities have to be somewhat hushed, this arrangement works for a while, until the karaoke bar is ordered to shut down for screening pornography. Sympathetic to Dazhuang's predicament, his co-workers leave the dorm room for a while when Zhaodi visits. This proves to be a good arrangement, until one of his co-workers, Qiangzi, drunkenly barges in during an intimate moment and becomes abusive, leaving Zhaodi feeling ashamed. She hurries off in a huff, leaving her husband feeling humiliated, and raging with red anger at his co-worker. The two get into a fight, which ends with Dazhuang hitting Qiangzi on the head with a stone, killing him instantly.

Screened on Shanghai Television in 2006, this is the storyline of Episode 2 of *Kewang Chengshi* (*Yearning for the City*),[1] a twenty-three-episode drama series centering on rural migrants' hardships and emotional struggles in the city. It is not surprising that the series has not been repeated on any television channels since its initial screening, despite the general trend of TV stations to recycle old films and TV dramas to fill up programming slots. After all, in the last decade and a half, the "main melody" of social harmony (see Chapter 2) has increasingly become an imperative for the Chinese media, especially since Xi Jinping took the reins in 2012. Along with many other stories in the same series, this story of Dazhuang and Zhaodi may strike many viewers as somewhat jarring.

This does not mean, however, that the social issues reflected in the *Yearning for the City* series and in "Night of the Spring Breeze" have vanished a decade later. Nor does it mean that the disappearance of narratives such as *Yearning for the City* from mainstream media has stopped people from accessing them. In fact, the emergence of a plethora of streaming platforms, especially those that have emerged in the past few years—such as Douyin,[2] which started in 2016—has made it profitable for streamers to (re)run video materials that are in demand but are no longer accessible via state media. *Yearning for the City* is one show that has enjoyed a comeback, thanks to these streaming platforms. As of March 2022, one such site on Douyin had garnered almost ten million views. And some of the comments posted in response to this particular episode are worth noting. Many viewers express sympathy for Dazhuang. "It's embarrassingly hard for a man without means," says one commenter; and others condemn his co-worker for lacking compassion. As for whether there is a viable solution to this problem, commenters are polarized. Some ask, "Why not rent a place?" or "How about getting a room in a hotel?" Others point out that renting is not realistic. "Rental properties tend to be far away from the construction site. It's not convenient to go to work. I am a *nongmingong*. I'm also a divorcée. I understand Dazhuang's situation." Another commenter, although he does not identify himself as a *nongmingong*, echoes this view: "Life is hard. Construction sites are usually far away from anywhere. It's hard to find a rental property nearby. Also, renting a place costs you at least three to four thousand *yuan* a month. With no car, you're bound to be late for work if you want to commute from home." The continuing popularity of shows such as *Yearning for the City* and the myriad comments left by reviewers are a clear indication that the issues reflected in such stories still resonate with migrant workers a decade and a half later.

Neither Dazhuang's bitter disappointment, embarrassment, shame, humiliation, and anger, nor Xiaohe's quiet yearnings, deep frustration, and profound sense of helplessness, are easily discernible in policy documents, media reports, and academic papers. If there were a "Dazhuang" who killed his co-worker in real life, his crime would most likely be narrated within the "law and order" framework. Rural migrants like Dazhuang stand in the shadows, under the bemused or judgmental gaze of the urban middle class—those rational, rights-bearing subjects with legitimate, socially approved desires for intimacy and dreams of fulfillment. Unable to relate to the attitudes of hope and optimism they are encouraged to adopt, many individuals from marginalized groups see a more realistic reflection of themselves in fictionalized accounts of their emotional struggles that are no longer in circulation.

As the chapters in this book have shown, rural migrants are used to seeing themselves represented in public discourses as a bifurcated figure. On the one hand, they are worthy, deserving, and, equally important, grateful recipients of urban middle-class charity. Many writers, photographers, and television producers do their best to give rural migrants their compassionate attention. Novelists, with subtlety or passion, write with touching pathos about individuals who are starved for intimacy. State television programs report on role models embodying positive attitudes despite their present hardships, and promise these displaced citizens a better future. Professional photographers take flattering pictures of factory workers wearing wedding gowns and suits on the factory's shopfloor, capturing a feeling of romance for those who otherwise could not afford their services.

At the same time, rural migrants are also the objects of governance. Their *suzhi* level is thought to be in need of improvement; their behavior is deemed to be in need of control and regulation; their unruliness—even criminality—is often presented as evidence of risk to the social order. Bureaucrats produce statistics from surveys that aim to indicate the extent of the "problem" of rural migrants, and state-funded sociologists and anthropologists answer the government's call to produce data about this group, publishing papers that identify causes and suggest remedies. Political leaders and policy makers at all levels—local, provincial, and national—ponder the potential ramifications of this problem for the nation's social harmony, political stability, and moral order, and struggle to come up with policy recommendations that may make a real difference, without undermining the hard-won achievements of China's middle class. While all the concerned parties frankly acknowledge rural–urban inequality and the systemic inequity caused by the *hukou* system as key factors in rural migrants' marital problems, most efforts that go into developing knowledge and ideas are motivated by anxiety about the likely undesirable consequences of inequality rather than by a moral concern about social justice. In the meantime, my conversations with young rural migrant workers from Foxconn in Shenzhen suggest that such bifurcated configurations of them have little buy-in from the very community that is being represented.

An Intimate Turn

I have argued in the past for a "cultural turn" in inequality studies (W. Sun 2013), and have suggested that the investigation of the cultural politics of inequality offers a new and potentially innovative pathway to understanding social inequality in China. I have further pointed out that this cultural turn hinges on the interplay between the *culture of inequality*, and the *inequality of culture*. In that earlier work, I define the culture of inequality as a set of moral, social, and political-economic values and assumptions that govern the ways in which inequality is rationalized, maintained, managed, and negotiated in institutional and organizational settings. The inequality of culture, on the other hand, refers to unequal access to an array of symbolic resources—the right to self-presentation, to have a political voice, to have one's stories and interpretations of social life heard and recognized as legitimate, as well as to the capacity to embody socially and politically appropriate sentiments and desires (W. Sun 2013).

The current book has been an attempt to embody that cultural turn, but it has also gone a step further, by arguing for an *intimate* turn in inequality studies. My study makes it abundantly clear that, in China as well as elsewhere (Clarke 2011; Illouz 1997), love and romance are often burdened with the task of mediating and negotiating structural and material inequality, and the domain of love and romance is a unique and key site of socioeconomic exchange. Furthermore, this research demonstrates that taking an intimate turn by no means leads to an intellectual retreat to the trivial, private, and personal. Rather, throughout the book, I have shown that the field of inequality studies has much to gain by addressing questions about the pursuit of social justice, dignity, and happiness at the level of personal affect. I have set out to write a book about inequality and intimacy, but this has not been a study of inequalities that exist in workers' incomes, labor contracts, working conditions, and industrial regimes; nor have I put migration, urbanization, *hukou* reform, and economic development front and center of my study. At the same time, I have shown that what goes on in each of these meta-processes of social change largely determines the extent of success or failure in the pursuit of dreams and intimate desires on the part of the rural men and women I study. Further, I have demonstrated that although people from all social classes experience "love troubles," an individual's capacity to enjoy fulfilling and warm feelings of love and to ward off such troubles and avoid "dark intimacy" often correlates with their socioeconomic position.

This study of the connection between inequality and intimacy in contemporary China has gone some way toward enhancing the analytic value of a number of concepts. It has brought to light the specific contours of this connection, and how it manifests itself in an increasingly authoritarian state that is in charge of running an extremely unequal society. A few insights regarding the connection between governmentality and individuals' desires have emerged from the analysis in the preceding chapters. First, the Chinese state does not just dictate the nation's policies on marriage, reproduction, and the legal framework of sexual conduct; it also decides which segments of society harbor desires that potentially threaten its political legitimacy, social stability, and moral order, and are therefore in need of top-down governing. Second, the state also functions to (re)invent new tropes of romance, to arbitrate "where, how, and by whom" certain aspects of people's private lives are "rendered problematic" (Rose 1998, 25), and to devise new boundaries of acceptable and legitimate desire. Third, no understanding of how governmentality functions through the regulation of desire in contemporary China is complete unless we take these two processes as co-dependent and mutually constitutive.

The analysis of discourses and practices of romantic consumption in the preceding chapters has also gone some way toward expanding and updating existing sociological insights about emotional capitalism. Sociologists have long argued that class positions are negotiated through romantic consumption, and the analysis of the relationship between class and consumption is particularly important for a society such as China in times of radical social restructuring. As argued in this book, while membership of the middle class is still in the process of being solidified, social change in China over the past several decades has also transformed the class structure of the socialist era. The lack of clarity regarding the class status of *nongmingong* certainly poses analytical challenges; but my analysis suggests that it has also brought fresh opportunities to uncover dynamic, complex, and sometimes unpredictable class-based practices. As this investigation shows, casting the rural migrant as a central empirical figure who nevertheless lacks analytical clarity—especially by juxtaposing this figure against the equally unstable category of the middle class—can be productive in our efforts to understand class inequality and the processes of class formation.

As I have argued in earlier chapters, rural migrants are an emotional precariat. Because of their socioeconomic disadvantage, rural migrant lovers and marital partners provide different kinds of emotional labor from urban middle-class individuals, and endure greater emotional anguish in their private lives. Yet, as lovers and practitioners of intimacy and romance, they are also expected to perform in front of the camera—be it for state television or professional photographers—in ways that lend support, legitimacy, and status to the state and the middle class. It is possible that well-intentioned agents of the state, including "thought workers" and academics who participate in state projects of moralization and socialization, are trying to help migrant workers, or at least they think they are. It is also possible that these individuals create and sustain social norms by encouraging conformity and discouraging deviance, as do moral opinion-leaders elsewhere, both inside and outside China. Nevertheless, by appearing in front of the camera, these migrant workers effectively generate surplus *symbolic* value that benefits the accumulation of political capital by a state that is keen to shore up its moral credibility—in addition to the central role they play in producing surplus *material* value that benefits the accumulation of transnational capital.

Finally, this study has filled a yawning gap in our existing knowledge about the intimate emotional consequences of social inequality in China. It is true that rural-to-urban migration, urbanization, and globalization have given rise to a neoliberal form of self-governance. What this amounts to is an aspiration to be able to make personal choices, to enjoy the freedom to live one's life as one chooses, to obtain the means and resources necessary to achieving fulfilling sexual intimacy, and to manage the risks of modern relationships competently— both practically and emotionally. However, China's compressed modernity has led to class-differentiated outcomes, and, as Yunxiang Yan (2009; 2010) argues, individualization without individuality is more prominently embodied in rural migrants. Like the migrant worker lovers in Dongguan who appear in the photo-essay I discussed in the introduction, the young women and men who talked to me in Shenzhen are caught at the crossroads between the urban and the rural; between the past and the future. Their existential predicament is encapsulated in a saying that has been widely circulated among rural migrant workers themselves: "Can't go back to the country, but can't settle down in the city." And in no other domain of their lives are these predicaments played out more painfully than in their intimate relationships. My conversations with rural migrant workers suggest that, in setting out to become modern urban individuals, many of them have paid a high emotional price for their ticket on that journey. Rather than fulfillment, they are more likely to inhabit an undesirable "emotional world," to use Hochschild's (2003) term. This is a world that is often tinged with quiet frustration, loneliness, and even despair, due to their inability to find a marriage partner. Also familiar in this world are feelings of being worthless, inferior, ashamed, or humiliated for being stuck in an exploitative, abusive, or even violent relationship. Their experience can also be infused with a sad, quiet longing for intimacy, as is the case for the newly married couple in *Yearning for the City*, or for Xiaohe, who can't stay in the hotel room with her husband: neither couple can afford accommodation that provides them with the privacy and comfort that are essential to the enjoyment of intimacy.

Another problem that contributes negatively to rural migrants' emotional make-up is the tension between rural marriage practices and urban sexual cultures. On the one hand, they are expected to date, court, and wed according to the traditional, characteristically rural, customs and rituals—the *xiangqin* (parent-arranged blind dates), betrothal gifts, and a preference to marry someone from close by, etc. On the other hand, they are also exposed to an urban consumption style, the allure of freer and more fulfilling ways of pursing intimacy, and the more relaxed sexual sensibility that is promoted in popular culture. To be sure, urban middle-class professionals may to some extent also face similar tensions; but this study has identified a number of key social, economic, and cultural obstacles that make it much more difficult, if not impossible, for rural migrants to overcome these obstacles. We are therefore able to predict with reasonable confidence that, unless such structural obstacles are removed, modernity's much-touted affective individualism will continue to produce strikingly unequal levels of emotional well-being and satisfaction, and these will largely be stratified along a rural–urban divide.

A Methodological Lesson

One important lesson that has emerged from this study is in relation to research methodology in inequality studies. I have become increasingly convinced that in order to learn how inequality impacts on intimacy we must conduct a different type of fieldwork, one that enables us to discover the invisible, to listen to awkward silences, and to understand absence and erasure in the narratives of marginalized individuals. Also, since an ethnography of the heart poses more challenges than conventional anthropology, we must forge new ethnographic partnerships. For example, taking a cue from anthropologists such as Judith Farquhar (2002), as well as from several sociologists of emotion (e.g., Illouz 2012), I have learned to excavate voices from a wide range of discursive sites—fictional or real, official, or grassroots. But I have also found that it is not only useful to hear what workers tell me about whom they want to date or do not want to date, or why they can or cannot find a lover, but also to find out how they engage in meaning-making while consuming different kinds of "love stories."

Of course, as I hope I have shown, this partnership—with writers and my research subjects respectively—has not enabled me to establish a hierarchy of truthfulness or authenticity, but it has to some extent enabled me to bring to light competing narratives and discourses. And I have managed to do so by asking questions about the political economy of cultural production: What are the power relations between those who speak and those who are spoken about? Who is the cultural producer, whose platforms deliver the content, where does the funding come from, who is the intended audience, and which social classes' sentiments, perspectives, and desires are considered "appropriate"? And most importantly, wherever possible, I have asked how and why marginalized groups' own voices clash, contradict, dovetail, or overlap with these cultural representations.

I hope it is clear by now that I chose the word "trouble" in the title of this book in order to signal my dual intentions in undertaking this study. First, I wanted to demonstrate the myriad ways in which political, social, economic, cultural, and moral forces conspire to cause troubles in rural migrant men's and women's pursuit of love and intimacy. But I also intended this study as an intellectual intervention, a "troubling" of the dominant paradigms of love, romance, and intimacy. I doubt very much that this "troubling" exercise will make much, if any, practical difference in terms of improving the marriage prospects of the rural migrant men who talked to me, or helping the migrant women in their everyday struggle to maintain intimate connections with their spouses, children, and parents despite separation. But I do hope that it opens up a new and useful analytical perspective in understanding how intimacy is deeply and intricately intertwined with inequality in societies such as contemporary China.

Finally, I want to say something about the image that appears on the cover of this book. It was taken by Zhan Youbing and published online under the pseudonym Jia Zheng in 2013, as part of the photo-essay "Rural Migrants' Love in Dongguan," which I have discussed at some length in the introduction. The photo, depicting a rural migrant couple dragging suitcases along a street of an industrial park in Dongguan, has a special hold on me because it seems to embody so many of the possibilities, as well as so many of the challenges, that face this particular social group. It raises questions such as: Where is this couple going, and where are they coming from? Have they just packed up to return to the village, or have they just arrived back in the city after a visit home? It is likely—although I cannot be certain—that the woman in the picture is pregnant. Are they married, and if so, what are they planning to do once the baby is born? Will they decide to send the child home to be looked after by one of the couple's parents? Will the mother and child leave the father and return to her rural home? If the child stays in Dongguan, will the parents be able to afford childcare? I also wonder what kind of accommodation the couple have: Do they live in a rental property, or separately in their respective factory dormitories? Are they saving every cent in order to buy a flat, like the couple who featured in CCTV's stories in Chapter 2? How difficult will it be for them to achieve the conjugal intimacy that is taken for granted by urban middle-class residents, and how prominently does this intimacy feature in the myriad family strategies and decisions they have to make? And, regardless of the choices they make, what kind of future, if any, does the city of Dongguan hold for this young couple?

Despite my lingering questions about this couple and about the entire young rural migrant worker cohort, it is my genuine hope that we are at least a step closer to understanding their predicament, and that we can start working toward a new analytical framework that takes the intimate consequences of inequality as given, and that consciously privileges human dignity and emotional justice over normative ideas and practices of love and romance.

NOTES

Introduction

1. All translations of Chinese in the book are my own, unless specified otherwise. All quotations of rural migrant workers and NGO employees in this and subsequent chapters are translated transcriptions either of audio recordings of interviews or conversations I conducted on various dates in the period 2015–2017, or of audio or text exchanges in WeChat from the same period or afterward.
2. In this chapter, and elsewhere in the book, I will usually refer to participants in my research with a two-letter code such as this, or a pseudonym such as "Xiao W" or "Liu YY," in order to preserve their anonymity. In some cases, participants have given me permission to use their actual names.
3. The photographer is Zhan Youbing, but he used the pseudonym Jia Zheng for his photo-essay "Rural Migrants' Love in Dongguan." Zhan's work should not be confused with the other photo-essay I also discuss in this book—Jia Dai Tengfei's "Love on the Assembly Line"—which was the inspiration for the CCTV series of the same, which I discuss in Chapter 2.
4. When citing authors writing in Chinese who share the same family name as another author, I have included the initial of their first given name *after* their family name. For authors writing in English whose names require disambiguation, I have included the initial of their given name *before* their family name. For authors whose names require further disambiguation, I have included their full first name, before or after the family name as appropriate.
5. Social scientists have produced a sizable—and still growing—body of work on China's widening social inequality. This literature has mostly been concerned with inequalities in welfare and living standards (Bian and Logan 1996; Davis 1995; Gerber and Hout 1998; Gustafsson, Li, and Sicular 2008; Nee 1989, 1991, 1996; Rona-Tas 1994; X. Zhou 2004), with particular emphasis on the causes of economic inequality, especially income inequality (Davis and Wang 2009, 15, 18).
6. For examples of scholarship that argues for and embodies the affective turn, see Clough and Halley (2007) and Gregg and Seigworth (2010).
7. The sociocultural construct approach asks about the relationship between emotion and social discourse—for instance, about how emotion gets its meaning and force from its location and performance in the public realm of discourse. It also involves asking how social life is affected by emotional discourse. This "emotion as discursive practice" approach takes texts, talk, and language as being "productive of experience and constitutive of the realities in which we live and truths with which we work" (Lutz and Abu-Lughod 1990, 9–11). This analytical focus on language requires researchers to pay attention to individuals' emotional experience as expressed in their own narratives, and to explain how talk about emotion becomes possible through the categories of certain cultural discourses (Lutz and Abu-Lughod 1990).
8. Going beyond the sociocultural construct approach, Nigel Thrift's (2007) "non-representational theory" argues for approaching affect, emotion, and feelings as

corporeal practices. Scholars following this approach argue for the need to attend to the movement and sensation of the body and a wide range of pre-linguistic and bodily expressions (Massumi 2002; Sedgwick and Frank 1995). The usefulness of this embodiment approach is evidenced in the ethnographic work of Ngai Pun (2005), who worked and lived with migrant women in an electronics factory in southern China, and witnessed first-hand the emotional anguish of some of her co-workers/research participants. Her attempt to make sense of a rural migrant woman worker's nightly screams alerts us to the possible "gap between the realms of consciousness and unconsciousness" (Pun 2005, 187), between language and the pre-linguistic, and between words and the body.

9 Among anthropologists working on social change in China, Judith Farquhar is by far the most explicit and insistent advocate of creative methodologies. On the one hand, like her colleagues in the field, she believes that knowledge regarding emotional experience can only become intelligible through the medium of "discourses" (Farquhar 2002), "stories," and "narratives" (Jacka 2006), and "public allegories" (Rofel 2007). On the other hand, she believes that cultural anthropology has sometimes been hasty in "turning from carnal life to representations, from bodies and practices to symbols and meanings" (Farquhar 2002, 7).

10 In my fieldwork, these texts serve as reliably useful conversational fodder to get at elusive data about two spheres: the intimate lives of migrant individuals; and how these individuals relate to and engage with ideas and views of love and romance in public discourses.

11 It is clear, then, that in this book I will use media and cultural material in ways and for purposes very different from the conventional method of cultural analysis or ethnography of media consumption, which was the main approach I adopted in *Subaltern China* (W. Sun 2014).

12 See, for instance, Li Zhang's work on the emergence of psychoanalysis and psychotherapy—what she calls "therapeutic governing"—as a critical tool for managing the population in a rapidly changing society (L. Zhang 2014, 2017, 2018; also see J. Yang 2015).

13 Originally agricultural settlements, these villages have now been swallowed up by urban and industrial development, and have expanded rapidly outside the scope of urban planning, mostly without adhering to prevailing building standards.

14 These tall buildings are called "handshake buildings" because they are so close to each other that occupants can virtually reach out their windows and shake hands with someone from the neighboring building. Built by local Shenzhen villagers on what was originally farming land, they are prominent features of the "village within the city" urbanization phenomenon, and are now mostly rented out to rural migrant workers by the local villagers. Some of the landlords of these buildings live on the premises, while others have moved out of the village.

15 "Gutter oil" is processed cooking oil that has been recycled from waste oil collected from various sources such as restaurant fryers, grease traps, and sewage drains. Although it was banned in the early 2010s, some restaurant owners in China continue to use it, hence the perennial news stories exposing such scandals. See, for example, S. Chen (2017).

16 The CPC is widely referred to in the West as the Chinese Communist Party (CCP), but this is not the officially endorsed name of the Party (English.gov.cn 2021), and it also carries negative connotations for many Chinese people (Quora 2020). Hence, I will use the acronym "CPC" throughout this book.

Chapter 1

1. For an extended discussion of the politics of naming rural migrant workers as *nongmingong*, see Chapter 1 of W. Sun (2014), "Configuring the *Nongmingong*."
2. The authors cited an official document released in 2010, so these percentages could be slightly different now.
3. As with the broader topic of the rural–urban divide, China's *hukou* policy and its discriminatory nature have been the subject of equally voluminous research. Chapter 1 in W. Sun (2014) includes an extensive review of the English-language academic literature on *hukou*. For some examples of the research on this topic since then, see Kam Wing Chan (2017).
4. In recent years, many popular cultural terms have emerged from the Chinese internet and social media to signify class differences, albeit in colorful and sometimes blatantly crude ways. See, for instance, my discussion of the term "*diaosi*" later in this chapter.
5. While "*diaosi*" began as a term of outright abuse in an online forum in 2010, it was quickly taken up as a self-deprecating identity by millions of poor and disenfranchised male rural migrant workers (Sum 2016), and subsequently by young people of all genders, to the point where today it almost has the status of a neutral description of someone who has been excluded from the benefits of China's growth (Kan 2013).
6. This is a popular expression on the internet meaning "instead of competing with others in one's own right, one uses one's father's achievement and wealth as a proxy."
7. The *People's Daily* article is sometimes unavailable online, but Baidu Baike (n.d., endnote 3) has a link to a screenshot of the original *People's Daily* page.
8. Although it is difficult to find published evidence confirming this claim, the observation is borne out by my personal communications with numerous social scientists in China.

Chapter 2

1. Six thousand *yuan* converts to approximately US$950 at the time of writing (2022).
2. Foxconn is a Taiwanese-owned electronics manufacturer that has plants in various parts of China, with its plant in Shenzhen being the earliest and biggest. As China's biggest global factory and manufacturer of parts for Apple and other electronics companies, Foxconn employs young and mostly unmarried workers, most of whom have rural *hukou* status. For discussions of labor conditions and Foxconn workers' experience with the industrial regime, see J. Chan and Pun (2010) and Selden, Pun, and J. Chan (2013).
3. I conducted these interviews as part of a larger, ongoing ethnographic project on the romantic experience of factory workers in the Pearl River Delta. From August to October 2015, I spent time with workers in the industrial complex of Longhua New District in Shenzhen, with a view to exploring how social inequality shapes their views on and experiences of romantic love and romantic consumption. During that period, I interviewed twenty-five Foxconn workers based in Shenzhen. These one-to-one interviews mostly lasted an hour and a

half, and were often in the small, crowded rental rooms where workers lived, or occasionally in a café located in the residential areas of the industrial complex often described as a "village within the city." In October 2016 and 2017 I returned to the same site and conducted follow-up interviews with eight of these interviewees. I also maintain regular contact with these individuals via WeChat, the most popular social media platform in China.
4. As mentioned in the introduction, my interest is not to produce an ethnography of workers' media consumption practices; readers who are interested in this topic can refer to my previous work (W. Sun 2014). Rather, I use these media texts primarily as an interview strategy in order to circumvent some of the difficulties involved in talking about emotions and relationships in a research setting.
5. QQ is an instant messaging service and web portal that is owned by WeChat's parent company, Tencent. While many users now prefer to use WeChat, QQ still boasted nearly six hundred million users as recently as 2020 (Thomala 2021).
6. See Brandtstädter and Santos (2009) for a discussion of kinship in China and the persistence of homosocial ties in Chinese society.

Chapter 3

1. According to Chinese folklore, this is the day when two mythical lovers, Niu Ling, an orphaned cowherd, and Zhi Nu, the weaving girl who is the youngest daughter of the Jade Emperor (ruler of heaven according to traditional Chinese religion), meet every year (Melton and Bauman 2010, 912–13).
2. For a detailed account of how bridal photography differs from conventional wedding photos, see Constable (2006) and Adrian (2006), in a special issue of *Visual Anthropology* on this topic.
3. Safety nets were installed outside the windows of tall buildings in Foxconn as a suicide prevention measure, after a number of Foxconn workers committed suicide by jumping from these buildings in 2010–2011.

Chapter 4

1. The names of the NGOs I discuss in this chapter and the individuals who work in them have been anonymized.
2. BB, personal interview, October 23, 2017. All subsequent quotes from BB are from this interview, unless specified otherwise.
3. Although the URL of the WeChat subscription account is available, I have decided to withhold it here, in order to protect the identities of the individuals concerned.
4. I am indebted to Meaghan Morris for suggesting this term.

Chapter 5

1. Ticket grabbing is a way of purchasing limited tickets online.

Chapter 6

1. For a good guide to scholarly works on the topic of China's rural migrants, see Pun (2016). Also, for an outline of how marital problems are discussed in the Chinese-language sociological literature, see W. Sun (2017).
2. "Lonely souls" is one of several colloquial expressions that are often used to refer to leftover men. Another such expression in common use is *guanggun* (bare sticks).
3. See more detailed discussions of *hukou* (residential permit) and its impact on rural migrant workers in Chapter 1 and at numerous other places throughout the book.
4. In this context, "distant love" refers to the fact that these northern women are from provinces that are different—and remote—from BH's home province, which is in southern China.

Conclusion

1. This series can be accessed from a number of Chinese video streaming sites, including https://tv.sohu.com/item/OTkyNDMy.html, and https://movie.douban.com/subject/21340776/.
2. Douyin is the Chinese version of the video-driven social media platform TikTok, which quickly achieved great popularity internationally when it merged with the lip-syncing service Musical.ly in 2018.

BIBLIOGRAPHY

ACFTU (All-China Federation of Trade Unions). 2010. "Zhonghua quanguo zong gonghui: Guanyu Xinshengdai nongmingong wenti de yanjiubaogao" ("All-China Federation of Trade Unions: Research Report into the Lives of China's New-Generation Rural Migrants"). Zhongguo fazhan menhu wang (China Development Portal), June 21. http://cn.chinagate.cn/reports/2010-06/21/content_20309952.htm.

ACWF (All-China Women's Federation). 2011. "Quanguo fulian: Zuo chengli ren chengwei Xinshengdai nongmingong chongjing" ("All-China Women's Federation: Young Rural Migrants Aspire to Become Urban Residents"). *Zhongguo qing nianbao* (*China Youth Daily*), December 9. http://news.sina.com.cn/c/2011-12-09/040323601684.shtml.

Adrian, Bonnie. 2003. *Framing the Bride: Globalizing Beauty and Romance in Taiwan's Bridal Industry*. Berkeley, CA: University of California Press.

Adrian, Bonnie. 2006. "Geography of Style: Taiwan's Bridal Photography Empire." *Visual Anthropology* 19(1): 73–85. https://doi.org/10.1080/08949460500374007.

Ahmed, Sara. 2010. *The Promise of Happiness*. Durham, NC: Duke University Press.

Anagnost, Ann. 2004. "The Corporeal Politics of Quality (Suzhi)." *Public Culture* 16(2): 189–208.

Anagnost, Ann. 2008. "From 'Class' to 'Social Strata': Grasping the Social Totality in Reform-Era China." *Third World Quarterly* 29(3): 497–519.

Appadurai, Arjun. 2004. "The Capacity to Aspire: Culture and the Terms of Recognition." In *Culture and Public Action*, edited by Vijayendra Rao and Michael Walton, 59–84. Stanford, CA: Stanford University Press.

Aying. 2014. "'Hunyin shougou' chuanqi: Jinqian zhida yo aiqing huancun" ("A Legend About a 'Marriage for Sale': Fast Track to Money While Love Awaits"). *Zhiyin* (Soulmate) 12, 36.

Baidu Baike. n.d. "Diaosi." https://baike.baidu.com/item/%E5%B1%8C%E4%B8%9D/1415463#3_2.

Bakken, Børge. 2000. *The Exemplary Society: Human Improvement, Social Control, and the Dangers of Modernity in China*. Oxford, UK: Oxford University Press.

Banyuetan (Bi-Monthly forum). 2011. "Xinshengdai nongmingong quefa qinggan zhichi" ("Second-Generation Rural Migrants Lack Support for Emotional Loneliness"), July 14. http://news.sina.com.cn/c/sd/2011-07-14/101422812600_2.shtml.

Bao, Hongwei. 2018. *Queer Comrades: Gay Identity and Tongzhi Activism in Postsocialist China*. Copenhagen: NIAS Press.

Bauman, Zygmunt. 2017. *A Chronicle of Crisis 2011–2016*. London: Social Europe Ltd.

Beck, Ulrich, and Elisabeth Beck-Gernsheim. 2002. *Individualization: Institutionalized Individualism and Its Social and Political Consequences*. Thousand Oaks, CA: Sage.

Beck, Ulrich, Anthony Giddens, and Scott Lash. 1994. *Reflexive Modernization: Politics, Tradition and Aesthetics in the Modern Social Order*. Oxford, UK: Blackwell.

Berlant, Lauren. 2011. *Cruel Optimism*. Durham, NC: Duke University Press.

Bian, Yanjie, and John R. Logan. 1996. "Market Transition and the Persistence of Power: The Changing Stratification System in Urban China." *American Sociological Review* 61(5): 739–58.

Boris, Eileen, and Rhacel Salazar Parreñas, eds. 2010. *Intimate Labors: Cultures, Technologies, and the Politics of Care*. Stanford, CA: Stanford University Press.

Bourdieu, Pierre. 1984. *Distinction: A Social Critique of the Judgement of Taste*. Cambridge, MA: Harvard University Press.

Brandtstädter, Susanne, and Gonçalo D. Santos. 2009. "Introduction: Chinese Kinship Metamorphoses." In *Chinese Kinship: Contemporary Anthropological Perspectives*, edited by Susanne Brandtstädter and Gonçalo D. Santos, 1–26. London: Routledge.

Brownell, Susan, and Jeffrey N. Wasserstrom, eds. 2002. *Chinese Femininities/Chinese Masculinities: A Reader*. Berkeley, CA: University of California Press.

Butler, Judith. 2012. "A Politics of the Street." Lecture given at the Peter Wall Institute for Advanced Studies, University of British Columbia, Vancouver, May 24. https://www.youtube.com/watch?v=v-bPr7t4tgA&ab_channel=PeterWallInstitutefor AdvancedStudies.

Butler, Judith. 2014. "Bodily Vulnerability, Coalitions, and Street Politics." In *Differences in Common*, edited by Joana Sabadell-Nieto and Marta Segarra (vol. 37 of *Critical Studies*), 97–119. Leiden, The Netherlands: Brill. https://brill.com/view/book/9789401210805/B9789401210805-s007.xml#:~:text=https%3A//doi.org/10.1163/9789401210805_007.

Cai Xiang. 2010. *Geming/xushu: Zhongguo shehui zhuyi wenxue wenhua xiangxiang (1949–1966)* (*Revolution/Narration: The Socialist Imagination in Chinese Literature and Culture (1949–1966)*). Beijing: Peking University Press.

Cai, Yong, and Wang Feng. 2014. "(Re)emergence of Late Marriage in Shanghai: From Collective Synchronization to Individual Choice." In *Wives, Husbands, and Lovers: Marriage and Sexuality in Hong Kong, Taiwan, and Urban China*, edited by Deborah S. Davis and Sara L. Friedman, 97–117. Stanford, CA: Stanford University Press.

Cao Guoxing. 2016. "Zhongguo Shekeyuan xuanbu: Jiang dui xueweilunwen jinxing 'yishixingtai shendu'" ("Chinese Academy of Social Sciences Announces That It Will Conduct 'Ideological Scrutiny' of Dissertations"). Radio France International, May 19. https://www.rfi.fr/cn/%E4%B8%AD%E5%9B%BD/20160519-%E4%B8%AD%E5%9B%BD%E7%A4%BE%E7%A7%91%E9%99%A2%E5%AE%A3%E5%B8%83%EF%BC%8C%E5%B0%86%E5%AF%B9%E5%AD%A6%E4%BD%8D%E8%AE%BA%E6%96%87%E8%BF%9B%E8%A1%8C%E2%80%9C%E6%84%8F%E8%AF%86%E5%BD%A2%E6%80%81%E5%AE%A1%E8%AF%BB%E2%80%9D.

Cao Rui, and Zhang Li. 2020. "Nongmingong hunlian moshi ershinian yanjiu zongshu" ("A General Assessment of Research on Rural Migrants and Their Marriage Patterns"). *Qingnian xianxiang yu wenti yanjiu* (*Research on Youth and Their Problems*) 229(5): 84–92.

Carlson, Benjamin. 2013. "The 7 Things You Can't Talk about in China." *Toronto Star*, June 30/July 2. https://www.thestar.com/news/world/2013/06/30/the_7_things_you_cant_talk_about_in_china.html.

Cartier, Carolyn. 2001. *Globalizing South China*. Oxford, UK: Blackwell.

CCTV (China Central Television). 2013. "Xinchun zou jiceng: 'Liushuixian shangde aiqing,' 'Xiaohan jiehun ji'" ("Spring Festival Grassroots Tour Reports: 'Love on the Assembly Line' and 'Xiao Han's Wedding'"), February 14. http://news.cntv.cn/2013/02/14/VIDE1360841230219396.shtml.

CCTV (China Central Television). 2016. "Nongmingong jincheng maifang yiyuanqiang jianlida" ("Rural Migrants Have Strong Desire for and Present Tremendous Potential for the Purchase of Real Estate in the City"), January 31. http://news.cntv.cn/special/jujiao/2016/210/index.shtml.

CCTV (China Central Television). 2019. "Xinchun zou jiceng: Kuayue 700 gongli de jingxi" ("Spring Festival Grassroots Tour Reports: Delightful Surprise That Comes from 700 Kilometers Away"), February 6. http://m.news.cctv.com/2019/02/06/ARTIE5rGzZLF0tKkMxZelodD190206.shtml.

Central Radio Network. 2015. "Li Keqiang: Rang pinkun jiating haizi you genduo shangsheng tongdao" ("Li Keqiang: Let Young People from Poor Families Have More Access to Upward Mobility"), March 15. http://news.cnr.cn/special/2015lh/zb/lkq/zy/20150315/t20150315_518005757.shtml.

Chan, Jenny. 2017. "Intern Labor in China." *Rural China* 14(1): 82–100. https://doi.org/10.1163/22136746-01401005.

Chan, Jenny, and Mark Selden. 2013. "Class, Hukou, and the New Generation of Chinese Rural Migrant Workers." Paper presented at the "Media and the Cultural Politics of Class in China" workshop, University of Technology, Sydney, December 4–5.

Chan, Jenny, and Ngai Pun. 2010. "Suicide as Protest for the New Generation of Chinese Migrant Workers: Foxconn, Global Capital, and the State." *The Asia-Pacific Journal* 37(2), September 13. http://japanfocus.org/-Jenny-Chan/3408.

Chan, Jenny, and Mark Selden. 2014. "China's Rural Migrant Workers, the State, and Labor Politics." *Critical Asian Studies* 46(4): 599–620. https://doi.org/10.1080/14672715.2014.960709.

Chan, Kam Wing, ed. 2017. *Urbanization with Chinese Characteristics: The Hukou System and Migration*. London: Routledge.

Chan, Kam Wing. 2021a. "China's Hukou Reform Remains a Major Challenge to Domestic Migrants in Cities." *World Bank Blogs*, December 17. https://blogs.worldbank.org/peoplemove/chinas-hukou-reform-remains-major-challenge-domestic-migrants-cities.

Chan, Kam Wing. 2021b. "What the 2020 Chinese Census Tells Us about Progress in Hukou Reform." *China Brief* 21(15): 11–17. https://www.researchgate.net/publication/353994952_What_the_2020_Chinese_Census_Tells_Us_About_Progress_in_Hukou_Reform.

Chan, Kam Wing, and Will Buckingham. 2008. "Is China Abolishing the Hukou System?" *The China Quarterly* 195: 582–606. https://doi.org/10.1017/S0305741008000787.

Chang Zizhong. 2010a. "Dangqian Xinshengdai nongmingong ze ou shengyu ji xiangguan fangmian de yanjiu" ("Research on New-Generation Rural Migrants' Decisions in Marriage, Reproduction, and Related Issues"). *Beifang jingji* (*Northern Economics*) 6: 20–22.

Chang Zizhong. 2010b. "'Nong erdai' de hunlian nanti: Qinggan queshi beihou de zhidu kunjing" ("Marriage Problems Facing "Second-Generation Rural Migrants": Structural Issues Behind the Absence of Love"). *Renmin luntan* (*People's Forum*) 280: 42–44.

Chang, Kyung-Sup. 1999. "Compressed Modernity and Its Discontents: South Korean Society in Transition." *Economy and Society* 28(1): 30–55.

Chang, Kyung-Sup, and Min-Young Song. 2010. "The Stranded Individualizer under Compressed Modernity: South Korean Women in Individualization without Individualism." *British Journal of Sociology* 61(3): 539–64. https://doi.org/10.1111/j.1468-4446.2010.01325.x.

Chen Kun. 2012. "Jifa Zhongguo qian xing di zuida liliang" ("The Great Force Propelling China Going Forward"). *Renmin ribao* (*People's Daily*), November 3. http://cpc.people.com.cn/18/n/2012/1103/c351073-19483801.html.

Chen, Mengxue, and Vladimir Canudas-Romo. 2022. "Urban–Rural Lifespan Disparities and Cause-Deleted Analysis: Evidence from China." *BMJ Open* 12: e050707. doi: 10.1136/bmjopen-2021-050707.

Chen, Minglu, and David S. G. Goodman, eds. 2013. *Middle Class China: Identity and Behavior*. Cheltenham, UK: Edward Edgar.

Chen, Stephen. 2017. "Chinese Restaurant Staff Jailed for Cooking with 'Gutter Oil.'" *South China Morning Post*, April 27. https://www.scmp.com/news/china/society/article/2091125/chinese-restaurant-staff-jailed-cooking-gutter-oil.

Cheung, Sidney C. H. 2006. "Visualizing Marriage in Hong Kong." *Visual Anthropology* 19(1): 21–37. https://doi.org/10.1080/08949460500373819.

China Labor Aid. 2016. "He Xiaobo qizi: Xiaobo tazai kanshousuo, shengbing le, zhongliu jun, jiu guanzhu" ("From He Xiaobo's wife: Xiaobo Held in Detention Center. Diagnosed with Tumor. Appealing for Support"), February 21 (accessed November 11, 2016).

Choi, Susanne Yuk-Ping. 2018. "Masculinity and Precarity: Male Migrant Taxi Drivers in South China." *Work, Employment and Society* 32(3): 493–508. https://doi.org/10.1177%2F0950017018755652.

Choi, Susanne Yuk-Ping, and Yinni Peng. 2016. *Masculine Compromise: Migration, Family, and Gender in China*. Oakland, CA: University of California Press.

Chongqing Report. 2010. "Chongqing nongmingong diaocha baogao: Si shenghuo shi xinzhong yongyuan de tong" ("Chongqing Report on Rural Migrants: Private Life is Forever the Source of Heartache"), March 26. http://cq.qq.com/a/20100326/000545.htm.

Chu Ruiya. 2013. "'90 hou' Xinshengdai nongmingong xiaofei zhuangkuang cha ai wanggou" ("Post 1990s' Rural Migrant Youths Like to Shop Online According to a Consumption Survey"). *Jinri zaobao* (*Morning News*), May 24. http://finance.ce.cn/rolling/201305/24/t20130524_17116912.shtml.

Ci, Jiwei. 1994. *Dialectic of the Chinese Revolution: From Utopianism to Hedonism*. Stanford, CA: Stanford University Press.

Ci, Jiwei. 2014. *Moral China in the Age of Reform*. New York, NY: Cambridge University Press.

Clarke, Averil Y. 2011. *Inequalities of Love: College-Educated Black Women and the Barriers to Romance and Family*. Durham, NC: Duke University Press.

Clough, Patricia Ticineto, and Jean Halley, eds. 2007. *The Affective Turn: Theorizing the Social*. Durham, NC: Duke University Press.

CNKI (China National Knowledge Infrastructure). n.d. "Academic Journals Database." https://oversea.cnki.net/kns?dbcode=CFLQ.

Constable, Nicole. 2006. "Nostalgia, Memory, and Modernity: Bridal Portraits in Contemporary Beijing." *Visual Anthropology* 19(1): 39–55. https://doi.org/10.1080/08949460500373892.

Constable, Nicole. 2009. "The Commodification of Intimacy: Marriage, Sex, and Reproductive Labor." *Annual Review of Anthropology* 38: 49–64. https://doi.org/10.1146/annurev.anthro.37.081407.085133.

Dagong bao (Workers' news). 2013. "Fushikang gonghui huiying 40 wan nügong jianzhi maiyin: Xi eyi wuru" ("Foxconn Labor Union Responds on Behalf of 400,000 Female Workers to Claims of Part-Time Prostitution: It's a Malicious Insult"), September 14. http://finance.takungpao.com/tech/q/2013/0914/1904951.html.

Davis, Deborah S. 1995. "Inequality and Stratification in the Nineties." *The China Revie* 11.1–11.25. https://www.jstor.org/stable/23453176.
Davis, Deborah S., and Sara L. Friedman, eds. 2014. *Wives, Husbands, and Lovers: Marriage and Sexuality in Hong Kong, Taiwan, and Urban China*. Stanford, CA: Stanford University Press.
Davis, Deborah S., and Feng Wang, eds. 2009. *Creating Wealth and Poverty in Postsocialist China*. Stanford, CA: Stanford University Press.
Delman, Jørgen. 2019. "Social Science in China: Between a Rock and a Hard Place." *eBioZoom*, October 6. https://ebiozoom.org/2019/10/06/social-science-in-china-between-a-rock-and-a-hard-place/.
Deng Kang. 2015. "Shei zangsong le Fushikang gongren de aiqing?" ("Who Killed Foxconn Workers' Chance for Love?"), August 21. http://www.wyzxwk.com/e/DoPrint/?classid=25&id=349998.
Deng Xiaoping. 1987. *Deng Xiaoping wenxuan disan juan* (*Selected Works of Deng Xiaoping*, volume III). *QSTheory*, July 31, 2019. http://www.qstheory.cn/books/2019-07/31/c_1119485398_76.htm.
Diamant, Neil. 2000. *Revolutionizing the Family: Politics, Love, and Divorce in Urban and Rural China 1949–1968*. Berkeley, CA: University of California Press.
Ding Wanqing. 2014. "Hunli chengle minglichang; aiqing hai neng zuo duo yuan?" ("Weddings Become a Vanity Fair; Is There Still Love?"). Qianzhan chanye yanjiuyuan wang (Qianzhan Industry Research Institute), May 13. http://www.qianzhan.com/analyst/detail/220/140513-8fd0f5b7.html.
Donner, Henrike, and Gonçalo D. Santos. 2016. "Love, Marriage, and Intimate Citizenship in Contemporary China and India: An Introduction." *Modern Asian Studies* 50(4): 1123–46. https://doi.org/10.1017/S0026749X16000032.
Driessen, Miriam, and Willy Sier. 2019. "Rescuing Masculinity: Giving Gender in the Wake of China's Marriage Squeeze." *Modern China* 47(3): 266–89. https://doi.org/10.1177%2F0097700419887465.
Du Ping. 2017. *Nangong he nügong: Dangdai Zhongguo nongmingong de xingbie, jiating yu qianyi* (*Male Workers and Female Workers: Gender, Family, and Mobility of Rural Migrants in Contemporary China*). Hong Kong: Xianggang Zhongwen daxue chubanshe (Chinese University of Hong Kong Press).
Du Ping. 2019. "Dagong Qingnian xingren yu qingmi guanxi yanjiu" ("A Study of the Link Between Trust and Intimate Relations among Young Rural Migrants"). *Zhongguo funü luncong* (*Forum on Chinese Women*) 152(2): 30–43.
Ebrey, Patricia B. 1991. "Introduction." In *Marriage and Inequality in Chinese Society*, edited by Rubie S. Watson and Patricia B. Ebrey, 1–24. Berkeley, CA: University of California Press.
Engebretsen, Elisabeth L. 2014. *Queer Women in Urban China: An Ethnography*. Abingdon, UK: Routledge.
English.gov.cn. 2021. "Full Text: Resolution of the CPC Central Committee on the Major Achievements and Historical Experience of the Party over the Past Century," November 16. https://english.www.gov.cn/policies/latestreleases/202111/16/content_WS6193a935c6d0df57f98e50b0.html.
Evans, Harriet. 1997. *Women and Sexuality in China: Dominant Discourses of Female Sexuality and Gender since 1949*. Cambridge, UK: Polity.
Fan Yechao. 2011. "Chuantong haishi xiandai: Xinshengdai nongmingong de hunlian zhuangkuang" ("Tradition or Modernity: Second-generation Rural Migrants' Marriages"). *Fazhi yu shehui* (*Law and Society*) 1: 180–81.

Farquhar, Judith. 2002. *Appetites: Food and Sex in Post-Socialist China*. Durham, NC: Duke University Press.

Farrer, James. 2014. "Love, Sex and Commitment: Delinking Premarital Intimacy from Marriage in Urban China." In *Wives, Husbands, and Lovers: Marriage and Sexuality in Hong Kong, Taiwan, and Urban China*, edited by Deborah S. Davis and Sara L. Friedman, 62–96. Stanford, CA: Stanford University Press.

Fincher, Leta Hong. 2014. *Leftover Women: The Resurgence of Gender Inequality in China*. London: Zed Books.

Fleischer, Victoria. 2013. "Chinese Factories Build Troubled Relationships." *PBS News Hour*, July 17. http://www.pbs.org/newshour/art/much-has-been-made-about/.

Foucault, Michel. 1977. "A Preface to Transgression." In *Language, Counter-Memory, Practice: Selected Essays and Interviews*, edited by Donald F. Bouchard, 29–52. Translated by Donald F. Bouchard and Sherry Simon. Ithaca, NY: Cornell University Press.

Gaetano, Arianne. 2015. *Out to Work: Migration, Gender, and the Changing Lives of Rural Women in Contemporary China*. Honolulu, HI: University of Hawaii Press.

Gerber, Theodore P., and Michael Hout. 1998. "More Shock than Therapy: Transition, Employment, and Income in Russia, 1991–1995." *American Journal of Sociology* 104: 1–50. https://doi.org/10.1086/210001.

Giddens, Anthony. 1991. *Modernity and Self-identity*. Stanford, CA: Stanford University Press.

Giddens, Anthony. 1992. *The Transformation of Intimacy: Sexuality, Love and Eroticism in Modern Societies*. Stanford, CA: Stanford University Press.

Goodman, David S. G. 2008. "Why China Has No New Middle Class: Cadres, Managers and Entrepreneurs." In *The New Rich in China: Future Rulers, Present Lives*, edited by David S. G. Goodman, 23–37. London: Routledge.

Grandey, Alicia A. 2000. "Emotional Regulation in the Workplace: A New Way to Conceptualize Emotional Labor." *Journal of Occupational Health Psychology* 5(1): 95–110. http://dx.doi.org/10.1037//1076-8998.5.1.95.

Gregg, Melissa, and Gregory Seigworth, eds. 2010. *The Affect Theory Reader*. Durham, NC: Duke University Press.

Guangming.com. 2021. "Guangming wang pinglun yuan: 'Xinshengdai nongmingong' weihe youren chayi[?]" ("Guangming.com Commentator: Why Are Some People Surprised by the 'New Generation Of Migrant Workers'?"). *Guangming ribao (Guangming Daily)*, August 18. https://guancha.gmw.cn/2021-08/18/content_35090395.htm.

Guilmoto, Christophe Z. 2012. "Skewed Sex Ratios at Birth and Future Marriage Squeeze in China and India, 2005–2100." *Demography* 49(1): 77–100. doi: 10.1007/s13524-011-0083-7.

Guo Junxia. 2016. "'Shanhun': Shehui liudong beijing xia de fu quan yu hunyin" ("'Hasty Weddings': Patriarchy and Marriage in the Context of Mobility"). *Yunnan Daxue xuebao (Research Papers of Yunnan University)* 6: 80–87. http://www.wkxb.ynu.edu.cn/html/2016/6/20160610.html.

Guo Lichang. 2013. "Xinshengdai nongmingong hunlian wenti ji duice" ("Problems and Solutions for the Marriage Problems of New-Generation Rural Migrants"). *Yibin xue yuan xue bao (Academic Journal of Yibin University)* 13(1): 87–90.

Guo, Yingjie. 2008. "Class, Stratum and Group: The Politics of Description and Prescription." In *The New Rich in China: Future Rulers, Present Lives*, edited by David S. G. Goodman, 38–52. London: Routledge.

Guo, Yingjie. 2012. "Classes without Class Consciousness and Class Consciousness without Classes: The Meaning of Class in the People's Republic of China." *Journal of Contemporary China* 21(77): 723–39.
Gustafsson, Björn A., Shi Li, and Terry Sicular, eds. 2008. *Inequality and Public Policy in China: Issues and Trends*. New York, NY: Cambridge University Press.
Han Chang, and Chang Guoshui. 2016. "Fangjia zhangle, heyue jiele. Hefei yi goufang zhe tiaolou shenwang" ("House Prices Soar, Contract Annulled, a Hefei Buyer Dies Jumping From a Building"). *Renmin wang* (*People's Daily Online*), Anhui channel, June 29. http://jx.people.com.cn/n2/2016/0629/c190316-28581125.html.
Hanser, Amy. 2008. *Service Encounters: Class, Gender, and the Market for Social Distinction in Urban China*. Stanford, CA: Stanford University Press.
Harrell, Stevan, and Gonçalo Santos. 2017. "Introduction." In *Transforming Patriarchy: Chinese Families in the Twenty-First Century*, edited by Gonçalo Santos and Stevan Harrell, 3–38. Seattle, WA: University of Washington Press.
Hassid, Jonathan, and Elaine Jeffreys. 2015. "Doing Good or Doing Nothing? Celebrity, Media and Philanthropy in China." *Third World Quarterly* 36(1): 75–93. https://doi.org /10.1080/01436597.2015.976019.
He Shuyao. 2022. "Shuju gaosu ni, daodi shi naxie yinsu zaochengle nongcun shengnan men de kunjing" ("Data Reveal the Key Factors Causing the Plight of 'Leftover Men' in Rural China"). *Shangguan* (*Shanghai Observer*), February 8. https://www.jfdaily.com/ news/detail?id=449728.
Hird, Derek. 2016. "Moral Masculinities: Ethical Self-Fashionings of Professional Chinese Men in London." *Nan Nü* 18(1): 115–47. https://doi.org/10.1163/15685268-00181p05.
Hird, Derek, and Geng Song, eds. 2018. *The Cosmopolitan Dream: Transnational Chinese Masculinities in a Global Age*. Hong Kong: Hong Kong University Press.
Hirsch, Fred. 2005. *Social Limits to Growth*, rev. ed. London: Taylor Francis.
Hochschild, Arlie Russell. 1983. *The Managed Heart: Commercialization of Human Feeling*. Berkeley, CA: University of California Press.
Hochschild, Arlie Russell. 2003. *The Commercialization of Intimate Life: Notes from Home and Work*. Berkeley, CA: University of California Press.
Hochschild, Arlie Russell. 2012. *The Outsourced Self: Intimate Life in Market Times*. New York: Metropolitan Books.
Hongxing xinwen (Red star news). 2021. "'Guli nüqingnian liuxiang jiejue dalingnan zeou nan' yin zhengyi, Hunan Xiangyin: Jinwei changdao" ("'Encouraging Young Women to Stay in the Hometown to Solve the Difficulty of Choosing a Mate for Older Men' Leads to Controversy, and Hunan Xiangyin County's Response Is: It's Merely a Suggestion"). *Pengpai xinwen* (*The Paper*), October 9. https://m.thepaper.cn/ newsDetail_forward_14826561.
Honneth, Axel. 2001. "Personal Identity and Disrespect." In *The New Social Theory Reader: Contemporary Debates*, edited by Steven Seidman and Jeffrey C. Alexander, 39–45. London: Routledge.
Hsu, Francis. 1948. *Under the Ancestors' Shadow: Chinese Culture and Personality*. New York, NY: Columbia University Press.
Huang Chuanhui. 2011. *Zhongguo Xinshengdai nongmingong* (*China's New-generation Rural Migrant Workers*). Beijing: Renmin wenxue chubanshe (People's Literature Press).
Huang Dan, and Ni Xiqin. 2020. "Langman ai yu xianshi hun jiafeng xia de Xinshengdai liudong nüxing hunyin celüe" ("Romantic Love and Marriage Strategies of Young Rural Migrant Women Who Are Caught Between Romantic Love and the Reality of Marriage"). *Qingnian tansuo* (*Youth Exploration*) 3: 83–90.

Huang Yingying, ed. 2017. *Wozai xianchang: Xinsheshehuixue tianye diaocha biji* (*I Was There: Fieldwork Notes in the Research of the Sociology of Sex*). Taiyuan Shanxi: Shanxi renmin chubanshe (Shanxi People's Press).

Huang Yingying. 2020. "Xiaojie yanjiu ershi nian" ("Twenty Years of Studying Prostitutes"). YiXi, June 7. https://www.yixi.tv/#/speech/detail?id=888.

Huang Yingying. 2021. "Zhuanfang Huang Yingying: Zhengyan kan xianshi shi yizhong nengli, nide buduan dui ziji tiwen" ("Interview with Huang Yingying: Opening Your Eyes to See Reality Is a Kind of Ability, You Have to Keep Asking Yourself Questions"). Interview by Zhang Xiong, July 20 (accessed November 30, 2021).

Hyde, Sandra Teresa. 2007. *Eating Spring Rice: The Cultural Politics of AIDS in Southwest China*. Berkeley, CA: University of California Press.

Illouz, Eva. 1997. *Consuming the Romantic Utopia: Love and the Cultural Contradictions of Capitalism*. Berkeley, CA: University of California Press.

Illouz, Eva. 2007. *Cold Intimacies: The Making of Emotional Capitalism*. Cambridge, UK: Polity Press.

Illouz, Eva. 2012. *Why Love Hurts: A Sociological Explanation*. Cambridge, UK: Polity Press.

Illouz, Eva. 2014. *Hard Core Romance: "Fifty Shades of Grey," Best Sellers, and Society*. Chicago, IL: University of Chicago Press.

Inner Mongolia Morning Post. 2012. "Nan nü xingbiebi shitiao Beida jiaoshou: San qianwan sheng nan cheng da wenti" ("Sex Ratio Seriously Out of Balance Says Beijing University Professor: The Problem of Thirty Million Leftover Men Is Serious"), March 13. http://news.sohu.com/20120313/n337567033.shtml.

Jacka, Tamara. 2006. *Rural Women in Urban China: Gender, Migration, and Social Change*. Armonk, NY: M. E. Sharpe.

Jacka, Tamara. 2009. "Cultivating Citizens: *Suzhi* (Quality) Discourse in the PRC." *Positions: East Asia Cultures Critique* 17(3): 523–35. https://doi.org/10.1215/10679847-2009-013.

Jeffreys, Elaine, and Gang Su. 2018. *Governing HIV in China: Commercial Sex, Homosexuality and Rural-to-Urban Migration*. Abingdon, UK: Routledge.

Jia Dai Tengfei. 2012. "Liushuixian shangde aiqing" ("Love on the Assembly Line"), February 16. http://blog.sina.com.cn/s/blog_5d08950b0100y611.html.

Jia Dai Tengfei. 2014. "Buyao rang nide zhaopian cuoguo zhege shidai" ("Make Sure Your Photographs Capture the Spirit of Our Times"), March 31. https://read01.com/jjy54x8.html#.Y4CLlb1BzIU.

Jia Zheng (aka Zhan Youbing). 2013. "Dongguan dagong zhe de aiqing" ("Rural Migrants' Love in Dongguan"), January 17. Online photo-essay. https://m.sohu.com/n/386381112/?pvid=000115_3w.

Jin Xiaoyi, Zhang Lu, and Yang Ting. 2016. "Shehui xingbie shijiao xia nongmingong de 'kua huji hunyin' yanjiu—jiyu Shenzhen P qu de diaocha faxian" ("Inter-Hukou Marriages of Rural Migrant Workers from a Gender Perspective: Findings from a Survey in P District of Shenzhen"). *Funü yanjiu lun cong* (*Journal of Chinese Women's Studies*) 2016 0(1): 30–38. http://www.fnyjlc.com/CN/abstract/abstract44.shtml.

Judd, Ellen. 2010. "Family Strategies: Fluidities of Gender, Community and Mobility in Rural West China." *The China Quarterly* 204: 921–38. https://www.jstor.org/stable/27917839.

Kam, Lucetta Yip Lo. 2013. *Shanghai Lalas: Female Tongzhi Communities and Politics in Urban China*. Hong Kong: Hong Kong University Press.

Kan, Karita. 2013. "The New 'Lost Generation': Inequality and Discontent Among Chinese Youth." *China Perspectives* 2013 (2): 67–73. https://journals.openedition.org/chinaperspectives/6190.

Kendall, Laurel. 2006. "Something Old ... Remembering Korean Wedding Hall Photographs from the 1980s." *Visual Anthropology* 19(1): 1–19. https://doi.org/10.1080/08949460500373777.

Kipnis, Andrew. 2006. "*Suzhi*: A Keyword Approach." *The China Quarterly* 186: 295–313. https://www.jstor.org/stable/20192614.

Kleinman, Arthur, Yunxiang Yan, Jing Jun, Sing Lee, Everett Zhang, Pan Tianshu, Wu Fei, and Jinhua Guo. 2011. *Deep China: The Moral Life of a Person*. Berkeley, CA: University of California Press.

Kong, Travis S. K. 2011. *Chinese Male Homosexualities: Memba, Tongzhi and Golden Boy*. Abingdon, UK: Routledge.

Lamont, Michele. 2000. *The Dignity of Working Men: Morality and the Boundaries of Race, Class, and Immigration*. Cambridge, MA: Harvard University Press.

Lee, Haiyan. 2006. "Nannies for Foreigners: The Enchantment of Chinese Womanhood in the Age of Millennial Capitalism." *Public Culture* 18(3): 507–29. https://doi.org/10.1215/08992363-2006-017.

Li, Chunling. 2013. "Sociopolitical Attitudes of the Middle Class and the Implications for Political Transition." In *Middle Class China: Identity and Behaviour*, edited by Minglu Chen and David S. G. Goodman, 12–33. Cheltenham, UK: Edward Elgar Publishing.

Li De. 2011. *Xinshengdai nongmingong hunyin baogao* (*A Report on the Marriage Problems Facing New-Generation Rural Migrants*). Shanghai: Shanghai Jiaotong University Press.

Li Hui, and Pu Kunhua. 2011. "Xinshengdai nongmingong de hunlian xinli chongtu tanxi" ("An Analysis of the Psychological Conflicts in New-generation Rural Migrants' Love Lives"). *Jiangxi nongye daxue xuebao* (*Journal of Jiangxi University of Agriculture*) 10(4): 55–58.

Li Le and Yu Qing. 2014. "Jiji xinlixue shijiao xia de Xinshengdai nongmingong hunlian wenti tanjiu" ("An Exploration of Young Rural Migrants' Marital Problems From the Perspective of Positive Psychology"). *Rencai ziyuan kaifa* (*Human Resources Development*) October: 40–42.

Li Lijing. 2016. "Guobuxia qu jiu li: Shei tou zou le Xinshengdai nongmingong de hunyin?" ("Divorce Is Inevitable if Marriage No Longer Works: Who Has Stolen the Marriages of New-Generation Rural Migrants?"). *Banyue tan* (*China Comments*), July 7. http://www.banyuetan.org/chcontent/jrt/201674/202297.shtml.

Li Peilin. 2003. *Nongmingong: Zhongguo nongmingong de jingji shehui fenxi* (*Rural Migrant Workers: A Social and Economic Analysis*). Beijing: Shehui kexue wenxian chubanshe (Social Sciences Academic Press).

Li Qiang. 2004. *Nongmingong yu Zhongguo shehui fengceng* (*Rural Migrant Workers and Social Stratification in China*). Beijing: Shehui kexue wenxian chubanshe (Social Sciences Academic Press).

Lin, Xiaodong. 2013. *Gender, Modernity and Male Migrant Workers in China: Becoming a "Modern" Man*. Oxford, UK: Routledge.

Lin, Xiaodong. 2014. "'Filial Son,' the Family and Identity Formation Among Male Migrant Workers in Urban China." *Gender, Place & Culture* 21(6): 717–32. https://doi.org/10.1080/0966369X.2013.802672.

Ling Qichao. 2011. "Hunsha sheying hangye fazhan fenxi" ("An Analysis of the Growth of the Wedding Gown Industry"). *Baidu*, October 21. http://wenku.baidu.com/view/5de91422dd36a32d7375815f.html.

Liu, Jianmei. 2003. *Revolution Plus Love: Literary History, Women's Bodies, and Thematic Repetition in Twentieth-Century Chinese Fiction*. Honolulu, HI: University of Hawai'i Press.

Liu Jiejie. 2011. "Yixiang de tamen ye kewang yifen ai: Xinshengdai nongmingong hunlian wenti yanjiu" ("They Are the Strangers in the City, but They Also Long for Love: A Study of New-Generation Rural Migrants and their Marriage Problems"). *Shehui yanjiu* (*Social Studies*) 6: 93–94.

Liu, Jieyu, Eona Bell, and Jiayu Zhang. 2017. "Conjugal Intimacy, Gender and Modernity in Contemporary China." *The Journal of British Sociology* 70(1): 283–305. https://doi.org/10.1111/1468-4446.12338.

Liu Jing. 2001. "Huji zhidu beihou: Dagongmei shengcun zhuangtai ji shehui xinli" ("Behind the Hukou System: The Living Circumstances and Social Psychology of Rural Migrant Women"). *Zhongzhou xuekan* (*Zhongzhou Academic Journal*) 9: 38–43.

Liu, Melinda. 2012. "China's Great Dream." *Newsweek*, March 17. https://www.newsweek.com/chinas-great-dream-63415.

Liu Sheng. 2011. "Zuo chengliren chengwei Xinshengdai nongmingong chongjing" ("To Become an Urban Citizen Is the Biggest Wish of New-generation Rural Migrants"). *Zhongguo qingnian bao* (*China Youth Daily*), December 9. http://zqb.cyol.com/html/2011-12/09/nw.D110000zgqnb_20111209_6-03.htm.

Liu Shu. 2013. "Ta de zhaopian chudong rende neixin" ("His Photos Touch People's Hearts"), January 9 (accessed September 19, 2016).

Liu, Tingting. 2020. "Wounded Masculinities: The Subaltern between Online Longings and Offline Realities." In *Love Stories in China: The Politics of Intimacy in the Twenty-First Century*, edited by Wanning Sun and Ling Yang, 113–30. Abingdon, UK: Routledge.

Liu Xiao. 2015. *Xinxing chengzhenhua Xinshengdai nongmingong hunlian yanjiu* (*A Study of Rural Migrants' Outlook on Marriage against the Backdrop of New Urbanization*). Xi'an: Sha'anxi fan Daxue (Sha'anxi Normal University Press).

Liu Yang. 2012. "Diaosi de laili yu hanyi" ("The Evolution and Connotation of the Term 'Diaosi'"). Liu Yang science network blog post, November 11. https://wap.sciencenet.cn/blog-1750-631481.html.

Louie, Kam. 2002. *Theorising Chinese Masculinity: Society and Gender in China*. Cambridge, UK: Cambridge University Press.

Louie, Kam. 2016. *Changing Chinese Masculinities: From Imperial Pillars of State to Global Real Men*. Hong Kong: University of Hong Kong Press.

Lü Xinyu. 2015. "Qingchun duandai shi: Cong 'rensheng' dao 'xiao shidai'" ("Discontinuous History of Youth: From *Life* to *Tiny Times*"). *Dianying yishu* (*Film Art*), October 23. http://www.globalview.cn/html/culture/info_6761.html.

Lutz, Catherine, and Lila Abu-Lughod, eds. 1990. *Language and the Politics of Emotion*. New York: Cambridge University Press.

Ma, Eric K. W. 2006. "Realizing Wedding Imaginations in South China." *Visual Anthropology* 19(1): 57–71. https://doi.org/10.1080/08949460500373975.

Marquis, Chris, and Zoe Yang. 2013. "Diaosi: Evolution of a Chinese Meme." *Civil China*, July 27. https://web.archive.org/web/20140123152346/http://www.civilchina.org/2013/07/diaosi-evolution-of-a-chinese-meme/.

Martin, Fran. 2016. "Overseas Study as 'Escape Route' for Young Chinese Women." University of Nottingham China Policy Institute Blog, June 22. https://theasiadialogue.com/2016/06/22/single-and-mobile-overseas-study-as-escape-route-for-young-chinese-women/.

Massumi, Brian. 2002. *Parables for the Virtual: Movement, Affect, Sensation*. Durham, NC: Duke University Press.

May, Shannon. 2010. "Bridging Divides and Breaking Homes: Young Women's Lifecycle Labour Mobility as a Family Managerial Strategy." *The China Quarterly* 204: 899–920. https://www.jstor.org/stable/27917838.

McClintock, Anne. 1995. *Imperial Leather: Race, Gender and Sexuality in the Colonial Contest*. Abingdon, UK: Routledge.

Melton, J. Gordon, and Martin Bauman, eds. 2010. *Religions of the World: A Comprehensive Encyclopedia of Beliefs and Practices*, 2nd ed. Santa Barbara, CA: ABC-CLIO.

Miao Tao. 2012. "Caili yu nongcun qingnian de hunlian kunjing" ("Betrothal Gifts and the Difficult Situation Facing Rural Youth"). *Keji wenhui* (*Science and Technology Digest*) 6: 205–6.

Murphy, Rachel. 2002. *How Migrant Labor Is Changing Rural China*. Cambridge, UK: Cambridge University Press.

Murphy, Rachel. 2004. "The Impact of Labor Migration on the Well-Being and Agency of Rural Chinese Women: Cultural and Economic Contexts and the Life Course." In *On the Move: Women and Rural-to-Urban Migration in Contemporary China*, edited by Arianne Gaetano and Tamara Jacka, 243–76. New York, NY: Columbia University Press.

Nanfang Weekend. 2014. "Waidiren: Beijing Shanghai bu huanying?" ("Migrants from out of Town Are Not Welcome in Beijing and Shanghai?"), May 22. http://www.infzm.com/content/100888.

NBS (National Bureau of Statistics). 2016. "2015 nian nongmingong jiance diaocha baogao" ("Report on the 2015 Survey of Rural Migrant Workers"), April 28. http://www.stats.gov.cn/tjsj/zxfb/201604/t20160428_1349713.html.

NBS (National Bureau of Statistics). 2021a. "Guanyu kaizhan 2021 niandu quanguo tongji kexue yanjiu xiangmu shenqing gongzuo de tongzhi" ("Notice of Applications for 2021 National Statistical Science Research Projects"), February 25. http://www.stats.gov.cn/tjgz/tzgb/202102/t20210224_1813972.html.

NBS (National Bureau of Statistics). 2021b. "Guanyu kaizhan nongcun qingnian hunyin guanxi diaoyan de tongzhi" ("Notice about Conducting Investigations into Rural Young People's Marriages and Relationships"), May 25. http://tjj.zj.gov.cn/art/2021/5/25/art_1562127_58949624.html.

NBS (National Bureau of Statistics). 2021c. "2020 nian nongmingong jiance diaocha baogao" ("Report on the 2020 Survey of Rural Migrant Workers"), April 30. http://www.stats.gov.cn/tjsj/zxfb/202104/t20210430_1816933.html.

Nee, Victor. 1989. "A Theory of Market Transition: From Redistribution to Markets in State Socialism." *American Sociological Review* 54: 663–81. https://doi.org/10.2307/2117747.

Nee, Victor. 1991. "Social Inequality in Reforming State Socialism: Between Redistribution and Markets in State Socialism." *American Sociological Review* 56(3): 267–82. https://www.jstor.org/stable/2096103.

Nee, Victor. 1996. "The Emergence of a Market Society: Changing Mechanisms of Stratification in China." *American Sociological Review* 101(4): 908–49. https://www.jstor.org/stable/2782234.

Ni Meng. 2020. "Wei nongmingong mianfei pai hunsha zhao, nü sheyingshi wennuan yiwan ren" ("Woman Photographer Warms the Hearts of Millions of People by

Offering Free Wedding Photoshoots"). *Cankao wang* (*Reference Network*), April 7. https://www.fx361.com/page/2020/0407/6534993.shtml.

Ong, Aihwa, and Li Zhang. 2008. "Introduction: Privatizing China: Powers of the Self, Socialism from Afar." In *Privatizing China: Socialism from Afar*, edited by Li Zhang and Aihwa Ong, 1–20. Ithaca, NY: Cornell University Press.

Ortner, Sherry. 2001. "Specifying Agency: The Comaroffs and Their Critics." *Interventions: International Journal of Postcolonial Studies* 3(1): 76–84. https://doi.org/10.1080/13698010020027038.

Pan Qing, and Ge Hongli. 2014. "Lun Xinshengdai nongmingong hunlianguan de bianqian" ("On the Transformation of Young Rural Migrants' Attitudes to Marriage"). *Chifeng Xueyuan xuebao* (*Chifeng Institute Academic Journal*) 35(11): 129–31.

Pan, Suiming. 2006. "Transformation in the Primary Life Cycle: The Origins and Nature of China's Sexual Revolution." In *Sex and Sexuality in China*, edited by Elaine Jeffreys, 21–42. London: Routledge.

Pun, Ngai. 2005. *Made in China: Women Factory Workers in a Global Workplace*. Durham, NC: Duke University Press.

Pun, Ngai. 2016. *Migrant Labor in China: Post-Socialist Transformations*. Cambridge, UK: Polity.

Pun, Ngai, and Jenny Chan. 2012. "Global Capital, the State, and Chinese Workers: The Foxconn Experience." *Modern China* 38(4): 383–410. https://doi.org/10.1177%2F0097700412447164.

Pun, Ngai, and Anita Koo. 2015. "A 'World-Class' (Labor) Camp/us: Foxconn and China's New Generation of Labor Migrants." *Positions: Asia Critique* 23(3): 411–35. https://doi.org/10.1215/10679847-3125811.

Pun, Ngai, and Huilin Lu. 2010. "Unfinished Proletarianization: Self, Anger, and Class Action among the Second Generation of Peasant-Workers in Present-Day China." *Modern China* 36(5): 493–519. https://doi.org/10.1177%2F0097700410373576.

Pun, Ngai, Shen Yuan, Guo Yuhua, Lu Huilin, Jenny Chan, and Mark Selden. 2014. "Worker–Intellectual Unity: Suicide, Trans-Border Sociological Intervention, and the Foxconn-Apple Connection." *The Asia-Pacific Journal* 12(11) no. 3, March 17. https://apjjf.org/2014/12/11/Pun-Ngai/4093/article.html.

Qianzhan Report. 2014. "2014–2018 Nian Zhongguo hunqing chanye shichang yanjiu yu touzi yuce fenxi baogao" ("A Report on the Market and Investment Pattern for China's Wedding Industry from 2014 to 2018"). http://bg.qianzhan.com/report/detail/cf9e74b3c7d14abc.html.

Qiu Ye. 2015. "Waichu yu guixiang: Yige nügongde qianyi shi" ("Leaving and Returning: A History of Mobility of a Rural Migrant Woman"). *Po tu* (*Groundbreaking*), November 24. http://groundbreaking.cn/yanyi/sannong/4522.html. Accessed August 3, 2016; this site has now been shut down.

Quora. 2020. "Should One Say CCP or CPC When Referring to the Chinese Communist Party?" (Question posed and answered on online forum.) https://www.quora.com/Should-one-say-CCP-or-CPC-when-referring-to-the-Chinese-Communist-party.

Ren, Hai. 2013. *The Middle Class in Neoliberal China: Governing Risk, Life-Building, and Themed Spaces*. London: Routledge.

Rocca, Jean-Louis. 2017. *The Making of the Chinese Middle Class: Small Comfort and Great Expectations*. New York: Palgrave Macmillan.

Rofel, Lisa. 2007. *Desiring China: Experiments in Neoliberalism, Sexuality, and Public Culture*. Durham, NC: Duke University Press.
Rona-Tas, Akos. 1994. "The First Shall Be Last?" *American Journal of Sociology* 100(1): 40–59. https://www.jstor.org/stable/2782537.
Rose, Nicholas. 1998. *Inventing Ourselves: Psychology, Power, and Personhood*. Cambridge, UK: Cambridge University Press.
Saunders, Doug. 2015. "Struggling to Succeed: Behind China's Crisis, Consumers Driven Underground—Literally." *The Globe and Mail*, August 21. http://www.theglobeandmail.com/news/world/the-ant-tribe-of-china/article26054666/.
Sedgwick, Eve Kosofsky, and Adam Frank. 1995. "Shame in the Cybernetic Fold: Reading Silvan Tomkins." *Critical Inquiry* 21(2): 496–522. https://www.jstor.org/stable/1343932.
Selden, Mark, Ngai Pun, and Jenny Chan. 2013. "The Politics of Global Production: Apple, Foxconn and China's New Working Class." *The Asia-Pacific Journal* 11(32/2), August 8. http://www.japanfocus.org/-Jenny-Chan/3981.
Seligman, Martin. 1991. *Learned Optimism: How to Change Your Mind and Your Life*. New York: Knopf.
Shao Haipeng. 2013. "Zheng Xie weiyuan Feng Gong: Lianai hunyin shi Xinshengdai nongmingong de 'Zhongguo meng'" ("Political Consultative Committee member Feng Gong: Love and Marriage Are the 'China Dream' of New-generation Migrant Workers"). Yicai.com, March 7. https://www.yicai.com/news/2537317.html.
Sharma, Yojana. 2019. "Ideological 'Rectification' Hits Social Sciences Research." *University World News*, December 12. https://www.universityworldnews.com/post.php?story=20191212160548739.
Shen Wenjie. 2007. "Chengxiang lianyin zaojiu chengshi xin yimin tan xi" (An Analysis of Marriage between Rural Migrants and Urban Residents). *Nanjing caijing daxue xuebao* (*Journal of Nanjing University of Finance and Economics*) 3: 87–91.
Shepherd, Christian. 2018. "China's Sina Weibo Reverses Gay Content Clean-Up after Outcry." *Reuters*, April 16. https://www.reuters.com/article/us-china-lgbt-censorship-idUSKBN1HN0KI.
Shi Leilei. 2015. "Qingnian nongmingong hunlian: Guannian, xinwei moshi jiqi bianqian licheng" ("Young Rural Migrants' Marriages: Views, Practices, and Patterns of Change"). *Qingnian taisuo* (*Youth Exploration*) 98: 75–80.
Shi, Lihong. 2017. "From Care Providers to Financial Burdens: The Changing Role of Sons and Reproductive Choice in Rural Northeast China." In *Transforming Patriarchy: Chinese Families in the Twenty-First Century*, edited by Gonçalo Santos and Stevan Harrell, 59–73. Seattle, WA: University of Washington Press.
Sina Technology. 2013a. "Caijing tianxia: Fushikang de yeshenghuo baodao zhenshi kekao" ("Economic Weekly: Foxconn's Night Life Report Is True and Reliable"), September 17. http://tech.sina.com.cn/it/2013-09-17/15308748142.shtml.
Sina Technology. 2013b. "Fushikang de yeshenghuo" ("Foxconn's Night Life"), September 13. http://tech.sina.com.cn/it/2013-09-13/09318736823.shtml.
Skeggs, Beverley. 2009. "The Moral Economy of Person Production: The Class Relations of Self Performance on 'Reality' Television." *The Sociological Review* 57(4): 626–44. https://doi.org/10.1111%2Fj.1467-954X.2009.01865.x.
Sohu. 2021. "Wei Houkai: Nongmin zeng shou shi cujin chengxiang gongtong fuyu de guanjian" ("Wei Houkai: Increasing Peasants' Income Is the Key if We Want Both Rural and Urban China to Prosper"). Presentation at the 2021 High-Level

Forum on China's Rural Development, December 2021. https://www.sohu.com/a/510485351_260616.

Solinger, Dorothy J. 1999. *Contesting Citizenship in Urban China: Peasant Migrants, the State, and the Logic of the Market*. Berkeley, CA: University of California Press.

Solinger, Dorothy. 2010. "The Urban Dibao: Guarantee for Minimum Livelihood or for Minimal Turmoil?" In *Marginalization in Urban China: Comparative Perspectives*, edited by Fulong Wu and Chris Webster, 253–77. Basingstoke, UK: Palgrave/Macmillan.

Sommers, Matthew H. 2000. *Sex, Law, and Society in Late Imperial China*. Stanford, CA: Stanford University Press.

Song, Geng. 2019. "Masculinizing Jianghu Spaces in the Past and Present: Homosociality, Nationalism and Chineseness." *Nan Nü* 21(1): 107–29. https://doi.org/10.1163/15685268-00211P04.

Song Li. 2019. "Liushuixian shang de aiqing kuaican" ("Fast-Food Romance on the Assembly Line"). *Zhongguo qingnian yanjiu* (*China Youth Research*) 7: 78–83.

Song Yueping, and Li Long. 2015. "Xinshengdai nongmingong hunlian ji shengzhi jiankang wenti tanxi" ("An Analysis of Marriage, Love, and Reproductive Health among New-Generation Rural Migrants"). *Zhongzhou xuekan* (*Zhongzhou Academic Journal*) 2015(1): 79–83. https://wf.pub/perios/article:190_doi%3A10.3969%2Fj.issn.1003-0751.2015.01.014.

Song Yueping, Zhang Longlong, and Duan Chengrong. 2012. "Chuantong, chongji yue tanbian: Xinshengdai nongmingong xinwei tanxi" ("Tradition, Cultural Shock, and Transformation: An Analysis of the Patterns of Marriage Behavior among New-generation Rural Migrants"). *Renkou yu jingji* (*Population and Economics*) 6: 8–15.

Stacey, Judith. 1984. *Patriarchy and Socialist Revolution in China*. Berkeley, CA: University of California Press.

Stallybrass, Peter, and Allon White. 1986. *The Politics and Poetics of Transgression*. Ithaca, NY: Cornell University Press.

Standing, Guy. 2011. *The Precariat: The New Dangerous Class*. London: Bloomsbury Academic.

Stiglitz, Joseph E. 2012. *The Price of Inequality: How Today's Divided Society Endangers Our Future*. New York: W.W. Norton & Company.

Sum, Ngai-Ling. 2016. "The Makings of Subaltern Subjects: Embodiment, Contradictory Consciousness, and Re-hegemonization of the Diaosi in China." *Globalizations* 14(2): 298–312. https://doi.org/10.1080/14747731.2016.1207936.

Sun Linlin. 2015. "2014 Zhongguo qing'an baogao" ("2014 Report on Love in China"). *Xin zhou kan* (*New Weekly*), February 4. http://blog.sina.com.cn/s/blog_490075660102vhh0.html.

Sun Peidong. 2012. *Shuilai qu wode nü'er? Shanghai xiangqin jiao yu "baifa xiangqin"* (*Who Is Going to Marry My Daughter? Matchmaking Corners in Shanghai and the "Dating Between White-Haired Parents"*). Beijing: China Social Sciences Press.

Sun Ruizhuo. 2010. "Xinshengdai nongmingong rongru chengshi luz ai hefang" ("What Lies Ahead for New-generation Rural Migrants' Desire to Belong to the City"). *Guancha yu sikao* (*Observation and Thinking*) 3(1): 44–47.

Sun, Wanning. 2004. "Indoctrination, Fetishization, and Compassion: Media Constructions of the Migrant Woman." In *On the Move: Women in Rural-to-Urban Migration in Contemporary China*, edited by Arianne Gaetano and Tamara Jacka, 109–28. New York: Columbia University Press.

Sun, Wanning. 2009. *Maid in China: Media, Morality, and the Cultural Politics of Boundaries*. London: Routledge.
Sun, Wanning. 2013. "Inequality and Culture: A New Pathway to Understanding Social Inequality." In *Unequal China: The Political Economy and Cultural Politics of Inequality*, edited by Wanning Sun and Yingjie Guo, 27–42. Abingdon, UK: Routledge.
Sun, Wanning. 2014. *Subaltern China: Rural Migrants, Media, and Cultural Practices*. Lanham, MD: Rowman & Littlefield.
Sun, Wanning. 2016. "Cultural Politics of Class: Workers and Peasants as Historical Subjects." In *Handbook on Class and Social Stratification in China*, edited by Yingjie Guo, 107–27. Cheltenham, UK: Edward Elgar Publishing.
Sun, Wanning. 2017. "Romancing the Vulnerable in Contemporary China: Love on the Assembly Line and the Cultural Politics of Inequality." *China Information* 32(1): 69–87. https://doi.org/10.1177/0920203X17733594
Sun, Wanning, and Wei Lei. 2017. "In Search of Intimacy in China: The Emergence of Advice Media for the Privatized Self." *Communication, Culture & Critique* 10(1): 20–38. https://doi.org/10.1111/cccr.12150.
Tan, Chris K. K., and Zhiwei Xu. 2020. "The 'Social Factory' of China's Male 'Virtual Lovers.'" In *Love Stories in China: The Politics of Intimacy in the Twenty-First Century*, edited by Wanning Sun and Ling Yang, 168–84. Abingdon, UK: Routledge.
Tao Haiqing. 2014. "*Zhiyin* chuanmei shangshi qianjing jihe?" ("What Are the Prospects for *Soulmate* in Going Public?"). *Zhongguo maoyi bao* (*China Trade News*), June 12. http://www.chinatradenews.com.cn/epaper/content/2014-06/12/content_17897.htm.
Taylor, Sandra. 2004. "Researching Education Policy and Change in 'New Times': Using Critical Discourse Analysis." *Journal of Education Policy* 19(4): 433–51. https://doi.org/10.1080/0268093042000227483.
Thomala, Lai Lin. 2021. "Number of Monthly Active Smart Device Users of Tencent QQ from 2014 to 2020." *Statista*, April 16. https://www.statista.com/statistics/227352/number-of-active-tencent-im-user-accounts-in-china/.
Thrift, Nigel. 2007. *Non-representational Theory: Space, Politics, Affect*. London: Routledge.
Tie Ning. 2010. "Chunfeng ye" ("Night of the Spring Breeze"). *Beijing wenxue* (*Beijing Literature*) 9: 38–47. https://caod.oriprobe.com/articles/25111079/chun_feng_ye_.htm.
Tomba, Luigi. 2014. *The Government Next Door: Neighborhood Politics in Urban China*. Ithaca, NY: Cornell University Press.
Tsang, Eileen Yuk-ha. 2020. "Being Bad to Feel Good: China's Migrant Men, Displaced Masculinity, and the Commercial Sex Industry." *Journal of Contemporary China* 29(122): 221–37. https://doi.org/10.1080/10670564.2019.1637563.
Veblen, Thorstein. (1899) 2007. *The Theory of the Leisure Class*. Oxford, UK: Oxford University Press.
Wallis, Cara. 2016. "Hukou Reform and China's Migrant Workers." *China Policy Institute: Analysis*, October 10. https://cpianalysis.wordpress.com/2016/10/10/hukou-reform-and-chinas-migrant-workers/.
Wang, David Der-Wei. 2004. *The Monster That Is History: History, Violence, and Fictional Writing in Twentieth-Century China*. Berkeley, CA: California University Press.
Wang, Fei-ling. 2005. *Organizing through Division and Exclusion: China's Hukou System*. Stanford, CA: Stanford University Press.
Wang, Pan. 2015. *Love and Marriage in Globalizing China*. London: Routledge.
Wang Shiyue. 2001. "Chuzu wu li de modao sheng" ("The Sound of a Cleaver Being Sharpened in a Rented Room"). *Zuopin* (*Literary Works*) 6: 4–10.

Watson, Rubie S. 1991. "Afterword: Marriage and Gender Inequality." In *Marriage and Inequality in Chinese Society*, edited by Rubie S. Watson and Patricia B. Ebrey, 347–68. Berkeley, CA: University of California Press.

Watson, Rubie S., and Patricia B. Ebrey, eds. 1991. *Marriage and Inequality in Chinese Society*. Berkeley, CA: University of California Press.

Weber, Max. (1922) 1978. *Economy and Society: An Outline of Interpretive Sociology*, edited by Guenther Roth and Claus Wittich. Berkeley, CA: University of California Press.

Wen Cong. 2013. "Dagong zhe de aiqing sui cuilei jie pai taren jiewen she qinquan" ("Dongguan Dagong Workers' Love May Move People to Tears but Photographing People Kissing May Infringe Their Right to Privacy"). *Yangcheng wanbao* (*Yangcheng Evening Post*), March 13: A24.

Whyte, Martin. 2010. *Myth of the Social Volcano: Perceptions of Inequality and Distributive Injustice in Contemporary China*. Stanford, CA: Stanford University Press.

World Press Photo Foundation. 2017. "Jia Dai Tengfei (2012 Joop Swart Masterclass)." YouTube, May 18. https://www.youtube.com/watch?v=IqjLzKuQoEo&ab_channel=WorldPressPhotoFoundation.

Wu Xiaoying. 2010. "From State Dominance to Market Orientation: The Composition and Evolution of Gender Discourse." *Social Sciences in China* 31(2): 150–64. https://doi.org/10.1080/02529201003794924.

Wu Xiaoying 2012. "Dai ji shiye zhong de 80 hou rentong" ("The Identification of the 1980s Cohort from a Generational Perspective"). *Jiangsu shehui kexue* (*Jiangsu Social Sciences*) 3: 38–44.

Wu Xiaoying. 2017. "Chengxiang qianyi de xingbie hua luoji jiqi jizhi" ("The Gendered Logic and Mechanism of Rural-to-Urban Mobility"). *Funü yanjiu lun cong* (*Journal of Chinese Women's Studies*) 143: 119–24.

Wu Xinhui. 2011. "Chuantong yu xiandai zhijian: Xinshengdai nongmingong de lian ai yu hunyin" ("Between Tradition and Modernity: Rural Migrants' Marriage and Love"). *Zhongguo qingnian yanjiu* (*Research on Chinese Youth*) 1: 15–18.

Wu Zhongmin. 2015. "Shehui gongzheng shi quanti renmin yiyuan zuida gongyue shu" ("Social Justice Is the Biggest Wish of the Population"). *Guangming ribao* (*Guangming Daily*), June 3. http://www.xinhuanet.com/politics/2015-06/03/c_127872922.htm.

Xi Jinping. 2012a. "Xi Jinping: Jinjin weirao jianchi he fazhan Zhongguo tese shehuizhuyi, xuexi xuanchuan guanche dang de shiba da jingshen" ("Xi Jinping: We Must Continue the Path of Developing Socialism with Chinese Characteristics, Promote the Party's Message from the Eighteenth Congress"). *Renmin wang* (*People's Daily Online*), November 17. http://cpc.people.com.cn/n/2012/1119/c64094-19615998-3.html.

Xi Jinping. 2012b. Xi Jinping zai changwei jianmianhui shangde jianghua ("Xi Jinping's Speech at the Meeting of the CCP's Standing Committee"), November 15. http://news.sina.com.cn/c/2012-11-15/121925587435.shtml.

Xi Jinping. 2016. "Xi Jinping zai zhexue shehui kexue gongzuo zuotanhui shang de jianghua" ("Xi Jinping's Speech to a Humanities and Social Sciences Conference"). Xinhuanet, May 18. http://news.xinhuanet.com/politics/2016-05/18/c_1118891128.htm.

Xiang Nan. 2015. "Diaocha cheng hunlian shi shoufang nongmingong zui jiaolü wenti, gaoyu gongzuo laolei" ("Survey Suggests That Marriage Problems Rank Higher Than

Being Overworked as the Most Worrying Aspect of Rural Migrant Life"). *Zhongguo qingnianbao* (*China Youth Daily*), May 7. http://www.chinanews.com/gn/2015/05-07/7257710.shtml.
Xiao Xiangmin, and Chen Aixiang. 2012. "Xinshengdai nongmingong hunlian guan jiqi jiaoyu duice" ("Young Rural Migrant's Attitudes to Love and Marriage and Policy Recommendations Regarding Their Education"). *Zhongguo jiti jingji* (*China's Collective Economy*) 25: 191–2.
Xie Li. 2014. "Diaosi shengcun xianzhuang: Yueshouru buzu sanqian yiri sancan jin hua 39 yuan" ("Current Living Situation of Diaosi: Monthly Income Is Less Than 3,000 *Yuan* and Spending as Little as 39 *Yuan* on Three Meals a Day"). *Renmin wang* (*People's Daily Online*), October 30. http://finance.people.com.cn/n/2014/1030/c1004-25935739.html.
Xinhuanet. 2016. "Nanzi wei maifang jia lihun jiaxi zhen zuo, ren fang liangkong hai pei 50 wan" ("Man Resorts to Fake Divorce in Order to Purchase Property, but Fake Divorce Becomes Real, Resulting in His Losing Spouse as Well as Half A Million"), April 4. http://news.xinhuanet.com/fortune/2017-04/04/c_1120748753.htm.
Xiong Jian. 2006. "Zhongguo nonge daxue jiaoshou Zhang Zhenghe tan Zhongguo chengxiang fazhan shiheng wenti" ("Professor Zhang Zhenghe from China Agricultural University Discusses the Issue of Development Imbalance between Urban and Rural China"). *Renmin ribao* (*People's Daily*), November 21. http://www.gov.cn/zwhd/2006-11/21/content_449061.htm.
Xu Chuanxin. 2006. "Xinshengdai nongmingong yu shimin tonghun yiyuan ji yingxiang yinsu yanjiu" ("New-Generation Rural Migrants' Willingness to Marry City People: A Study of Various Factors"). *Qingnian yanjiu* (*Youth Research*) 9: 38–43.
Xu Jiaming and Wei Ran. 2018. "Nanxing Xinshengdai nongmingong de ze ou kunjing ji jiehun celüe—jiyu Subei C cun de diaocha yu fenxi" ("The Mate Selection Dilemma and New-generation Rural Migrant Men's Marriage Options and Strategies—based on the Investigation and Analysis of C Village in Northern Jiangsu"). *Zhongguo qingnian yanjiu* (*China Youth Research*) 1. http://www.zgqnyj.com/index.php?m=content&c=index&a=show&catid=201&id=3033.
Xu Jing, and Zheng Yingying. 2012. "Hanguo sheyingshi yuan jiceng dagong zhe hunsha meng" ("Korean Photography Studio Helps Realize Rural Migrants' Dream of Wearing a Wedding Gown"). *Sina*, November 25. http://news.sina.com.cn/o/2012-11-25/164425658484.shtml.
Yan Dan, and Su Jianjun. 2013. "Zai yali zhong chengzhang zai mimang zhong jianshou de Fushikang nü" ("Foxconn Women Maturing under Pressure and Persevering Under Disorientation"). *Zhongguo funü bao* (*China Women's News*), November 6, A03.
Yan, Hairong. 2008a. "Neoliberal Governmentality and Neohumanism: Organizing Suzhi/Value Flow through Labor Recruitment Networks." *Cultural Anthropology* 18(4): 493–523. https://doi.org/10.1525/can.2003.18.4.493.
Yan, Hairong. 2008b. *New Masters, New Servants: Migration, Development, and Women Workers in China*. Durham, NC: Duke University Press.
Yan, Yunxiang. 2009. *The Individualization of Chinese Society*. Oxford, UK: Berg.
Yan, Yunxiang. 2010. "The Chinese Path to Individualization." *British Journal of Sociology* 61(3): 489–512. https://doi.org/10.1111/j.1468-4446.2010.01323.x.
Yan, Yunxiang. 2016. "Intergenerational Intimacy and Descending Familism in Rural North China." *American Anthropologist* 118(2): 244–57. https://doi.org/10.1111/aman.12527.

Yang, Jie. 2015. *Unknotting the Heart: Unemployment and Therapeutic Governance in China*. Ithaca, NY: Cornell University Press.

Yang Li, and Shu Renhua. 2010. "Xinshengdai nongmingong hunlian de xiandai xin yanjiu" ("A Study of the Modern Attitudes of New-Generation Rural Migrant Workers to Marriage"). *Shanxi nongye daxue xuekan* (*The Academic Journal of the Shanxi Agricultural University*) 3: 279–81.

Yang, Xueyan, Shuzhuo Li, Isabelle Attané, and Marcus W. Feldman. 2017. "On the Relationship between the Marriage Squeeze and the Quality of Life of Rural Men in China." *American Journal of Men's Health* 11(3): 702–10. https://doi.org/10.1177%2F1557988316681220.

Yanow, Dvora. 2007. "Interpretation in Policy Analysis: On Methods and Practice." *Critical Policy Studies* 1(1): 110–122. https://doi.org/10.1080/19460171.2007.9518511.

Yao Peng. 2013. "Geng zhide guanzhu de shi nügong de neixinshijie" ("It Is Worth Paying More Attention to Women Workers' Inner World"). *Zhongguo funü bao* (*China Women's News*), September 25, A02.

You Fengwei. 2002. *Niqiu* (*Loach*). Shenyang: Chunfeng wenyi chubanshe (Chunfeng Literature and Art Publishing House).

Zavoretti, Roberta. 2016. "Is It Better to Cry on a BMW or Laugh on a Bicycle? Marriage, 'Financial Performance Anxiety,' and the Production of Class in Nanjing (PRC)." *Modern Asian Studies* 50(4): 1190–219. https://www.jstor.org/stable/24734807.

Zelizer, Viviana A. 2005. *The Purchase of Intimacy*. Princeton, NJ: Princeton University Press.

Zhang, Everett. 2011. "China's Sexual Revolution." In *Deep China: The Moral Life of the Person*, edited by Arthur Kleinman, Yunxiang Yan, Jing Jun, Sing Lee, Everett Zhang, Tianshu Pan, Fei Wu, and Jinhua Guo, 106–51. Berkeley, CA: University of California Press.

Zhang, Jun, and Peidong Sun. 2014. "'When Are You Going to Get Married?' Parental Matchmaking and Middle-Class Women in Contemporary Urban China." In *Wives, Husbands, and Lovers: Marriage and Sexuality in Hong Kong, Taiwan, and Urban China*, edited by Deborah S. Davis and Sara L. Friedman, 118–46. Stanford, CA: Stanford University Press.

Zhang, Li. 2001. *Strangers in the City: Reconfigurations of Space, Power, and Social Networks within China's Floating Population*. Stanford, CA: Stanford University Press.

Zhang, Li. 2002. "Spatiality and Urban Citizenship in Late Socialist China." *Public Culture* 14(2): 311–34. https://muse.jhu.edu/article/26289.

Zhang, Li. 2008. "Private Homes, Distinct Lifestyles: Performing a New Middle Class." In *Privatizing China: Socialism from Afar*, edited by Li Zhang and Aihwa Ong, 23–40. Ithaca, NY: Cornell University Press.

Zhang, Li. 2010. *In Search of Paradise: Middle-Class Living in a Chinese Metropolis*. Ithaca, NY: Cornell University Press.

Zhang, Li. 2014. "Bentuhua: Culturing Psychotherapy in Postsocialist China." *Culture, Medicine, and Psychiatry* 38(2): 283–305. https://doi.org/10.1007/s11013-014-9366-y.

Zhang, Li. 2017. "The Rise of Therapeutic Governing in Postsocialist China." *Medical Anthropology: Cross-Cultural Studies in Health and Illness* 36(1): 6–18. http://dx.doi.org/10.1080/01459740.2015.1117079.

Zhang, Li. 2018. "Cultivating the Therapeutic Self in China." *Medical Anthropology: Cross-Cultural Studies in Health and Illness* 37(1): 45–58. https://doi.org/10.1080/01459740.2017.1317769.

Zhang Li, Zhou Zhou, and Zhang Yizhe. 2012. "Xinzhi wei chengshu jiehun you shengzi: 90 hou buru hunyin weicheng" ("Psychologically Immature Yet Already Married and Having Children: Those Born in the 1990s Are Entering the Walled City Called Marriage"). *Zhejiang ribao* (*Zhejiang Daily*), August 16. https://zjnews.zjol.com. cn/05zjnews/system/2012/08/16/018740599.shtml.

Zhang Ning. 2013. "*Zhiyin* ti yu diduan wenhua shangpin de shengchan he xiaofei" ("The *Soulmate* Genre and the Production and Consumption of Low-End Cultural Products"), October 3. http://blog.sina.com.cn/s/blog_a353266f0101rcrs.html.

Zhang Qianqian. 2013. "Dang aiqing zhaojin xianshi: 'Xinchun zou jiceng': 'Liushuixian shangde ai': 'Xiaohan jiehun ji' shouji" ("When Love Shines through Reality: Production Notes on 'Grassroots Reports,' 'Love on the Assembly Line,' and 'Xiao Han's Wedding'"). *Dianshi yanjiu* (*Television Research*) 6: 48–49.

Zhang Xiao. 2016. "Chunjie linjin, daling qingnian zhongchou 'fan bihun guanggao' toufang Beijing ditie" ("As Spring Festival is Round the Corner, Young People of Marriageable Age Crowd-Source Funds to Place 'Anti-Marriage Advertisements' on Beijing's Subway"). CQNews, January 22. http://news.cqnews.net/html/2016-01/22/content_36251233.htm.

Zhao Lu. 2013. "Shilun Xinshengdai nongmingong de hunlianguan: Yi shehui hudong wei shijiao" ("A Preliminary Discussion of New-Generation Rural Migrants' Attitudes to Marriage from the Perspective of Social Interaction"). *Shehui yanjiu* (*Social Studies*) 19: 129–30.

Zhao, Yuezhi. 2010. "Chinese Modernity, Media, and Democracy: An Interview with Lu Xinyu." *Global Media and Communication* 6(1): 5–32. https://doi.org/10.1177%2F1742766510362017.

Zheng, Tiantian. 2022. *Violent Intimacy: Family Harmony, State Stability, and Intimate Partner Violence in Post-Socialist China*. New York: Bloomsbury Academic.

Zheng Xiaoqiong. 2012. *Nügong ji* (*Stories of Female Rural Migrant Workers*). Guangzhou: Huacheng chubanshe (Huacheng Press).

Zheng Xiuguo. 2013. "Zhencheng: Dida he chuji linghun de qinggan zhiji: Qianxi yangshi xinchun zou jiceng, liushuixian shangde aiqing deng xilie baoda" ("Sincerity Is the Key to Reaching the Authentic Soul: An Analysis of the 'Grassroots Reports' and 'Love on the Assembly Line' Series"). *Dianshi yanjiu* (*Television Research*) 6: 46–8.

Zheng Xupeng, and Zheng Wenxi. 2013. "90 hou nongmingong diaocha: Xiaofei dou shuaka yue ru si qian yueguang'" ("Survey of Rural Migrants Born in the 1990s: They Mainly Use Their Bank Card When Shopping, and Spend All Their Monthly Income of 4,000 *Yuan*"). *Chongqing shangbao* (*Chongqing Daily*), August 2. http://finance.people.com.cn/money/n/2013/0802/c218900-22418411.html.

Zhou Tingyu, and Qiu Hongjie. 2005. "Youyuan qianli lai xianghui—Zhongguo zehun banjing buduan kuoda" ("Destiny Will Bring Lovers to Meet Even if They Are 1,000 Miles Apart—in China the Sphere for Choosing a Marriage Partner Is Continuously Expanding"). Xinhuanet, October 7. http://3g.66wc.com/1843.html.

Zhou, Xueguang. 2004. *The State and Life Chances in Urban China: Redistribution and Stratification 1949–1994*. New York: Cambridge University Press.

Zhu Guannan. 2012. "Chuantong dao xianzai: Xinshengdai nongmingong de hunlian zhuanxing yu kunjing" ("From Tradition to Modernity: Dilemmas in New-generation Rural Migrants' Marriage Prospects"). *Xinjiang shehui kexue* (*Xinjiang Social Sciences Research*) 3: 130–34.

Zou Yuan, and Li Xin. 2020. "Jianzhu gongdi pai hunsha zhao Changsha qidui nongmingong fuqi ying langman Qixi" ("Construction Company Offers Wedding Photography and Seven Rural Migrant Construction Site Workers Get a Taste of Romance on the Double Seven Festival"). Rednet, August 25. https://hn.rednet.cn/content/2020/08/25/8252184.html.

Zukin, Sharon, and Jennifer Maguire. 2004. "Consumers and Consumption." *Annual Review of Sociology* 30: 173–97. https://doi.org/10.1146/annurev.soc.30.012703.110553.

INDEX

academic research
    Chinese Communist Party and 35–6
    from outside China 42–3
    as serving the state 45
Adrian, Bonnie 76, 81, 83, 90
Ahmed, Sara 83
Anagnost, Ann 43
assembly lines, impact on workers 84–5
at a distance government 51

Bauman, Zygmunt 29
"Bed-Warming Project" 23
Bell, Eona 140
Berlant, Lauren 10, 51–2, 53
betrothal money *(caili)* 124, 127, 137–8, 144
Boris, Eileen 119
Bourdieu, Pierre 10, 74–5
bridal photography *see* wedding photographs
Butler, Judith 29, 32

Cai Xiang 63
capitalism and emotions 10
Chan, Kam Wing 27
Chang Zizhong 38–9, 41
"Chen Huan's Choice" on CCTV 52
China Central Television (CCTV)
    discourse of governing 48
    government position and policies on 47–8
    Grassroots Reports 48
    Li Yongsheng's story 47, 48
China Dream 33
China Women's News
    optimistic article on Foxconn women workers 102–3
    reaction to "Foxconn's Night Life" article 101–2
    transgressive *versus* normative framework 103

Chinese Communist Party
    academic research and 35–6
    love lives of rural migrants and 33
Choi, Susanne Yuk-Ping 82, 143
"Chunfeng Ye" ("Night of the Spring Breeze") 159–60
Ci, Jiwei 51–2
class
    consciousness of, rural migrants and 60
    consumption and 74–6, 91, 164
    economic reforms and 27–9
    emotional experience and 10
    meaning of consumption items and practices 72
    positions, consumption and 72
    precariat class 29–32
    privilege, and access to love 106
    Titanic (film), discussion about 1–3
cold intimacy 99
cold violence 131
colloquial language, use of 3
commercialization of intimacy 99
commodification of intimacy 10
communication in marriage 129–32, 140
compressed modernity 11
Constable, Nicole 76, 77
consumption
    class and 74–6, 91, 164
    class positions and 72
    diaosi and 31
    inequality and 90
    as leveling force 75–6
    low levels of rural migrants 55
    middle class and 75
    positional goods 75
    realistic level of 54
    "revolution-plus-love" formula, shift away from 63–5
    and rural migrants, link between 58–9
    rural-urban inequality 26
    see also wedding photographs

counseling service *see* marriage and relationship counseling services
cover image 166–7
cross-class love in *Titantic* (film), discussion about 1–3
cross-*hukou* marriages 37–8
cultural values, deinstitutionalization of intimate life and 119–22
culture, language use and 3
culture of inequality 162–3

dark intimacy
  cold intimacy and 99
  difficulties of researching 94
  fictional and media texts used for research 94–5
  as intrinsic bad 99
  Loach (You Fengwei) 109–11
  NGO, perspective from 95–7
  power imbalance 98–9
  research into lives of 93–4
  second-hand ethnography of 113
  "*The Sound of a Cleaver Being Sharpened in a Rented Room*" (Wang Shiyue) 107–9
deinstitutionalization of intimate life 119–22
Delman, Jørgen 36
Deng Xiaoping 32
Deng Xiuzhen 71
diaosi, use and meaning of term 30–2
diceng, use of term 27–8
divorce 120, 139
Dongguan lovers *see* "Rural Migrants' Love in Dongguan" photo essay
Du Ping 109

economic redistribution, middle class and 33–4
Economic Weekly, "Foxconn's Night Life" article in 100–3
education, rural-urban inequality and 25–6
emotional capitalism 10, 164
emotional labor 119, 164
  falling in love as 107
  "Love on the Assembly Line" photo-essay (Jia Dai Tengfei) 86–7
  see also intimacy work

emotional loneliness, migrant life and 34
employment, rural-urban inequality and 26
ethnography of emotion, love stories and 8

fake divorces, investment in housing and 50
Farquhar, Judith 94
Farrer, James 122
Feng Gong 33, 34–5, 50
fengzi chenghun (marriage by having a child) 154
fieldwork 12–4
Foucault, Michel 98, 108
"Foxconn's Night Life" article in *Economic Weekly* 100–3
Foxconn Workers' Union
  reaction to "Foxconn's Night Life" article 101
  silence of on crucial issues 102
  transgressive *versus* normative framework 103
future
  blind faith in, skepticism about 55
  hope of a better future 56, 59
  imagining a better 65
  optimism regarding 51–2, 55, 56, 60, 66–7
  politics of the 51–2

Ganji.com, report by 30
Giddens, Anthony 10–1
government
  policy changes needed 45
  research into love life of rural young people 23–4
  responsibility of re. happiness of migrants 38–9
governmentality and desire 9–10, 163
Gow, Mike 36
Guo, Yingjie 28

happiness of the Chinese people 33
health care access, rural-urban inequality and 26
He Xiaobo 61–2
Hirsch, Fred 75
historical perspective 62–4
HIV/AIDS, cultural politics of 98

Hochschild, Arlie 99, 107, 165
"Home Is Where You Are" on CCTV 52, 59, 65
homosexuality 120
housing
    class inequality and 50–1
    fake divorces, investment in housing and 50
    owning as a pipe dream 54–5
    spatialization of class 75
    vacant, *hukou* system and 50
Huang Ying 55–6
hukou system
    as contributing to marriage problems 37
    as discriminatory 25
    inequality and 46
    reforms 27, 43–4
    rural-urban inequality 26–7
    rural-urban marriages 37–8
    success in marriage market and 29–30
    vacant housing and 50
Hunang Yingying 93–4
Hyde, Sandra 98
hypergamy in the marriage market 144

idiomatic language, use of 3
Illouz, Eva 10, 72, 75, 86, 94, 99, 118, 140
income disparity, rural-urban 25, 26
individualization 164
    affective individualism 120–1
    modernity and 11–2
inequality
    consumption and 90
    culture of 162–3
    emotional consequences of 164
    housing and 50–1
    hukou system 46
    and intimacy, conceptual framework for 9–12
    intimate consequences of 7, 9
    intimate life, link with 29–30
    intimate turn in studies of 162–5
    love, discourse of as managing 49
    love as deployed to manage 66–7
    "Love on the Assembly Line" photo-essay (Jia Dai Tengfei) 74
    men and 155–8
    political challenges posed by 33
    research from outside China 42–3
    socioeconomic framework for understanding 112–3
    suzhi (personal qualities) 40–1, 45–6
internet
    idioms, use of 3
    love and sexuality discourses on 40
intimacy
    conceptual framework 9–12
    deinstitutionalization of intimate life 119–22
    modernity and 10–2
intimacy work
    capacity to aspire for higher level of intimacy 138–9
    inequality and 119
    inequality as background for decisions on 140
    MB's story 129–32
    meaning of term 119
    PC's story 132–7
    as resting with women 118–9
    state, market and tradition as backdrop for women 137–8
    WJ's story 123–6
    XM's story 126–9

Jacka, Tamara 43
Jia Dai Tengfei 72, 83
    see also "Love on the Assembly Line" photo-essay (Jia Dai Tengfei)
Jiang Wenlai 23–4
jiejie see sex work/workers
Jing Tiankui 144
Judd, Ellen 122

Kendall, Laurel 77
Kewang Chengshi (Yearning for the City) television series, Episode 2 160–2
Kleinman, Arthur 90

labor activists, love between 61–2
language, colloquial and idiomatic 3
Lee, Haiyan 63, 66
leftover men 143–5
life expectancy, rural-urban inequality and 26
Li Keqiang 33
Liu, Jieyu 140

Liu Jianmei 62–3
living standards in lowest income bracket 30
Li Yongsheng 47
Li Zhang 50
Loach (You Fengwei) 109–11
love
  lost faith in 64
  love as different for men and women 61
  type of focussed on in book 8–9
"Love on the Assembly Line" photo-essay (Jia Dai Tengfei)
  accolades for 87
  backdrop, choice of 83
  emotional labor by participants 86–7
  as "giving love" 85–7
  inequality and 74
  meaning of photos for participants 83
  modernization of China and 74
  political usefulness of 90–1
  production of photographs 73–4
  response to 72
  rural migrants' responses to 88–90
love stories on CCTV
  class consciousness, rural migrants and 60
  complexity of responses to 57
  consumption and rural migrants, link between 58–9
  ethnographic approach 49
  "Home Is Where You Are" 52, 54–5, 59, 65
  ideology-in-the-making shown in 66
  "Love on the Assembly Line" 49–50
  marriage, emphasis on 58
  message promoted by 59–60
  moral template, inequality narration and 59
  parental opinions *versus* own desires 56–7, 58
  political objectives of 66–7
  responses to of Foxconn workers 53–5, 56–7, 67
  sexuality of men and women in 60–1
  use of 49
  "Xiao Han's Wedding" 52, 57, 59–60, 64–5
"Love Troubles" as title, choice of 8, 166

Lu, Huilin 28
Lü Xinyu 65
Ma, Eric 76–7
marriage
  communication in 129–32, 140
  competitive culture of in villages 127–8
  deinstitutionalization of intimate life 119–22
  emphasis on in love stories on CCTV 58
  fengzi chenghun (marriage by having a child) 154
  hypergamy in the marriage market 144
  ideal married life 127
  MB's story 129–32
  parental opinions *versus* own desires 123–6, 127, 138
  PC's story 132–7
  pressure to get married 121–6, 127–8
  rural migrants, difficulties faced by 38
  rural-urban 37–8
  state, market and tradition as backdrop for women 137–8
  WJ's story 123–6
  XM's story 126–9
marriage and relationship counseling services
  increased use of 121
  office 117
  services offered 117
  training course at 117–8
marrying up 144
Marx, Karl 74
masculinity
  complexity of 112
  scholarship on 143
  see also men
May, Shannon 122
MB's story 129–32
media
  love and sexuality discourses on 40
  see also China Central Television (CCTV); love stories on CCTV
men
  betrothal gifts, demands for 156
  BH's story 152–5
  class-based oppression and 157
  complexity of masculinity 112

factors impacting masculinity 144–5
future research 156
inequality and 155–8
in the intimacy market 109–11
JH's story 149–52
leftover men 143–5
masculine compromise 143
masculine grievance 155–8
odds as against migrant men 146–7
purchasing sex/sexual domination as unacceptable 156
80s and 90s cohorts, differences between 145–55
scholarship on 143, 145
sex ratio, imbalance in 144
sexual frustration and low self-esteem 38
sexuality in love stories on CCTV 61
"*The Sound of a Cleaver Being Sharpened in a Rented Room*" (Wang Shiyue) 107–9
triple oppression of state, capital and patriarchy 156
YY's story 147–9
ZB's story 141–2, 146–7
middle class
consumption and 75
economic redistribution and 33–4
instability of 75
mobility, traditional family structures and relationships and 152
modernity
intimacy and 10–2
as uneven in China 11
modern/traditional attitudes and practices
deinstitutionalization of intimate life 119–22
suzhi and 42

National Bureau of Statistics (NBS), love life of rural young people research 23–4
national television *see* China Central Television (CCTV); love stories on CCTV
"Night of the Spring Breeze" ("*Chunfeng Ye*") 159–60
nongmingong
defined 24
precariat class and 29–32

optimism 51–2, 55, 56, 60
Ortner, Sherry 140

parental opinions *versus* own desires 56–7, 123–6, 127, 138
Parreñas, Rhacel Salazar 119
PC's story 132–7
Peng, Yinni 82, 143
personal qualities *see suzhi* (personal qualities)
policy changes needed 45
political stability, love lives of rural migrants and 32–5
positional goods 75
precariat class 29–32, 150, 152, 164
privatization of social order 9–10
propaganda, affective adjustment via 53
prostitution *see* sex work/workers
psychological self-adjustment, migrants lack of 41–2
psychotherapy, increased use of 121
public funds investment, rural-urban inequality and 26
Pun, Ngai 28

qualities of human bodies and their conduct *see suzhi* (personal qualities)

redistribution, middle class and 33–4
research
aims 8
difficulties and complexities of 7–8
emotional side to data gathering 14
fieldwork 12–4
focus groups 13
materials used 8
methodology 165–7
Village Q 12, 13–4
"revolution-plus-love" formula 62–4
Rocca, Jean-Louis 75
"Rural Migrants' Love in Dongguan" photo essay 166
images shown 4
publicity received by 4
questions raised by 6–7
reactions to 4–6
rural migrant workers
as bifurcated figures in public discourses 162

characteristics related to marriage
problems 37
as consumers, expectations of 50
death of love for 65
difficulties finding marriage
partners 50
first-generation 25
married, difficulties faced by 38
as nongmingong 24
population growth 24
"Rural Migrants' Love in Dongguan"
photo essay 3–7
second-generation 25
wedding photographs 77
rural-urban inequality
consumption levels 26
educational level 25–6
employment 26
health care access 26
hukou system 26–7
income disparity 25, 26
life expectancy 26
as migration driver 26
public funds investment 26
rural-urban marriages 37–8
rural/urban practices, tension between 165

second-generation rural migrant workers 25, 28
wedding photographs 81
self-awareness, migrants lack of 41–2
self-governing, encouragement of 9–10, 51, 59
self-reflexivity, capacity for 11
sex ratio, imbalance in 144
sex-related crimes, repressed sexuality and 32–3
sexuality in love stories on CCTV 60–1
sexual loneliness of men
"The Sound of a Cleaver Being Sharpened in a Rented Room" (Wang Shiyue) 107–9
see also men
sex work/workers
cultural politics of 97–100
difficulties of researching 94
fictional and media texts used for research 94–5

"Foxconn's Night Life" article in *Economic Weekly* 100–3
Loach (You Fengwei) 109–11
love and romance, continuing belief in 96
NGO, perspective from 95–7
as non-permanent profession 96
research into lives of 93–4
"The Sound of a Cleaver Being Sharpened in a Rented Room" (Wang Shiyue) 107–9
traditional ideas about sex 96
transgression and 97–8
transnational capital and 103
social harmony, love lives of rural migrants and 32–5, 44
social media, love and sexuality discourses on 40
social order, privatization of 9–10
social science research
Chinese Communist Party and 35–6
from outside China 42–3
as serving the state 45
socioeconomic inequality, intimate consequences of 7, 9
Song of Youth (Yang Mo) 60
Soulmate (Zhiyin)
compressed modernity of China in 105
narratives of 104
pedagogic agenda 104–7
success of 103–4
"The Sound of a Cleaver Being Sharpened in a Rented Room" (Wang Shiyue) 107–9
stability
diaosi as cause for concern 31–2
love lives of rural migrants and 32–5, 44
Stallybrass, Peter 98
Standing, Guy 29, 150
state
discourses on love and intimacy 9–10
policy changes needed 45
research into love life of rural young people 23–4
state media *see* China Central Television (CCTV)
state television *see* love stories on CCTV
suzhi (personal qualities)

defined 39
inequality and 40–1, 42–3, 45–6
modern/traditional attitudes and practices and 42
post-socialist governance and control 43
as problem or solution 39–42
self-awareness, migrants lack of 41–2

Taiwan, wedding photographs in 76, 81
Titanic (film), discussion about 1–3
title of this book, choice of 8
traditional/modern attitudes and practices
　deinstitutionalization of intimate life 119–22
　suzhi and 42
transgression 97–8
transnational capital 103
triple oppression of state, capital and patriarchy 111–2, 137, 156

utopianism 51

Veblen, Thorstein 75
Village Q 12, 13–4

Wang, David Der-Wei 63
Weber, Max 74
wedding photographs
　assembly lines, impact on workers 84–5
　bridal dresses, meaning of 84
　class, consumption and 91
　consumption, inequality and 90
　familial and social expectations 82
　free photoshoots 81–2
　growth of industry 76–7
　as key component of weddings 78–9, 81
　as legitimating the marriage 82
　range of prices 77
　rural migrant workers 77, 80–3
　second-generation rural migrant workers 81
　status and identity as shaping motivation for 83
　Taiwan 76, 81

urban professionals' perspective 77–80, 82, 83
Xu Aiguo and Deng Xiuzhen 71
see also "Love on the Assembly Line" photo-essay (Jia Dai Tengfei)
Wei Houkai 26
Wellford, James 74
White, Allon 98
WJ's story 123–6
women
　agency over marriage and family 112, 122, 139–40
　child factor 139
　cross-hukou marriages 37–8
　parental opinions *versus* own desires 123–6
　sexuality in love stories on CCTV 60–1
　state, market and tradition as backdrop for 137–8
　WJ's story 123–6
Women's Federation *see China Women's News*
Wu Xiaoying 28, 155

"Xiao Han's Wedding" on CCTV 52, 57, 59–60, 64–5
Xi Jinping 33
XM's story 126–9
Xu Aiguo 71

Yan, Hairong 42–3
Yan, Yunxiang 11
Yang Min 61–2
Yang Mo 60
Yearning for the City television series, Episode 2 160–2
Yunxiang Yan 120, 164

Zhang, Everett 122
Zhang, Jiayu 140
Zhang Qianqian 64–5
Zhao Lu 41
Zhao Shuli 63
Zheng, Tiantian 98
Zheng Xiaoqiong 85
Zheng Xiuguo 59–60

Printed in the USA
CPSIA information can be obtained
at www.ICGtesting.com
LVHW012047080324
773937LV00003B/390